HOME IS A ROOF OVER A PIG

HOME IS A ROOF
OVER A PIG

An American Family's Journey in China

AMINTA ARRINGTON

THE OVERLOOK PRESS
NEW YORK, NY

This edition first published in the United States in 2012 by
The Overlook Press, Peter Mayer Publishers, Inc.
141 Wooster Street
New York, NY 10012
www.overlookpress.com
For bulk and special sales, please contact sales@overlookny.com

Cataloguing-in-Publication Data is available from the Library of Congress.

Design and typeformatting by Bernard Schleifer
Printed in the United States of America
1 3 5 7 9 10 8 6 4 2

ISBN 978-1-59020-899-1

To my husband,
who read and lived each page
with me;
who called me a writer
before I ever
thought of myself as one.

And to my father
who pushed me to dig deeper
in writing
and in life;
whose pride in me
has always let me feel
I had no boundaries.

Contents

✾

Chapter 1

门'

GATE

❁

T HE CHINESE WRITER ZHANG AILING SAID THAT EVERY BUTTERFLY IS A dead flower flying back to look for her lost life.

Perhaps that explains why I found myself arriving in China with a husband, three children, nineteen pieces of luggage, and a contract to teach at a local university. Three years before, my husband Chris and I had traveled to one of China's poorer provinces to adopt a beautiful baby girl. We named her Grace Amelie—her middle name French like her older sister's, her given name Grace because she was a heaven-sent gift. But as we finished up the paperwork and prepared to fly home, something began to nag at me.

It started at the hotel, when we took off her layers of clothes and the rag that served as a diaper, and replaced them with the cutest outfit we had brought with us and a fresh Pampers. For I knew I was changing her. And I was changing her yet again when I gave her her first bath, put her in a high chair, and babbled to her in English. It nagged at me when we boarded the airplane, landed her on U.S. soil, and happily told her she was now an American. For even though we were giving her a family and a place to belong, I knew I was changing her identity. And she was losing something.

Yes, the truth was, I had come to China, in part, looking for the life my daughter had lost.

❁

From the moment we got off the plane in Beijing, people stared at us. One woman walked to within a few feet, set down her bags, put her hands on her hips, and openly gawked.

As we stood in line to board our next flight, the deplaning passengers filed past, separated by a glass partition. Suddenly, one of them caught sight of the five of us and motioned to the others. The passengers all crowded in, noses to the glass, pointing and unabashedly taking us in, as they might a rare white Bengal tiger at the Beijing Zoo.

We were dropped off in front of our new home in the middle of the night. We walked up two flights of bare concrete steps to a tiny two-bedroom apartment that didn't have enough beds for the five of us.

"There's no running water," Sally from the university's foreign affairs office said apologetically. "It gets turned off every evening."

We left the unpacking till morning and huddled together in the available beds, exhausted.

The next morning I tripped over open suitcases and made my way to the window for my first daylight look at our new surroundings. Outside I saw a long red line of contiguous courtyards. They were affixed to a drab contemporary apartment block, making them even more striking: an explosion of red brick and verdant vines, of character and history. Inside the courtyards, elderly women chatted on stools or tended small gardens. The courtyards looked like pieces of the village, a part of the old world taken with their residents to the city when they had come seeking a better life.

Each courtyard had a gate. Like the courtyards, the gates were all slightly dissimilar, some with tile roofs, others with wrought-iron doors. Faded red paper couplets adorned with Chinese calligraphy marked the sides and tops of most of them. Each gate, though composed of worn bricks and aging tiles, managed to look grand, as if to say boldly and with just the slightest amount of condescension: Is one really making an entrance if one doesn't pass over a threshold and under a roof?

In old China, women rarely went beyond gates such as these. They remained in seclusion, guarded from prying eyes, retaining their mystery at the expense of their freedom. The gate also defined insiders from outsiders, family from strangers. Where one stood in relation to the gate defined who one was.

I knew this society clearly defined me. I was a stranger. I was a foreigner. I stood outside the gate.

❀

Chris had gone for a walk and came back with a smile on his face. "It's China out there," he said. "We are in the real China."

The real China. That was what I had wanted. A China of raising children, taking crowded buses to work, sitting on stools playing Chinese checkers, hand-washing laundry and hanging it out the window. A China of homemade dumplings, acupuncture, and the ancient and remarkably accurate Chinese medicine. A China that would astound me with its history and civilization, and force me out of my American conveniences and show me a way of life unchanged by the centuries. I wanted to experience the China that my daughter came from. This was the China I had wanted.

Twice before I had traveled here, once with my mother-in-law, visiting the top tourist attractions in the big cities; once with my husband when we adopted Grace. Both times I saw hints of the real China—a mother holding her baby over a dumpster while he peed through split pants, sunburned peasants selling fruit on the street, a dark alley visible through a circular doorway teeming with activity—but for the most part I had been safely ensconced with other foreigners in high-end hotels that served buffet breakfasts with English muffins and French pastries. This time I wanted a China not sanitized for the consumption of Western tourists. But now, as I faced the noises, the stares, the smells, the crowds, I was less sure.

I've always been one to fall for romantic and ideal notions. I married my husband because I had found my soul mate. Practical considerations, such as our ten-year age difference or utter pennilessness, didn't factor in. I chose my college major, political science with an emphasis on international relations, because I was fascinated with it. I had no idea how it would ever translate into future earnings. I dreamed of fighting poverty in the third world, of bringing Muslim and Christian women together, of owning a family farm. I cried when the orphaned Oksana Baiul won the Olympic gold medal in figure skating, and cried again when Princess Diana died. Cynicism and I cannot breathe the same air. I expect the best of everyone and dislike reading news reports, watching movies, or believing stories that might suggest otherwise.

I'm a small-town girl. Lynden, Washington, my hometown, has a church on nearly every block and the majority of its families, including my own, are descended from Dutch immigrants who left their big families and small farms in the Netherlands in hopes of opportunity in the larger expanses of America, eventually settling in Michigan, Iowa, South Dakota, and Washington State. In Lynden, as in other Dutch communities, everyday life is centered on the Christian school and the Reformed church, whose ethic is "work is worship." I attended school with the children of my parents' own classmates, secure in my identity as Roger and Marlene's daughter, and Lue and Lucy's granddaughter. Life was happily busy for my three little brothers and me—a pattern of high school basketball games, summers working in the strawberry and raspberry fields, and potlucks after church on Sunday with grandparents, aunts and uncles, and cousins. I went to college in the Midwest, as my parents had, not able to imagine higher learning without flat landscapes and bitter winters.

After Chris and I married, I immediately started graduate school in international relations in Washington, D.C., and happily (albeit naively) became the instant mother of his two sons, precious fifth- and sixth-grade boys, each with a mop of naturally curly hair just like their father, each of whom opened their heart to me and allowed me the privilege of being their mom. For five years we were a family of four. Life revolved around Chris's career in the U.S. Army, along with ball games, swim meets, and Boy Scouts. With my master's degree in hand, I dreamed of making my mark on the world of diplomacy. Instead I held a variety of low-paying, under-stimulating jobs, feeling typecast as a military wife and limited by our numerous moves.

Two months after 9/11, I gave birth to Katherine. Three months later Chris deployed to Afghanistan, leaving me with a baby, two rebellious teenagers, and a raging case of postpartum depression. When Chris returned the boys graduated from high school and we began the lengthy process of adopting from China. The day we finished the adoption paperwork, after months of visits with doctors, social workers, and notaries, we found out I was pregnant with Andrew. He was born in September of 2003; we received our referral for Grace six weeks later. The following year we traveled to China to adopt Grace, said good-bye to our oldest son as he shipped out to begin his own army career, moved once again, watched as our second son struck out on his own, and prepared for Chris's yearlong deployment to Iraq. While he was gone I stayed at Fort Stewart, Georgia, with our three little ones, none of whom was potty-trained. It wasn't that big of a deal. Military families do stuff like that all the time.

Chris returned home safely with his unit in January 2006. It was now August, and we were in China.

❁

"You should go out and explore," Chris said, trying to encourage me. He had grown a beard to celebrate his retirement from the army, but he still possessed the bearing of a soldier.

"I think I'll stay here and continue unpacking," I said, not wanting to leave our tiny sanctuary.

"I'll unpack and watch the kids. You just go."

"Are you sure?" I asked.

"Of course I'm sure. Besides, we're hungry. I found a small grocery store and you could pick up some things we need."

He escorted me to the door, nearly pushing me outside. A steady flow of older people, arms filled with large onions and cabbages, walked along the quiet alley in front of our building. The campus had the feeling of an old neighborhood: old people, old trees, old streets, old courtyards. Cars were few; bicycles, plentiful. Along the quaint streets, people stopped to chat or poked their heads out of their courtyards to say hello to neighbors.

I stared at the building I had just exited—the foreign teachers' apartment building. It was a four-story rectangular block. The closest color to describe it would probably be a grayish-brown, but it seemed to have no intentional color at all, like dishwater. The building's best feature was a modest courtyard decorated with a few potted plants and trees. Other than the courtyard, it looked identical to the other buildings surrounding it.

Across the street I spotted a small, rather unkempt park. But at its center was a Chinese pavilion, its tile roof flowing down into curves like the skirt of a pirouetting Cinderella, a jewel of traditional Chinese simplicity in a setting of drab apartment blocks and 1970s-era academic buildings.

I left the campus, stepping along the faded sidewalk tiles of dusty Ying Sheng Road. There on the next corner, just as Chris had described, was the Jiayuan (pronounced Jah-ywen) supermarket, really more of a small grocery. Inside, chicken feet were prominently displayed at the counter, next to purplish "thousand-year-old" eggs, fresh tofu, and seaweed. What would I feed my hungry children? There were no tater tots, no cream of mushroom soup, no cheese ravioli. In fact, there was no cheese at all. And no butter. After walking the aisles, I picked up some peanut oil (the only cooking oil to be found), a five-kilogram bag of rice, a carton of long-shelf-life milk, and some vegetables.

I wanted to buy eggs, but I didn't know how. There were no egg cartons—only a plastic milk crate filled to the top with brown and speckled eggs, with a few downy feathers and chicken dung mixed in. I posted myself a few feet away and, while pretending to consider the array of vegetables, watched a woman ask for a plastic bag, carefully pick out her eggs, then hand the bag to the woman behind the meat counter who weighed it and attached a price. As soon as she finished, I copied her every move and was rewarded with a dozen eggs. Feeling more confident, I took my groceries and headed for home. I still had no idea what to expect in the coming days, but at least today we would be able to eat.

A few days later, we walked our three children to the local kindergarten. Outside the gate were bicycles, motorcycles, three-wheeled carts, electric bikes, and a few scooters. Grandfathers smoked while their grandchildren played at the playground. The lobby was packed as everyone tried to register—no lines, no order, only a swarm of hands and arms and legs pushing forward.

Inside dimly lit classrooms we saw rows and rows of tables, crowded with rows and rows of black-haired children, reciting in unison. My daughters held my hands and I squeezed them tightly, assuring them that all was well.

Our older daughter Katherine Mireille, four, looked up at us with shocked eyes when boiling hot water was poured into her metal drinking cup. I gave her a reassuring smile and helped her find her chair at the table where the teacher indicated she could sit. She raised her eyebrows accusingly when she heard about naptime, but her father just patted her on the back.

In another class, we sat Grace, three, and Andrew, two, on little orange chairs with chipped paint and told them if they needed to go potty, they could just use the room to the right with its raised trough over which several boys and girls were all squatting together in one straight line. I smiled at our children, letting them know this would be just fine.

We watched the different classes do their synchronized morning exercises, raising their hands and clanging shakers, which were made from old beer cans filled with tabs and taped over. We smiled at the other parents and grandparents, so curious about the foreign family in their midst. We purchased blankets and linens for naptime and paid extra money for their lunches.

Then my husband indicated that the teachers wanted to start their day, that we were in the way, that we should probably go.

"What?" I said to him.

"I said we should go. The kids are settled. It's time."

And I looked up at him, thinking, you mean we are supposed to leave our children here? Our babies? Alone in this school where they don't understand a word and everything is so different? Stuck in classrooms with more than forty children? This is their education we are talking about, I implored.

"At least let me try to talk to Grace's teacher," I said.

"About what?" my husband said.

I need to tell her about Grace, I thought. I need to tell them that though she looks Chinese, she's an American. She doesn't understand their language. She doesn't know their customs.

But I looked at my daughter and realized that my anxieties had not transferred to her. She was oblivious to the fact that she was in a room full of children who looked like her. She didn't seem the least bit perturbed that they were babbling in an incomprehensible tongue. The room was filled with new playmates and that was all she needed to know.

"Come on," Chris said, reaching out for my hand. "It's time to go."

Monday morning I taught my first class. Our medical college lay nestled beneath the famed Taishan (pronounced Tie-shawn), or Mount Tai, the foremost of China's five sacred mountains and the pride of the city of Tai'an, even all of Shandong province. We lived on the university's old campus at the foot of Mount Tai, just at the edge of downtown Tai'an. But we taught most of our classes on the new campus, located outside the city and built about five years before our arrival.

The new campus announced itself with its main gate, a lone structure, jutting three stories high from an otherwise flat, barren landscape. The gate was a simple angular structure of two sides and a roof, devoid of any decoration except the five Chinese characters across the top: 泰山医学院. Translated, those characters meant Taishan Medical College, although in its English-language publicity materials it was always upgraded to Taishan Medical University. Unlike the quaint courtyard gates outside our living-room window, this colossal gate was a hollow structure, a faux-marble-plated monstrosity. Sally from the university's foreign affairs office proudly told us it was the third largest gate in Shandong province.

In traditional Chinese, gate is written 門, a vivid representation of the courtyard gates outside my window. But in 1950, Mao began to simplify the Chinese characters. His great task was to modernize China's masses, which meant the masses needed to be literate. It was a difficult task: China had one of the world's most complex writing systems, and a population of 500 million, most of whom were peasants. Literacy at that time was an abysmal 20 percent. Over the 1950s and 1960s, about one-third of the Chinese characters were made less complicated and had their number of strokes reduced.

China is now quite proud of its 85 percent literacy rate and the simplification campaign is considered a success. But when Mao simplified the characters, 門 became the deflated 门, not nearly as evocative. 門 drew me inside, beckoned me to see for myself what lay beyond. I wanted to enter that traditional world of courtyards, hear grandparents telling stories, see three generations making dumplings together, smell the cabbage and garlic and peppers simmering over an outdoor wok. 门, in contrast, seemed flat and functional, the modern China of monochrome matchbox buildings, garish facades, factories, pollution, and cement.

門

GATE

(traditional)

门
GATE
(simplified)

Weeks later, a student described the impression the university's massive modern gate made on her when she first arrived at the university. For her, walking through this gate meant a new life as a university student. That was fitting, because in Chinese this same character 门 also means "turning point." She was leaving the village behind, using education to propel her to a bright future in the modern China.

However impressive the students found it, the gigantic university gate never captured my imagination. Despite its size, it was new and flat. It was just a 门; it didn't beckon me in, like the 門 of the China of old. But I knew that to truly understand China, I had to pass through both gates: the old and the new, the ancient civilization and the aspiring modern one.

I walked into the classroom and eagerly looked at the faces of about thirty students. At my entrance, they all stopped talking, gave a collective involuntary "Oh!" and burst into applause.

Buoyed by their response, I launched into my carefully planned first day. I told them I was from America and hung up a map on the blackboard, pointing to my hometown. I told them about my family and passed around a large family photograph. My audience was rapt, so curious about this new foreign teacher.

After a brief presentation I paused. "I thought you might want to know a little more about me," I said.

"Yes!" they answered enthusiastically.

Chinese students are notoriously shy, so I divided them into groups of three or four students with the task of coming up with questions in English to ask me. After about five minutes, we launched into question-and-answer time.

A girl raised her hand. "One of your children looks like a Chinese girl."

I had expected this. But I still felt unprepared. Would they be angry with me for taking away one of their children? Would they attribute to me some kind of high-minded altruism that I knew I just didn't possess? Would they feel ashamed that another country had stepped in to take care of their orphans?

"Yes," I said to the student. "In fact she is Chinese. She is adopted."

This was followed by murmuring and many more questions. How many countries have you been to? How many languages can you speak? What was your major? Have you climbed Mount Tai? Can you sing us some popular American songs? Why have you come to China?

I paused to collect my thoughts before answering the last question.

"Well, why not come to China? You are a great country. You have five thousand years of civilization."

They nodded in agreement.

"You know that we have a Chinese daughter. We thought that some-day she would want to return to the country of her birth. Wouldn't it be a pity if she returned to China, but couldn't understand the language and couldn't appreciate the culture?"

"But why did you come to Tai'an and not a big, developed city like Beijing or Shanghai?" asked the students.

"Well, we came to China with an organization, and they assigned us a city and a university. But the other cities they send teachers to are large and cosmopolitan. We wanted to experience the real China. We think this is the real China. What do you think?"

They agreed.

"Besides, Shandong people are famous for being friendly and warm-hearted." They nodded their heads and smiled.

We had time for one more question and a tall, lanky student raised his hand. "You are American. You have freedom and liberty. We Chinese have traditions and history. What will you do about this gap?"

To tell the truth, I had no idea. But the more I thought about it, I knew the student was right. If I wanted to truly understand China, if I hoped to give my daughter back something of that fascinating culture she had left behind, I had to make up for these differences. It was this gap, between my young nation and their ancient civilization, between my American mind-set fixated on freedom and the Chinese mind-set tied to centuries of traditions and customs, between my American individualism and their love of collective harmony, it was this gap, with all its inherent tensions, that I needed to bridge.

Chapter 2

HOME

❀

I FELL IN LOVE WITH CHINA THROUGH ITS LANGUAGE.
And my love affair with the Chinese language began with one word. Home.
My friend Wenxin wrote "home" on the blackboard:

HOME

"In this character you can see a roof"—here he pointed to the top of the character: ⼧ —"over the classical Chinese character for pig," he said, indicating the portion below the roof: 豕.

"In ancient China," he continued, "the life of man and his swine were so bound up together that the pigs just wandered through the house. You can see this history and culture reflected in the character for 'home'—a pig with a roof over it."

I was astounded. What I had thought were mere strokes and dashes suddenly came alive on the page. These characters were a porthole through which I had a direct view into the China of more than three thousand years ago.

It was the year 2000, and Wenxin (pronounced Wun-sheen) and I were classmates in the beginning Japanese class at Waseda University in Tokyo. The army had sent Chris to Camp Zama, a small base just outside of Tokyo. Our boys were in high school and our three younger ones hadn't yet been born. Since my days were free, I took this chance, my first opportunity to learn firsthand about Asia, to jump into the culture. I studied Japanese every morning in a class of eight students. There was Bettina from Germany, François from France, and, in addition to Wenxin, four other students from China. I was the only American.

For the Europeans and me, this was our first experience in Asia. For the Chinese, with the exception of Garlum from Hong Kong, this was their first time out of China, their first airplane ride, their first real contact with Japan or the West. Amazingly and wonderfully, the eight of us formed a tight bond. During the course of the year, over miso soup lunches, at kabuki plays, or during dorm parties where we made dumplings and cheesecake, we talked about East and West, about Mao and missing chads in presidential elections.

On our first day of class, Wenxin told me he had recently graduated from a university in Xi'an (pronounced Shee-ahn).

"Where is Xi'an?" I asked him.

"It's the city famous for the Terra Cotta Warriors," he told me. I was embarrassed to admit that I had never heard of the Terra Cotta Warriors, which were excavated from the tomb of China's first emperor.

Wenxin pulled out his notebook and drew a cartoonish map of China, looking as it does like a rooster.

"Here is Beijing," he said, "My city, Xi'an, is also in the north of China, but west of Beijing."

But I hardly heard him. I was focused on the last item he had drawn: a small oval off the rooster's breast, signifying Taiwan. I drew in my breath, sure that he was making a deliberate political statement.

Later, at the end of our year of study together, I asked him about this.

He laughed. "It was just reflex," he told me.

Wednesday afternoons we had kanji class, kanji being the Japanese word for the Chinese characters, which the Japanese had borrowed from China centuries before, when Japan had no written language. This class was essential for Bettina, François, and me; for our Chinese classmates, it was like a return to kindergarten. They sat patiently while we tediously wrote out the characters stroke by stroke, learning to write each line at the correct angle and each dash with appropriate flourish.

It was during one of those Wednesday afternoons that I learned the character for "home," and began a journey of discovery about the ancient culture of China that I could see reflected so succinctly in these tight bundles of dashes and strokes. As the weeks passed we learned more characters. Wenxin and my other Chinese friends continued to supply commentary and explanation.

"Imagine you are looking at a horse cart from a bird's-eye view," Wenxin said, pointing to the character for "car." "See the wheels on each side?"

CAR
(traditional)

Other characters were so vivid they required no explanation. We could feel the drizzle in the character for "rain," and see the farmers laboring for centuries in the terraced rice fields shown in the character now simply meaning "field."

RAIN

田

FIELD

"Cowry shells were used as currency in ancient China," another classmate told me, giving the character for "shellfish," 貝, added meaning. "That's why many characters having to do with money have the character for shellfish as one of their components. She wrote other characters on the board: "to buy" 買, "to sell" 賣, and "expensive" 貴.

I was hooked from that moment on. What other language could give such insight into culture and history? Certainly not the phonetic ones I had previously studied.

As my passion for all things Chinese continued to grow, my interest in Japanese began to fade. I realized that the aspects I found most interesting about Japanese culture actually came from China, "the Middle Kingdom," as I learned its name meant when expressed in characters:

MIDDLE

KINGDOM

CHINA

"The Country at the Center of the World." History told China that its rightful place was as the heart and hub, never subservient or on the periphery. This idea has been part of the Chinese mind-set for centuries, particularly during the Tang Dynasty (AD 618–907) when Central Asians came along the Silk Road seeking trade, kings from as far-flung places as Kashmir and Nepal came paying tribute, and Japanese and Koreans came to study. When the students returned home, they brought the Chinese characters with them, which is why I was learning Chinese characters in Tokyo. But I soon grew frustrated studying them once removed; I longed to go to the source.

❁

Five years later, Chris called me from Baghdad.

"It's time for me to retire from the army," he said. "I'm tired of being away from you and the kids. If I stay in the army, I'll just get sent back here again. You've followed me around the world. You've done everything in support of my career. I've had a great twenty-six years in the army and it's your turn now. We'll move where you want to move and do what you want to do."

It was quite an offer. That summer we would celebrate our tenth anniversary. In our first five years of married life we had moved five times, crossing two oceans to live on three continents. In the second five years Chris deployed twice to war zones. All my dreams, hopes, and ambitions (of which I have plenty), for the past ten years, had been necessarily suppressed under the banner of "duty, honor, country." But now, suddenly, the restrictions were gone and the world abounded with choices.

"We've talked about moving to China someday," I told him. "Maybe someday is now."

"I know this is your dream. But how would we support ourselves?" he asked. My husband was the practical one.

"We could teach English. I've heard that if you have a master's degree, you can teach at a university in China. Besides, I've taught English in Germany and Japan. I have experience."

"Well, the children are still in preschool, they are young enough to adapt," he admitted.

"Not just adapt," I added. "They are at the perfect age to learn the language and the culture."

"You're right," he said. "It would be a great experience for them. Completely expand their worldview. But could we really just up and move to China?"

"With you retiring from the army, we'd be going through a major life transition anyway," I said.

"That's true. And if we wait, we'll soon be settled into another career, into another community."

"If we're going to do this, it has to be now."

I began researching our options. Chris and I discussed as much as we could during the ten-minute phone conversations we were allowed. I sent him websites to check out, and he e-mailed me back his opinions. We found there were organizations that sent American teachers to China, and I fired off several e-mails. They came back with quick responses: we don't accept families, or, it would be too difficult with three young children. Others didn't respond at all. We found one organization that was supportive of sending families to China, but they were Mennonite and we were disqualified because of Chris's army career. Others required that we raise a substantial amount of financial support. I despaired that we would ever get to China.

I remembered that my high school biology teacher had spent several years teaching in China after his retirement, so I called him. He and his wife listened to my ideas and answered my questions. They told me about Educational Resources & Referrals—China (ERRC), a small organization headed by a Chinese-American woman named Martha Chan.

I called Martha and she honestly laid out the difficulties. University apartments in China were small, too small for a family with three children. Not only that, but many universities would not be willing to take on a family, concerned about the potential complications. Medical care outside of the larger cities was substandard. But all of that notwithstanding, she was willing to take us on.

That spring she began looking for a placement for us. One university after another turned us down. She finally found a well-known teacher training university in Guangzhou, southern China, which promised a three-bedroom apartment if Chris and I both taught there. We happily accepted. We bought Cantonese-learning tapes, prepared for life in a subtropical climate, and imagined spending weekends in nearby Hong Kong. Chris processed his retirement from the army. We put all of our household goods into storage and began driving across the country from Fort Stewart, Georgia, to my hometown in Washington State, saying good-bye to friends and family along the way.

As we drove through Illinois, Martha called. The university in Guangzhou had fallen through. They only had one teaching opening, and without both of us teaching there, we couldn't live in the family apartment. It was now June and we were scheduled to go to China in August. We had no house, no job, no alternate plan. We did the only thing we could do: get back on the road.

In Wyoming Martha called again. She had found another university. This one was in a smaller city, and not so prestigious. It could offer only a two-bedroom apartment, but was willing to accept our family. I hastily scribbled down the information as Chris drove down the freeway: Taishan Medical College, in the city of Tai'an, Shandong province. It was about midway between Beijing and Shanghai, Martha told us.

"So much for the subtropics," Chris said. "I guess we should have thought twice before putting all our winter clothes in storage."

I didn't care. We were going to China.

Although the first day had been unsettling, Chris and I were still thrilled our children had this chance to attend kindergarten in China. Chris had been a linguist in the army. He could, in varying levels of proficiency, speak Farsi, Dari, German, Japanese, and Spanish. I was a language enthusiast as well, though not nearly as gifted. But I knew the advantages for children of being immersed in a foreign language at a young age.

But Chinese wasn't just a foreign language. It was Grace's birth language. And language is perhaps the greatest portion of our identity, an indelible imprint upon the brain, the medium we use to compose our ideas and formulate our thoughts. Loving words from parents, exhortations from teachers, letters from pen pals, chats with friends—all are sent in a certain language. We were determined that if nothing else, Grace would be able to speak her birth language, allowing her to understand her birth culture authentically—without translation.

But we didn't take one child to China, we took three. Grace's adoption gave a Chinese heritage to our whole family, and this journey was one our family would take together. And that's where the Chinese language came in again. Unlike Grace, Katherine and Andrew were not born in China, and don't remotely resemble Chinese. We hoped that just as Grace's adoption into our family gave her an American identity, that common facility in language would spread her Chinese heritage over all three children—giving them not only a shared form of communication, but a shared identity.

The local Chinese kindergarten presented our children with many adjustments. Mornings began with synchronized morning exercises; lunch was steamed bread and tofu soup; and for those bathroom times, they soon became comfortable with the raised coed trough. But there was an even more fundamental change: their names. In the kindergarten, our children were known by their Chinese names.

Grace was naturally the first one in the family to have a Chinese name. When we adopted her, she was called Fu Zhi Chun, the name given to her by the orphanage in Fuzhou city of Jiangxi (pronounced Jyong-shee) province. Fu was the family name given to all the children of Grace's orphanage. I'm not sure why they picked this character, for it's not a traditional Chinese family name. But perhaps they chose it not only to give these babies their best wishes (this character carries the meaning "blessing" or "happiness"), but also to remind them of their hometown in China. Fu (pronounced Foo) sounds like the first syllable in Fuzhou, although the characters are written differently. Grace was born in February around the time of Spring Festival, and her given name Zhi Chun (pronounced Juh Chwen) means "to know that spring is coming."

When we took Grace to America, she became an Arrington, just like us. So when we went back to China, we all adopted her original surname, Fu. In China, the order of names is reversed. The family name is said first; the individual name, last. Perhaps it's a metaphor, since one should think of one's family before oneself.

Katherine, our oldest daughter, had attended a Chinese school on Saturdays in Savannah, Georgia, and we had asked her teacher to give her a Chinese name. Since Grace's name had to do with the season of spring, we decided to continue this theme for her siblings. Katherine's November birthday gave the inspiration for Rui Xue (pronounced Rwee Shway), meaning "the first blanket of snow in winter," as yet untrodden—pure, clean, and white. When we added the Fu for our family name, her complete name became Fu Rui Xue.

That left us with Andrew, our red-haired boy. I e-mailed Wenxin asking for advice.

"How about Fu Qiu Hua (pronounced Foo Choh Hwah)," Wenxin suggested. "*Qiu* means "autumn," and *Hua* means "blooming" or "brilliant.""

"I like that," Chris said. "I like the double meaning. Brilliant in color and brilliant in mind. That's my boy."

And his name was in keeping with the pattern. Now all of our children's names reflected the seasons of their birth.

On days Chris and I didn't have classes, we would drop the kids off at their kindergarten, then spend the day exploring our new town. Tai'an is a medium-sized city in the heart of largely rural and conservative Shandong province. Perhaps its most striking (and endearing) feature, other than its sacred mountain, is its very ordinariness. Farmers arrive at daybreak with a load of melons to sell on the street; locals do most of their shopping in the early morning hours, haggling with street vendors over freshly caught fish or various cuts of pork, cabbage heads or tree fungus, tofu squares or pickled eggs. Donkey carts share the road with shiny black Volvos. Most people still shop at corner grocery stores or open-air markets. Mao amulets swing from the rearview windows of taxis, and posters of Mao hang in the homes of grandparents, who care for the children as the parents go off to work to support the generations above and below.

Modernization began to make its way to Tai'an in the 1970s. But it came in an unkind way, bringing nondescript, rectangular apartment blocks that demonstrated China's former fondness for Soviet-style architecture, along with coal smokestacks bellowing smoke, dust, and grime. But if you peered down certain packed-dirt alleys or rode past an old neighborhood, you could still see the old Tai'an: circular doorways opening into traditional courtyard homes, small shacks with sagging tile roofs, cracked concrete walls exposing the original bricks, stones, and tiles. Although modern thinking was creeping in inevitably as the city developed, most people in Tai'an had been peasants only a generation ago.

We walked along the streets near our campus, finding one alley that contained nothing but stalls selling fruit and vegetables. Another dark entry just across the street from the campus sold *shaobing*, flat round biscuits, fresh out of the black iron oven, delicious, and only costing three mao (each mao worth a dime). We also discovered an open-air market within walking distance, with chickens in cages, clothing, and vegetables. We began to get an idea of what a fair price was—and when we were being cheated.

We ventured out to eat in restaurants, usually guessing at menus we could not comprehend. If we ordered chicken, which we thought was a safe choice, it arrived in a stew of its own juices, an entire chicken hacked to pieces, bones and all, with the head adorned on top like a maraschino cherry. Chicken was also never complete without that delicacy, the feet, usually prominently accompanying the head with one foot poking out at its right hand and the other at its left. The fish, with staring eyes and tingly tail, looked like it had swum right from the ocean and leaped onto our platter, making only a momentary pit stop in a hot oiled wok to pick up some spices and marinade. Pork and tofu were universal staples, it seemed, arriving with nearly every entree.

We found our town's McDonald's. Tai'an scored a "3" on the

McDonald's/KFC globalization index: one McDonald's and two KFCs. From McDonald's second-floor window we ate Big Macs and double cheeseburgers and watched the steady current of cars, buses, scooters, motorcycles, and donkey carts.

From some American students in town we learned how to purchase a bus pass. From then on, instead of jamming one-yuan notes into the collection box at boarding, we relished flashing our bus pass, a trapping of legitimacy that let everyone already boarded—who were certainly staring at us—know that we belonged. That pass was like a badge of courage; with it we began to take the bus boldly around town. When there was a line to get on the bus, we found we needed to be a little aggressive to keep our place. We also realized our allowance of personal space had greatly shrunk.

We found department stores we liked, and learned that if the price discount was marked as an "8," it actually meant 20 percent off. We discovered a bigger supermarket, similar to a Walmart in its layout, a short bus ride away. We went up and down the aisles, aware that our fellow shoppers were staring curiously at the contents of our shopping cart. Not only did this store have butter, which we had been doing without, but it also sold something similar to Kraft cheese slices. Our favorite comfort food then became a grilled cheese sandwich (fried in a wok, of course), both sides liberally slathered with butter, fried golden brown, and served with hot and sour soup. We had it so often Chris dubbed it Menu Option A.

In our apartment, we had to learn to live as five people in a very small space. We wedged the small kitchen table between the wall and the easy chair, at least allowing the three children to sit at the table. In their room, the girls each slept on a twin bed with Andrew sleeping on the floor at the foot of Katherine's bed. We tripped over one another in the narrow, tunnel-like kitchen, and our backs ached from bending over the low sink to wash dishes. To have hot water for dishwashing, we carried a basin into the bathroom and filled it using the showerhead. We got in the habit of putting on shoes before using the bathroom, as the floor was often wet from morning showers.

We found that peanut oil worked just as well as olive oil, and soon hardly noticed the nutty aroma it lent to all our food. But we decided that rice noodles were a poor substitute for the pasta we were used to. I experimented with various dishes at home: chicken and broccoli over rice, stir-fried rice, dumplings over rice.

Gradually, we pieced our lives together again, and began to feel that this place was our home. But I wondered about the homes of the Chinese around us. Of course an ordinary Chinese home no longer contained a pig, but what did it contain? I wondered about the routines of the household and the structure of relationships, for the home is the fount of culture, where cultural upbringing begins.

As a foreigner, I could explore streets and shops, I could ride in trains and taxis, and I could even work and go to school; but the home was an inner sanctuary, a place I could not go without invitation. Yet my knowledge of this culture would be hopelessly incomplete should I never find a way in.

Chapter 3

教书
TEACH

Everyone has the same correct answer.
—my student Christina

❀

"SOMETHING STRANGE HAPPENED THIS MORNING," CHRIS SAID TO ME. We were having lunch in Iwakuni, Japan, and the date was August 8, 2002—easy to remember because it was Chris's birthday. Chris, nine-month-old Katherine, and I had taken the bullet train down to southern Japan from our home near Tokyo for a few days' vacation.

"I was watching Katherine sleep while you took a shower. Suddenly, a thought popped into my head: 'We should adopt a sister for her from China.'"

I felt a flash of electricity go up my spine. I dropped my chopsticks into my ramen and looked right at him. "Yes, that's exactly what we should do."

In that one split second, I had never been more sure of anything. It was like the scales fell from my eyes and suddenly I saw that my whole life had prepared me to do just this. Three of my cousins are adopted, one of whom I am particularly close to—the matron of honor at our wedding. Another was adopted from Korea. I had recently completed my year of Japanese study with my Chinese classmates, whom I now counted among my close friends. I had grown to admire Chinese culture, and during my visit to China had even purchased paintings of Chinese children for the nursery.

Chris and I knew nothing about adoption. Even though Katherine had been conceived on a round of fertility drugs, we had never considered adoption. After all, we had our boys, and we were satisfied parenting them. Would we be allowed to adopt? We already had children, we lived in Japan,

Chris was in the military, and we didn't have a lot of money. All seemed grounds for disqualification.

For the rest of our vacation I thought about adopting. When we returned home I obsessively occupied the computer, searching for information about adoption from China. I learned that there were thousands of baby girls in China's orphanages. I learned that China was the biggest source country for U.S. adoptions. And I learned that we were qualified to adopt. On August 31, we began the paperwork.

Along Ying Sheng Road we became a daily spectacle: one or two parents herding three children to and from the kindergarten. On the way to school we often saw grown women squatting in the dirt along our street relieving themselves and countless children wearing split pants peeing onto the trees; no one raised an eyebrow, even when stray urine got on their clothes or hands.

Dust turned our air into a brown haze; the poor air quality often made our famous mountain seem but a dim silhouette. Some days just walking the children to school meant a change in clothing right afterward. At times, due to the pollution, we rode into the main gate of the new campus unable to see the library directly ahead of us.

The omnipresent flies and bugs were regular guests at restaurants, attracted by the smells. Garbage was thrown onto the street. Bare cement floors were considered adequate for homes and guests. Even businesses seemed primitive. The driving on the streets seemed to have no rules. Overcrowding was the expected norm at any public venue, from church to bus to train.

Yet at the same time, life here had a vitality that seemed inversely proportionate to this lack of cleanliness and sophistication. I had noticed this phenomenon in Europe. Northern Europe was clean, but also sterile; no one seemed allowed to step outside of his ordered, circumscribed box. Southern Europe was less clean and more chaotic, yet also more open. Japan was much cleaner and more refined than China. Yet, in Japan no one seemed to look our way or bother with us.

In China people were always talking to me on the street, from students to passersby to street cleaners. Because they seemed unconcerned about the language barrier, I felt less apprehensive as well. I quickly learned how to say "adopted," "three children," and "no, she's not one of your Chinese, she's our daughter and she's Chinese-American." People often touched and stroked the children, commenting on their appearance or their hair. I sensed no barriers separating people one from another. Closeness, even intimacy, felt dynamic and life-giving and perfectly natural. I felt my connection with society as I went about my business, talking with teachers, purchasing food on the street, waving to the retired folk. I felt alive! I would take this connectedness over a more "civilized" world any day.

But while I delighted in my newfound connection with those around me, Chris was having the opposite reaction.

"Take a picture, it'll last longer!" he would mutter to whoever was staring as we walked down the street.

The previous week he was taking the trash out on his way to work when the bag, made of plastic so thin it was nearly sheer, burst open, spilling coffee grounds, aluminum cans, used milk cartons, and a dirty diaper onto the floor.

"More made-in-China crap," he grumbled as he walked out the door, leaving me with the mess to clean up. My temper surged within me but I bit back my sore words and, clenching my teeth, swept up the floor.

Besides these little frustrations, the dust and pollution were constantly bothering his sinuses, and he frequently had to occupy the bathroom for lengthy periods due to gastrointestinal upset. It was easy to blame the problem on unclean Chinese cooking practices. As the weeks went on, Chris found more things to blame China for: unexpected power outages, pushy crowds, and putrid garbage heaped everywhere, among others.

Initially I was nervous about our girls getting used to the bathroom situation in China. Katherine had shown some skittishness using outhouses at county fairs in the United States and I knew this would be a big thing to get used to. It started already in the airport in Beijing. There were only "squatties," porcelain holes in the bathroom stalls. My girls refused to use them.

But my concerns abated quickly. This was one cultural difference they easily got used to. In fact, they became too comfortable. Our kids soon felt completely normal squatting anywhere and everywhere. I came to accept the expediency of this procedure, but Chris wasn't thrilled. "What is Grandma going to say at home this summer when your daughters do that while walking down Front Street?" he asked.

The kids may have adjusted quickly to new bathroom rules, but other things took much longer, particularly Katherine's adjustment to full immersion in Chinese kindergarten. Andrew and Grace, then both three years old, were young enough to avoid a full, head-on collision with culture shock. Our youngest, Andrew, had always focused on the written word. He began learning the Chinese language not only with enthusiasm, but with outright glee. He often asked us how to say something in Chinese, and once told that particular word it became entrenched in his vocabulary—tone and all. Grace was able to charm everyone with her smile and the playful gleam in her eye. She was often the focus of curious questions, but thankfully was oblivious to it. Grace communicates physically—with her smiles and eyes, with running and jumping, with skipping and laughing. She seemed unaware that she spoke a different language. And since Grace had never turned down food of any sort, the change in diet caused no problem for her.

Our oldest, Katherine, on the other hand, had always had precocious powers of perception and analysis. At nearly five, she was fully aware of her position as the lone English speaker in a class of over thirty students. When I asked if she had made any friends she replied, "Mom, I can't make any friends here. They speak Chinese and I speak English." Katherine was more inclined to inform others of her opinions and observations than to listen to what others had to say. She was a raconteur whose voice had been taken away. And since she was not much for listening, her progress in picking up the language was quite slow. She was old enough to be tremendously affected, yet too young to have developed the needed coping skills.

Observing her in the classroom, we found she would tune out completely and retreat into her own private world, an impenetrable bubble. We listened to the deafening noise as her class of preschoolers faced the teacher and recited in unison at the top of their voices. Katherine had her head down, concentrating on something she was doodling, appearing to not even hear them. Retreating within at school meant acting out at home; we had to contend with tantrums, willfulness, neediness. We were glad we had purchased a homeschooling curriculum with a heavy emphasis on reading out loud. It helped to spend each evening listening to stories, with our younger ones curled up and Katherine's head on my shoulder.

❁

Our children were getting used to their new life as American children taught by Chinese teachers. Chris and I had a parallel new life: as American teachers instructing Chinese students. For our entire family, life was centered in the classroom.

I enjoyed teaching from the first day. In my two previous trips to China I rarely had contact with the Chinese people themselves. Apart from tour guides, all of whom seemed well versed in the official line, I was mostly among other Western tourists as I was shuttled from one major tourist attraction to another. But teaching put me in front of dozens of eager and expectant faces every class. I got to face the real China every time I went to work.

I found my students fascinating. They were mostly young women, as women formed the preponderance of English majors. Most were not only from Shandong province, but also had never traveled outside of Shandong province. The majority came from the small villages that were so common in our largely agricultural province. While I thought they would be only children, in fact this was not so. Most had at least one if not two or three siblings. They told me the one-child policy was enforced more laxly, as well as unevenly, in the countryside. The head of one village might look the other way if the policy was violated; another might charge a fine, such as 1,000 yuan (about $125); a third might tear down their house.

They had been raised at least partly by grandparents, or their grandparents had lived nearby. One student told me her house did not feel right without her grandmother. Our students knew they too would care for their parents. This knowledge gave them a serious quality I have never observed in students from the West. The sense of responsibility gave them confidence, yet at times also weighed them down. They spoke with gratitude of the sacrifices their parents had made for them; they did not feel they had a right or claim to it. Invariably, they had parents who pushed and encouraged them to get this far in their education, and sacrificed so they could do so.

My students loved their country. They talked about their devotion to their "motherland" and declared that they must develop themselves now so that they could better serve China.

I noticed immediately in my classes that if I referred to a certain cultural or historical figure, either the entire class knew the person, or none of them knew.

"Richard Nixon?" —Everyone nodded and smiled.

"Abraham Lincoln?" —"Of course. He is famous for the war between the South and the North."

"Martin Luther King Jr.?" —"I have a dream!"

"Jimmy Carter?" —Blank looks.

"Sigmund Freud?" —Quizzical expressions.

"Sting?" —"Who is that?"

There was a body of common knowledge, the bounds of which were determined by the college entrance examination—the once-per-year examination that determined which university they would be allowed to attend, if any at all. That which was on the exam, whether useful or not, was read, recited, tested, memorized, regurgitated; all other knowledge, completely ignored. I often heard my students say: "As everyone knows . . . and then follow it with a statement such as ". . . the invasion of China by Japan was an aggressive nation invading a peaceful one"; or "As we all know, since joining the WTO English has become important for China's development . . ." This was no hyperbole on their part. Either everyone knew, or nobody knew. Rarely was the knowledge unevenly spread.

The vehicle for learning this testable knowledge was the textbook. As there was one test for all, there was necessarily also one textbook for all. This meant there was only one version of history. I had heard about textbook controversies in Asia; in particular, that China was upset about the particular wording of Japanese textbooks relating to the Japanese invasion and occupation of China in the 1930s. At the time I couldn't understand why the wording of one textbook was causing such an uproar. Now I understood: it was because there was only one textbook. In such exam-based societies as Japan, South Korea, and China, the textbook is powerful, as are its authors. The textbook contains the Truth for a generation, and it is understandable that people will fight for the right to decide what the Truth is.

In fact, the Truth is a political matter. Tiananmen Square is scantly mentioned in Chinese history textbooks. Susan Shirk, in her book *China: Fragile Superpower*, reported that during a textbook revision in 2001, reflecting China's changing foreign policy priorities, the language regarding the United States softened. But that same revision made Japanese atrocities from the occupation of Manchuria to the atrocities in Nanjing even more vivid, replacing dry descriptions with poignant phrasing and pages of gruesome photos.

"The textbook is like the Bible," Chris wryly observed. "Challenging the textbook is like saying you don't believe the infallibility of Scripture."

We would chuckle at this. But after reflection, it no longer seemed a joke. There are no scriptures, per se, for the Chinese people. Mao's little red book might have fulfilled this function during the Cultural Revolution, but no more. *The Analects of Confucius* perhaps, but unlike the Buddha, Confucius had remained a mortal man, and his writing at various times fell in and out of fashion. Although Buddhism and Daoism and even Christianity had quite a number of adherents, in fact, there was no religion that had achieved national status in China, and thus no sacred text to define Truth for the Chinese. So for our students, Truth was defined by the textbook.

I had heard before I arrived that Chinese students memorized their textbooks. I thought it was an exaggeration. It was not. Every morning when I left for the school bus I saw the students, textbook in hand, reading out loud to memorize the text.

The textbook was the sun, moon, and stars; teachers, lectures, and any other sources of knowledge were only accessories to help one gain the knowledge in the textbook. This was reflected in the Chinese language. The Chinese verb "to teach," 教, is made up of two parts called radicals. The radical on the right side, 攵, is believed to be a picture of two hands holding a stick. (Interestingly, this same radical is also on the right side of the character for government: 政.)

教
TEACH

政
GOVERNMENT

But what I found even more interesting than the embedded idea of corporal punishment was that this verb, "to teach," is often accompanied by the object "books." So in a sentence, if a teacher is asked about his work, he would say, *wo jiao shu*, 我教书, "I teach books."

I asked for a parent-teacher conference at the kindergarten to assess the children's progress, with Sally from the university's foreign affairs office to translate. Grace and Andrew's teachers had no issues to bring up; they thought the transition was going well. Grace, in particular, had picked up the language with amazing speed.

"Mom, I can speak a lot of Chinese, right?" Grace ended the majority of her sentences with "right?"

"You do. You speak a lot of Chinese."

"Better than Katherine and Andrew, right?"

It was true. The Chinese had begun to flow from her mouth much faster than we had expected and more rapidly than her siblings, a point of pride for Grace. We had adopted her ten days before her first birthday, before she was talking at all. Nevertheless, it seemed for her that Chinese-language study had not begun; rather, it had been reawakened.

Katherine's transition, both linguistic and otherwise, was not proceeding as smoothly. My research about the benefits of second-language acquisition at a young age and my own high-minded ideals about how it would help bind the two cultures of our family together ran directly into my headstrong four-year-old daughter who had no intention of cooperating. It just wasn't happening. As her teacher kept repeating in the conference, Katherine had "her own ideas, her own ideas."

The principal of the kindergarten suggested that when I pick Kather-

ine up I come early, stay in her class, and model how I wanted her to inter-
act. And so I became completely absorbed in the Chinese education system.
Mornings I taught in the university, the top tier of China's education system; afternoons I sat in a small orange chair in kindergarten. I usually
stayed for about an hour, observing the class, helping Katherine color, being
friendly to all her classmates, just making her feel more comfortable with
my presence. Her classmates quickly became used to my afternoon arrival;
they would scoot over to make room for me at the table, and greet me with
ayi, hao (hello auntie). I would return the greeting, saying *ni hao* (hello) to
her classmates. When we left, I did as the other children did, saying *laoshi,
zaijian* (good-bye, teacher), and would expect Katherine to do the same.

Despite all this effort, more mornings than not she collapsed into tears
when we dropped her off. And as we walked home in the afternoon she
talked about our old home in Georgia, and all that she had left behind: a
spacious and comfortable home, her toys and her backyard, her cousins
and friends. We had read about the culture shock process and its different
phases. But with Katherine the entire process was exaggerated as she had
to acclimate to a new culture without the benefit of much life experience.
Precocious personality and indomitable will notwithstanding, she was still
just a child. I wondered if I was expecting too much. I wondered if we
would fail utterly.

Chapter 4

人口
POPULATION

There are a billion people in China. It's not easy to be an
individual in a crowd of more than a billion people. Think
of it. More than a BILLION people. That means even if
you're a one-in-a-million type of guy, there are still a thousand guys exactly like you.
                              —A. WHITNEY BROWN, *The Big Picture*

❀

SOMETIMES I THINK I SHOULD HAVE SUBTITLED THIS BOOK "A THREE-Child
Family in a One-Child World." Walking down the street in the early days
one of the first Chinese phrases I picked up was *san ge haizi*, meaning "three
children." In fact, it could have been my Chinese name, for when I heard *san
ge haizi* I instinctively turned to the speakers. I knew they meant me.

For us, China's one-child policy was an issue of some emotional im-
port, as Grace would likely not be in our family were it not for this policy.
We knew that the one-child policy, together with poor social security networks and cultural preference for sons, led to the abandonment of thousands of baby girls each year. It was easy to view it as one of the evils of
the Communist Chinese government. But as with many cultural differences,
it was not so simple.

My Oral English textbook had a unit entitled "Is it a Good Idea to Control Population Growth in the World?" In Chinese, population is expressed
人口, literally meaning "people mouths." These two characters are among
the most common and basic of the thousands of Chinese characters.

The first character has two strokes, the second three. They are characters Chinese students learn in kindergarten. But put them together, and
they austerely, yet uniquely, express the challenge China has long faced: a
large population means more mouths to feed.

人

PEOPLE

口

MOUTHS

POPULATION

The textbook had more units than I had classes, so I could pick and choose which units to teach. I decided to skip the population unit. I didn't feel confident I could handle this subject in an impartial way. As the mother of a Chinese child who had been abandoned shortly after birth, I didn't want to come across as critical of Chinese culture, or in any way superior.

Fridays Chris and I both finished our classes at noon, so we began having regular lunch dates, trying out the local cuisine at nearby restaurants. That Friday I stared at my husband across the table from me. Chris's last army haircut had been in May. After twenty-six years of weekly haircuts and daily shaves, Chris forswore any tonsorial equipment applied to his hair or face. By the time we arrived in China in August, he had a full beard and a mop of curly hair. By October, his beard was overgrown and unkempt.

"You look like a mountain man," I told him.

"Perfect. That's exactly the look I'm going for," he replied. "Kind of a cross between Osama bin Laden and Nostradamus."

The problem was that Chris's beard was not trimmed. He refused, out of some warped sense of principle, to shave around the neck or tame the hair crawling up his cheekbones.

"All natural," he said proudly.

Worse, although Chris's hair is a handsome salt-and-pepper gray, his beard grew in reddish above his lip, black in other places, and with long white tendrils extending down his chin.

I hated it.

But I could say nothing, for he derived a perverse pleasure from my displeasure, and only grew more obstinate every time I mentioned it.

Although he wouldn't admit it, it wasn't just about the convenience of not shaving. By becoming a foreign grizzly, he was keeping the new culture at arm's length, making himself unapproachable, distant; it was a mask he wore, covering nearly his entire face, allowing him to retreat within.

For Chris, the initial excitement of living in China had worn off. He was tired of eating rice. He was tired of being stared at. He was tired of the crowds and tired of the pollution. After all, seeing a baby wearing split pants peeing on the sidewalk is cute the first few times; after that, one only notices the smell of urine.

Since China was my passion much more than his, I began to take his displeasure and irritation personally. In fact, this beard felt like a wall keeping me out as well. I tried to look directly into his eyes and find my husband in that hairy ogre. Only in the dark of night, when I could not see him, but could feel his arms around me and hear his familiar voice, did I feel the man I married was still there.

After we ordered our dishes I told Chris my decision not to teach the textbook's unit on population, but he refused to let me off the hook.

"It's a great chance for the students to truly examine this topic," he said. "Perhaps even go beyond the official line they've heard for years."

I had to admit he was right.

"You shouldn't pass up this opportunity," he said.

That made sense, for I had personally added to my job description the task of helping the students learn to think critically, viewing it as almost of equal importance with improving their English ability. Since my students had rarely been exposed to an opposing opinion, whether in history, politics, or even mundane matters, I felt part of my job was to present them with a different viewpoint from the established one, just so they couldn't say, "As everybody knows" one more time. Here would be my first chance.

I started work on a lesson plan. I decided to use several articles from *China Daily*. This way I was politically safe, as *China Daily* was the official government English-language newspaper. I did a search on their website and found about ten articles published in the previous two months relating to the one-child policy. I read each article and constructed five or six discussion questions. The articles were on various aspects of the one-child policy and its ramifications, many of which I had never thought about before. One discussed the economic effects as the only children began to enter the job market, and a smaller workforce had to support a larger number of retired persons. Another looked at the effects on the family when a married couple, both of whom were only children, struggled to support both sets of parents. I read about some nuances to the policy, for example, in Beijing if two only children got married, they could have two children instead of one. There were also articles on how the one-child policy was firmly adhered to in urban areas, but in rural areas, because of less developed social security networks and more traditional thinking, farmers were allowed to have a second try to get a boy if their first child was a girl.

One topic not covered in any newspaper article was the unintended side effect that most of my students seemed completely ignorant of: the abandonment of baby girls.

I reached my classroom, more than a little nervous.

"What do you think is the most famous thing in China to people in the West?" I asked the students. They were always interested in Western perceptions of China.

"The Great Wall," they answered correctly.

"How about the second most famous thing?" I asked.

"The Terra Cotta Warriors."

"No."

"The Forbidden City."

"No."

"Tiananmen Square."

"Close . . . but, no."

Blank looks.

"The second most famous thing about China to the West is the one-child policy."

They smiled and laughed. Glad my introductory humor had gone well, I passed out the articles. After giving them time to discuss the articles in their groups, I had each student pick one of the discussion questions and answer it for the class.

One question was "Is it fair that only children in Beijing can have two children, and others cannot?"

The student wrinkled his brow, then answered, "I don't think it's really a question of fair or not fair. It's about the right policy for the situation. Beijing has maintained a low birth rate for a long time. Now it has the pressure of an aging population."

His answer surprised me. Many of the questions I had written were about fairness. Is it fair that farmers can have two children if their first is a girl? Is it fair that ethnic minorities are allowed two or three children? Is it fair that rich people are not dissuaded by the fines and can easily have more than one child? Questions of fairness came automatically to me. But my students didn't think that way. In their minds what was best for the city, the region, or the country as a whole was the most important question.

Question: "Why are farmers who have a girl as their first child allowed to have a second child?"

Answer: "In traditional Chinese thought, the family line is the most important thing. In a family, the great-grandfather gave birth to the grandfather, the grandfather gave birth to the father, the father to the son. If you have a girl, the family line will stop. It is a dead branch on the family tree. We Chinese have an ancient saying that giving birth to a girl is like pouring out water, you never get it back. This is why the Chinese prefer boys to girls."

I didn't touch this, other than to say that it wasn't proper English to describe men as giving birth.

Question: "In some provinces there is a great gender imbalance, for example, in Jiangxi province the sex ratio is 119 newborn baby boys to 100 baby girls. What are the implications of this imbalance?"

Answer: "Well, basically, young men in Jiangxi province will have a hard time finding wives in the future."

This was the standard answer I had heard or seen in print whenever the gender imbalance was mentioned in the Chinese press, and it infuriated me. "Yes, I know we are all concerned about these poor boys in Jiangxi who may not be able to find a wife, but what about the girls, the missing girls?"

The students looked at me strangely. I went to the board and wrote "119:100" and below it "103:100." I continued: "If left to nature, the sex ratio would be one hundred and three baby boys born for every hundred girls. But in Jiangxi the ratio is one hundred and nineteen boys for every hundred girls. What has happened to these missing girls?"

A girl stood up. "What do you mean, missing girls?"

I took a deep breath. "If the natural birth rate is 103:100, but the actual birth rate is 119:100, then for every hundred girls born, sixteen are missing. It's just the math! Sixteen have not been given life at all. They have either been aborted, or left outside by the side of the road, or something. But they are gone."

Passion was gaining over objectivity, and I was on shaky ground. Because my students had never considered the missing girls, I felt I had to bring it up. Yet doing so meant criticizing their society.

"Okay, enough for that article. Let's move on to the next group," I said quickly.

One of the students to answer was Hope. Chris had dubbed him "the boy named Hope." Thankfully, later in the semester he changed his English name to George. I hadn't taken much notice of Hope until then. As a rule, the few boys in the class always sat together in the back and didn't speak much. Hope chose this question to answer: "If you are an only child, will you choose to move to Beijing and marry another only child just so you can have two children?"

Hope, with simple conviction, stated, "Yes, I will do this."

The class grew quiet. Hope continued. "I am an only child. My parents both worked and were busy with their jobs. I was often home alone, and I was lonely."

This was perhaps the first time Hope had spoken in English in front of such a large audience. He was noticeably uncomfortable, yet his passion propelled him. "When I get married, I want to have two children: a little boy, and a little girl. Then, I can say to my son, you must take care of your little sister and watch over her. And I can say to my daughter, look up to your older brother, and learn from his example. My two children will always have each other to talk to, and they will never be lonely."

The whole class stared at him, amazed by his zeal and eloquence. "I have already told my mother, and she supports this idea. She thinks I should do it too," he added. I never thought of Hope/George in the same way again.

Another question I asked was: "By allowing farmers to have another child if their first is a girl, isn't the government acknowledging that boys are better than girls?"

A female student chose to answer. "No, our government believes that all children are precious. But it's simply compromising their policy with the traditional thought that is still strong in the countryside."

"How does this make you feel?" I asked the class, most of whom were women. "When farmers are allowed to have a second child if their first child is a girl, doesn't this really mean that in the government's eyes, girls are inferior?"

But these questions were raised by my Western mind, by a mind that in childhood grew up hearing of equal rights, the glass ceiling, and the failure of the Equal Rights Amendment. The girls didn't get their dander up, as I was kind of hoping. They simply felt their government and their family viewed everyone as equal, and they understood, without being offended, the traditional Chinese preference for sons. I wondered if their daughters would feel the same.

In our city of Tai'an, the preference for sons was tacitly understood in any conversation, and assumed without a hint of embarrassment. But in the countryside, traditional thinking remained even stronger. The preference for sons had not faded away, as witnessed by the "missing girls."

One female student wrote this to me in a journal entry:

> It is not rare in the countryside of China that the vast majority of people have a preference for boys over girls. So it does not take too much stretch of the imagination to realize that my grandma and grandpa did not like me at all. Worse still, they even decided to abandon me. How could they do that? But it is true. Luckily, that "perfect idea" was rejected by my parents. So, here I am now an independent girl, a mature girl, a girl possessing dreams and hopes.

My second year of teaching I decided to have a spontaneous conversation with students, one-on-one, as their final exam for Oral English class. In previous semesters my students had written and memorized speeches for their final, and this I hoped to avoid. So instead I asked these fifty-five students some questions about their family, hometown, and hopes for the future.

One girl, with the English name of Jessica, shifted uncomfortably when I asked about her family.

"My family is unlike the families of my classmates," she said. "I was raised by my grandparents because my parents had three daughters."

I looked at her questioningly. "But why were you raised by your grandparents?"

"Well, you know about the one-child policy. I guess my father was embarrassed to have three children in his house. So one of us had to go live somewhere else."

"Are you the youngest?"

"No, I'm the middle child."

"But why were you the one to go?"

"I'm not sure," she replied. "I've never asked them. I don't know why it was me."

"How about this summer?" I asked. "Will you live with your parents?"

"No, my grandparents. That is my home. I don't feel comfortable in my parents' home. I just don't feel like I belong there."

She thought for a moment. "Perhaps this summer I will buy my mother a present and try harder to have a relationship with her."

That evening I told Chris about Jessica's story.

"If they had to send a child away, why did they send the middle child, and not the youngest one?" I asked him. It seemed the birth of the youngest was what turned the tolerable two into an unacceptable three.

The following week I had oral finals for the second half of the class. Crystal, a shy girl who usually had her hair pulled back in an awkward ponytail, gave me the answer I was seeking. When I asked her about her family, she gave me the formulaic response I was used to:

"My family has four persons: my father, my mother, my younger brother, and me."

We continued to discuss her family for a few minutes. She told me about the wheat and corn her parents grew on their small piece of land, and stated that her brother was a student. Then she mentioned her sister.

"But wait, you never mentioned a sister," I said.

"Well, actually, I also have a sister. She is one year younger than me. In the countryside you can have two children if the first is a girl. But my parents wanted to have a boy, so they sent her to live with another family."

I immediately remembered Jessica, and the pain this situation had caused her. "But what about your sister?" I asked. "Was she happy growing up with this family?"

"Oh yes," she said. "This family is related to our family. She told me she loves her parents very much. They would often bring her to my house to play with me."

But then she thought a little bit. "But I think my parents have regret over this. A few days ago my sister found out she failed the college entrance exam. When my father called to tell me, he was drunk. I think he feels a lot of regret."

Jessica and Crystal stayed on my mind for several days. I wondered how many others had stories like theirs. Or how many had other stories, stories they would never share, stories never talked about in their family. But stories everyone knew.

Later that week I told these two stories to our babysitter Hong, a recent graduate of the local agricultural university whose hometown was in Hunan province. She nodded her head throughout. When I finished, she told me her story:

"When I was a little girl—I still have vivid memory of this—my grandmother always told my mother she should send my little sister away. You see, I was the oldest, then two more girls, finally the fourth one was a boy.

"But then my mother got pregnant with twins, one girl and one boy. It was hard to feed a family of six children, so my grandmother always nagged my mother to send my youngest sister away. One morning, I woke up and my sister was gone. I starting screaming and crying; in fact, I refused to calm down. My mother could not control me. Finally, she went to the village and got my sister back."

At this point, Hong pulled some family photos out of her purse— baby pictures of the twins, and more current pictures showing a beautiful sixteen-year-old girl with a striking resemblance to Hong. "This is her, this is the one my grandmother wanted to send away," she said.

I was dismayed. It seemed it was the women themselves, especially the headstrong grandmothers, who perpetrated the preference for sons. Chinese society would never shed its gender inequality if the women themselves held on to such traditions.

❀

One day in my office we discussed the recent news reports that the family of Confucius had decided to add female descendants to its family tree. This was significant, for Confucian thought was often blamed for China's traditional view of women. Although mostly women showed up at my office, one male student, Lucas, came faithfully. He was a serious and articulate student hailing from a small village in northwest Shandong. His surname was Li, the same surname of most of the people in his village.

"In my village, the family tree is also important. Every year it is updated for Spring Festival, and we go to a special shrine to honor our ancestors."

"Are women on the Li family tree?" I asked.

"Yes, they are there. Next to the husband's name, the wife's name is put in parentheses." He then drew on a piece of paper how it might look.

"Okay," I said. "Now suppose this husband and wife have two sons and one daughter. How does this appear on the family tree?"

Lucas took out his pencil and wrote the two sons under the husband and the wife. "They will be shown like this."

"But what about their daughter?" asked one of the female students, a city girl. "Isn't she on the family tree?"

"Yes, she's on the family tree. But she goes on a different family tree. The family she marries into."

"Ah," said the female student, "But she doesn't go on the Li family tree. Because she's not really part of the family."

I was reminded of a scene in Amy Tan's novel *The Joy Luck Club*. The parents of a two-year-old girl, Lindo, complete the arrangements for her marriage to the son of the Huang family. Lindo, now an adult and a mother herself, narrates her story:

> Because I was promised to the Huangs' son for marriage, my own family began treating me as if I belonged to somebody else. My mother would say to me when the rice bowl went up to my face too many times, "Look how much Huang Taitai's daughter can eat." My mother did not treat me this way because she didn't love me. She would say this biting back her tongue, so she wouldn't wish for something that was no longer hers.

❁

After all the students had read their articles and answered their questions, we had a general discussion about the one-child policy. Many students were highly in favor. They had been repeatedly taught that China's vast number of people was a drain on a country not only trying to develop, but also hoping to regain the prestige it once had. A country couldn't develop if it used all its resources simply feeding all the mouths.

But the population problem affected them personally as well. They had been competing with China's masses for almost as long as they could remember for slots at the best middle school, the best high school, and finally for the opportunity to attend university. Now, as they realized that in the next few years they would enter the job market, where the unemployment rate for new college graduates hovered at around 30 percent, they still felt the population pressure. I overheard some students once: "If only China didn't have such a large population, then all our dreams could come true." With this mind-set, reducing the population, even by coercive measures, was something they understood. They applauded their government.

Others felt differently. "Every coin has two sides," they said, translating a Chinese proverb. They appreciated the benefits, but wondered about the side effects this artificial intervention was having on their society. On a personal level, they worried about the "little emperors," those only children with two parents and four grandparents who were solely focused on one child. While most of my students had siblings, they had already observed this phenomenon in their young cousins or neighbors.

Others worried about the added stress of putting one's only child in an education system rife with competition. Already the exam system produced a great deal of pressure. Now factor in that each family had one and only one child to put all their hopes, dreams, and life savings into, and competition was explosive. It also took an emotional toll on these children. Getting their (one) child the best education possible, to include elite schools and extra classes in music, ballet, or English, had become a national obsession for urban families. In Shanghai, families spent an average of 25 percent of their salaries on their child's education (compared to 10 percent in industrialized countries, such as the United States).

After class, I went to the kindergarten, bundled up my three children, and took them home. Grace begged me to stop at a roadside stand and buy a hot dog on a stick. Hot dog in hand, Grace skipped most of the way home. With her penchant for pleasure, that was her favorite mode of transport.

"Mom, I'm Chinese, right?"

"Yes. Aren't you lucky? Because Chinese people are so beautiful." Grace's dark chocolate hair, which had finally started to grow long and thick, was cut in a fashionable pageboy. Her tresses sprang up and down as she skipped.

"And you're American too. You're Chinese-American."

"Yep. I'm Chinese-American, right?"

She took a bite of her hot dog and skipped on ahead. I was grateful that she was so much less complex than her older sister. At least for now, in her three-year-old mind, the issue was settled.

I thought back to that morning the adoption agency had called us, telling us we had been matched with a little girl, and that they had already e-mailed us her picture. Chris should have been at work by then, but had been delayed. As such, we were both present for The Call.

"Don't check e-mail until I get downstairs too!" I hastily called to him.

We stood there together before a computer screen and watched a picture of a Chinese child, our daughter, take shape. The first thing I saw was her dark, penetrating eyes. And complete lack of hair. About two months later we flew to China to pick her up. There, just like her picture, was a bald little girl whose eyes stared unwavering, unflinching, with an inborn confidence and sense of presence that could only have come from heaven.

I thought about her laugh, utterly contagious, making everyone around want to join in the fun of this little girl completely abandoned to mirth. China's surplus mouth had become my surplus joy.

Chapter 5

学
LEARN

Each horizontal stroke is like a mass of clouds in battle formation, every
hook like a bent bow of the greatest strength, every dot like a falling
rock from a high peak, every turning of the stroke like a brass hook,
every drawn-out line like a dry vine of great old age, and every swift
and free stroke like a runner on his start.

—WANG HSICHIH (AD 321–379),
describing the written Chinese language

❀

WITH THE CHILDREN'S ROUTINE SET AND MY TEACHING SCHEDULE FALL-
ing into place, it was time to get serious about learning Chinese.
The Chinese character meaning "to learn" or "to study" is one that has been
simplified. While it is now written 学, previously it was written 學. One
source I read stated that the traditional character shows two hands 臼 writing characters 爻 on a board above the head of a child, 子. Another said
there were two hands reaching through a covered mind to teach.

LEARN
(traditional)

LEARN
(simplified)

I found both of these views remarkable. The first showed the importance
of learning to write the characters in the course of study for any child. In the

primary school years, writing held primary importance over reading. In later years, most scholars were also calligraphers; writing and study were inextricably intertwined. The second view, with two hands reaching into a child's mind, sadly, emphasized the top-down view of education that I was struggling with in China. It was also an accurate depiction of a culture that viewed education not as teaching the mind to think for itself, but rather, stuffing in as much information as possible. This character told me that this was not a problem unique to the People's Republic; it had been occurring for centuries.

I was no longer a child, but I still had come to China to learn, and the first step in that process was to study Chinese. I had made an attempt to learn the language in preparation for our trip to China to adopt Grace. However, just as soon as we had finished the loads of paperwork required and settled in to wait the several months for the Chinese government to match us with a baby, we found out I was pregnant with Andrew. I quickly discovered one could not both study Chinese and grow a child at the same time; both activities demanded all of one's strength and oxygen. It was either one or the other. I dropped Chinese.

A few years later, while Chris was deployed to Iraq, I tried again. I listened to a half-hour of Pimsleur Chinese on the CD player while I made the children breakfast; then practiced writing Chinese characters while the girls were at preschool and I was home with only Andrew. During the summer I hired a tutor once a week. But for the most part I was on my own.

Now I was ready to pick up my studies. I asked Sally from the foreign affairs office if she could help me find a tutor. She found Zhang, a member of the English faculty, who lived in the same dormitory for single women teachers as Sally. Zhang was in her late twenties, an impeccably dressed teacher with long hair usually pulled back in a stylish ponytail. She met me after one of my classes and we compared schedules, arranging to meet twice weekly for two hours per session.

I had been practicing tones on my own, repeating faithfully what I heard on the CDs. However, with no one to correct me, it was not surprising that Zhang declared my tones were atrocious. Mandarin Chinese is a tonal language. Syllables are inflected with one of four tones. The first tone is high and level, as if singing the word instead of saying it. The second tone rises, much like we might do at the end of a question. The third tone, falling and then rising all in one syllable, produces that signature Chinese sound; finally the fourth, falling, similar to how we might give a command or say something with particular emphasis, such as the *now* in "Do it right now!" Tones are critical in speaking Chinese; using the wrong tone changes the meaning entirely. *Ma* spoken with the first tone, *mā*, means "mother"; spoken with the third tone, *mǎ*, means "horse."

It seems like every language has some sort of linguistic blind spot. For my students learning English, they continually, even after years of study, used the pronoun "he" when telling a story about their mother, or "she" when pointing to their male classmate. In Chinese, both "he" and "she" are pronounced the same, *ta*. In Japanese, the "r" and "l" sounds are interchangeable. This creates enormous difficulty when learning English, where they are not interchangeable. My Japanese students made such humorous statements as "For lunch I usually eat sushi and lice." For those of us English speakers learning Chinese, the tones are our blind spot. I would repeatedly ask for something, sure I was using the proper word, but a slight difference in tone prevented understanding.

Zhang drilled me repeatedly, but it had little effect, for I could hear no difference between my incorrect tones and her correct ones. The situation was dire, so she pressed for a radical cure: stop speaking altogether. I kept my mouth shut and began to listen. I listened to snippets of conversations in the grocery store, listened to dialogues on television, listened to the Chinese teachers chatting as we rode the bus to and from the new campus. All the while I tried to train my ear to heed something it had never been required to pay attention to before.

I realized that I had focused on each individual tone; but actually, the tones were usually combined to form multisyllable words. Each combination was pronounced with its own short melody; stringing the words together into sentences created a piece of music. Slowly, I began to pick up on nuances I was previously oblivious to, until the hitherto harsh-sounding Chinese gradually became altogether pleasant. Before, it had felt like my entire time in China I was listening to the orchestra tune up. Suddenly, the symphony had begun and I could hear melody instead of cacophony.

My ears attuned, Zhang could start in again on the drills, until my tongue could produce what my ear could now hear. I confidently took my burgeoning skills into my real-world classroom, using Chinese when buying groceries, interacting with teachers in the kindergarten, and ordering food in restaurants.

Chris and I had looked at a linguistic map of China before arriving, and we were pleased we were coming to Shandong province. While the written language was standard throughout China, there were a number of spoken dialects, most mutually unintelligible. We greatly enjoyed southern China and had been genuinely excited at our initial assignment, but living there would have posed a dialect problem. The Cantonese of Hong Kong and Guangdong province is vastly different from standard Mandarin Chinese. If posted there, we would learn Mandarin in the classroom, but then hear something completely different on the street. Since Mandarin is based on the Beijing dialect, the closer to Beijing, the closer the dialects are to standard Mandarin. Fortunately for us, the local Tai'an-hua (Tai'an dialect) was quite similar to Putonghua, the common language, or Mandarin. So I was able to learn *pingguo*, *putao*, and *boluo*, then walk out of the classroom onto the street and buy some apples, grapes, and a pineapple. I could study the terms "left," "right," "intersection," and "straight ahead," then hop in a taxi, confidently giving the driver directions.

But while I was making progress with Chinese, Katherine continued to struggle with her immersion into Chinese kindergarten. One weekend a breakthrough came. We ran into one of her classmates at the park across the street. Her classmate shouted "Rui Xue!" (Katherine's Chinese name) and ran toward her. They played together while I spoke with the girl's mother. We learned that her daughter's name was Le Le. Now Katherine not only had a friend, but even knew her name. On Monday when we walked to school, Le Le rode past us on a motorcycle with her father and again called out "Rui Xue!" Katherine grinned and when we got to school went happily to meet Le Le, forgetting all about her usual morning tantrum.

After running a few errands, Chris and I walked past the kindergarten on our way home. Music was piped through the loudspeakers, and the teachers and students were lined up doing their choreographed morning exercises. Passersby stopped to watch the children obviously enjoying themselves. Except for Katherine. She was the only one not doing the motions. Instead, she stared at a man nearby sawing a branch off a tree. When he finished, she remained withdrawn, still not participating with the rest of the class. Then she sat down on the ground. At that point I went through the gate into the playground to encourage her, but she refused to stand up or participate. I finally left her in the care of her teacher, who was also trying to encourage her, and Chris and I departed to do other errands. I worried about her all day. Something in her personality was putting up a block, re-fusing to accept this culture and this language.

That afternoon when I picked Katherine up, I said, "Come on, let's go say good-bye to Le Le." We searched out Le Le, found her, and made a showy *zaijian*! Then I said *zaijian* to any other classmate of hers looking my way, as well as to Katherine's other nameless friends. Then some of her other friends said *zaijian* and we responded to them. Then the entire class waved and said *zaijian* to us. Katherine left with a big grin on her face. So we had a big victory in the morning, followed by a sense of defeat, but then more positive signs in the afternoon. Each step of integration and transition was so difficult, so much work.

Once we got home, we sat in the courtyard with Mr. Jia, as we often did. Our foreign teachers' building had a duty office manned by our "min-ders" twenty-four hours a day. Mr. Jia was one of them. He was tall and thin, gray hair (or black hair when he dyed it) cut short, usually smoking, filled with no-nonsense advice for any situation. Mr. Jia's three children all lived in Tai'an; they each had one child. Mr. Jia and his wife picked up their grandchildren from school, brought the oldest to her dance class, and often cared for the younger ones throughout the course of the day. More often than not, two-year-old Feng Xin (pronounced Fung Sheen) could be seen trailing his grandfather as Mr. Jia putzed around the courtyard, water-ing the plants or sweeping away the leaves.

Mr. Jia spoke clear and slow Mandarin, and he loved children. On his own initiative, he taught our children Chinese while he played with them in the courtyard.

"*Zhe shi shenme yanse?* (What color is this?)," he would ask, pointing to Andrew's blue trousers.

"*Lanse!*"

"*Zhe shi shenme yanse?*" he would repeat, this time pointing to Grace's red shirt.

"Hongse!"

In this simple, nonthreatening way, my children learned their colors in Chinese. Mr. Jia continued to teach them in the safety of our courtyard, building their confidence for the rigors of the schoolroom.

While the children and I focused on learning how to speak this frustrating tonal language, my first love, the characters, continued to captivate me as my Chinese studies progressed. Apart from simply being fascinating, I hoped these ancient pictographs would help unlock the mysteries of this old civilization. I hoped they would give me greater understanding of the culture that had produced my daughter.

As an art form, Chinese calligraphy reflects proportion, harmony, and balance. Each character, when boiled down, is an artistic rendering of nature. For some characters this is particularly easy to see, for example, "mountain," 山, or "river," 川. Ultimately, at least until the advent of the computer age, every literate Chinese was a practitioner of calligraphy.

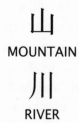

MOUNTAIN

RIVER

A picture has a much longer life than a word. Unlike our capricious English words, which can be conjugated, suffixed, prefixed, made plural, or otherwise adapted, a Chinese character remains an encapsulated singular morpheme, not allowing such impulsive mutation. Each character, a completed work of art—mounted, framed, and hung on the wall—cannot be then modified. Granted, some evolution has occurred, but much more sluggishly than in languages with words made up of mere letters.

The Chinese language must be considered in both its forms: spoken and written. Unlike most other world languages, written Chinese does not specify how the words are pronounced. Thus, the spoken language has been completely free to live whimsically and impetuously, not having the responsibility of written words to keep it from straying too far from home. Completely independent from its script, oral Chinese historically has never been tied down, adopting different forms from region to region and even from village to village.

The characters, unlike those freewheeling spoken words, have been the steady workhorses of the Chinese language, plodding along, rarely deviating to the left or right. They have managed to carry upon their shoulders the same meanings almost since their creation. To gaze upon a character is to have a window into the China of three thousand years ago, as I had first learned when meeting 家, the character for "home." Our English words find it hard to carry their history along with them, and etymology must be studied to be understood, but not so Chinese. Their characters present their history plainly in distinct brushstrokes and flourished dashes.

The English language, in contrast, has been subject to foreign takeover and invasion since its inception, and, as a result, easily takes in new words and makes them its own, from pork to pizza. The dynamic nature of the English language is bound with the tumultuous history of Europe. Each invasion, each voyage of discovery, and each technological advance marked and shaped our lingua. The Roman invasion of Britannia introduced Greek and Latin words into our Saxon dialect, and when the Normans conquered England in 1170 we began to demand as well as ask, to reply as well as answer, and to smell odors as well as smells. The Industrial Revolution gave us not only trains, cogs, pulleys, and engines, but also the words by which to call them. And the expansion of the British Empire meant we, borrowing words from Tamil and Hindi, slept in pajamas and ate curry.

Unlike English, it is the nature of the Chinese language to not allow such foreign intrusions (although that has changed somewhat recently, as Deng Xiao Ping's opening to the world has allowed the introduction of such popular items as *kele* ("cola") and *kafei* ("coffee"). While the twenty-six letters of English invite infinite creative couplings, the few hundred allowable Chinese syllables have about as much mobility as overloaded cars on a freight train.

But I think the principal difference is that seemingly more than in other languages, each Chinese character carries not only the dispassionate meaning, but also a living culture. My earliest exposure to this came with our daughter Grace, whose original given name is Zhi Chun, written 知春. As soon as our adoption agency told us her name, I e-mailed my Chinese friend Ruby and asked her the meaning.

Ruby, a beautiful girl from Taiyuan, in Shanxi (pronounced Shahn-shee) province west of Beijing, had been one of my closest friends during my days studying Japanese in Tokyo. When she first introduced herself, I thought she must have chosen her English moniker out of patriotism for "Red" China. I later learned that "Ruby" was a direct translation of her Chinese name, Chengyu. And after her lawyer father's death in a mysterious car accident, Ruby had certainly become the least "red" of my five Chinese classmates.

Ruby responded that Zhi Chun meant "to know that spring is coming." We were thrilled with such an optimistically expectant meaning, but I wondered how such a long meaning could be derived from only two characters. When I looked up their meanings in my Chinese-English dictionary, I found 知 was a verb meaning "to know." 春 meant the season of spring. So together the meaning was clear: "to know spring." But Ruby told me the meaning was "to know spring *is coming*." Where did the rest of the meaning come from? I was delighted with the meaning—for the remaining words certainly added a poetic and hopeful element—but I was a little suspicious because those extra words simply weren't present.

Perhaps Ruby added this on her own, I thought, so I asked a number of my friends and students. But they all told me the same meaning. How was this additional feeling of hope added? How did they all know this? When I asked them, they would simply shrug their shoulders.

Words in English may also carry connotations, certain feelings about the word in addition to the neutral meaning. "Housewife," for example, is a loaded word, and its very mention can bring up the entire women's movement of the past decades. When one says this word, in some circles, it can be tantamount to inserting the words "she's only a" in front of "housewife," although they've actually not been said at all.

But the Chinese language does this to a far greater extent than English. In addition to feelings, whole phrases, even sentences and paragraphs are attached to a single morpheme, going back to Tang Dynasty (AD 618–907) poetry, Chinese proverbs from the Spring and Autumn period (770–

476 BC), or key events in history. For every word written or spoken, thousands of others swirl around in the mist, unsaid yet understood.

In reading *My Country and My People* by Lin Yutang, I came across a passage that explained this to me. The author notes that each character also includes a word picture that is intrinsically part of the character, but is almost completely untranslatable. It is as if each individual character represents the beautifully painted object in the center of a picture. Surrounding this object is a dramatic misty landscape enhancing the ambience and character of the entire painting. Here I imagined the works of the Dutch Masters, such as *The Milkmaid* by Vermeer. The milkmaid herself is exquisite and one's eye is drawn immediately to her, but she is much better understood perfectly placed in her surroundings of white plaster walls, high multipaned windows, and Dutch tiles. Unfortunately, it is only after long years of studying Chinese, reading Tang Dynasty poetry, and knowing the history of these characters that these ethereal surroundings of each Chinese character can be known. For the rest of us, it remains unfathomable.

Such a language where each character is not only a picture, but also a word picture, creates vivid imagery and a poetry we have difficulty equaling with our phonetic language. However, the Chinese pictographs do give their language a weakness for expressing abstract concepts. It is easy to draw a picture of a tree, 木, a mouth, 口, or even bamboo, 竹. But how do you draw a picture of "achievement," illustrate a sentiment like "boring," or sketch an idea like "contentment"?

The ancient Chinese came up with ways to describe such intangible concepts by combining two tangible pictures. One of the first words I learned was "something," which is 东西, comprised of the two characters meaning "east" and "west."

EAST

WEST

SOMETHING

As far as "achievement," the Chinese term is 建树, "build a tree," which is quite an achievement indeed. "Boring" combines the classical character for "no," 无, with the character for "chatting," 聊, making 无聊, which does seem rather dull and tedious. And the idea of "contentment" is expressed in Chinese by combining the character "full," 满, with the character "feeling," 意, as perhaps feeling full is the definition of contentment, recalling days when food was not always so plentiful. Even in today's China the standard rhetorical greeting is not "How are you?" but rather "Have you eaten?"

满
FULL

意
FEELING

CONTENTMENT

In my Oral English classes I was fond of role-plays, which allowed the students to use English in a free way aided by the props of drama and make-believe. After dividing one class into groups of five or six students, I gave them two weeks to choose a Chinese proverb and prepare a role-play to be performed in the class. These particular tourism majors had a dramatic bent, and when I walked into class on role-play day I immediately saw swords and other props. One student had a crown made of the branches of a weeping willow upon his head.

I was then treated to a series of dramatic reenactments of four-character proverbs, known in Chinese as *chengyu*, most of which came from the Spring and Autumn or Warring States (475–221 BC) periods, but some from later times. One group performed a story based on the proverb 铁杵磨针 (*tie chu mo zhen*): "turn the iron rod into a pin." In this proverb, the Tang Dynasty poet Li Bai observed a woman's painstaking work polishing a rod of iron until it became a sharp pin. The students were shocked to find I had never heard of Li Bai. "But he's a famous poet!" they implored. One student, anxious to demonstrate the importance of Li Bai to his uncomprehending teacher, leaped to the blackboard and proceeded to write from memory one of Li Bai's most famous poems:

白日依山尽,	The white sun sets behind the mountains,
黄河入海流,	The Yellow River flows into the sea
欲穷千里目,	You will widen your view one thousand *li*,
更上一层楼.	By climbing further up one flight.

The other students of the class helped me along in the translation, but surprisingly, I had little difficulty with it, and was even able to get the gist of the first two lines myself. These were characters I used in daily life, such as "day," 日, "mountain," 山, "enter," 入, "1,000," 千, and "building," 楼. This meant I, an American with only a few years of Chinese study under my belt, could almost read this piece of Tang Dynasty poetry, and could understand it completely with the help of my nineteen- and twenty-year-old students. At the same time, the mysteries of *Beowulf*, written in my own ever-changing language about the same time as the poem above, were completely lost on me.

This ever-changing nature of the English language means even relatively recent literary giants, such as Shakespeare (1564–1616) or Milton (1608–1674), are becoming increasingly remote, even alien and inaccessible. But the hieroglyphic wisdom of the poets of the Tang Dynasty is timeless and close, a treasured family heirloom that still finds daily use, still uttered while washing dishes, sitting on the bus, writing at one's school desk, or going about the innumerable facets of ordinary daily life.

❁

In one of my Chinese-language sessions with Zhang I learned the Chinese word for "poem." The word was *shī* (pronounced shuh), said with a high level tone.

"This is so frustrating," I said to Zhang. "Every word in Chinese sounds alike! *Shī, shí, shǐ, shì*; every Chinese word has *shi* in it. I've already learned *shi*, which means 'is,' the *shi* in *bangongshi*, which means 'office,' the *shi* in *kaoshi*, which means 'test,' as well as *shi* said with a rising tone, which means 'rock.'"

Written, each of these meanings had its own Chinese character to represent it. This was a great advantage, and often the meaning would leap from the page when I saw the character. However, with the spoken language the characters were nonexistent. One of the most difficult parts of Chinese for me was understanding the spoken language, an inherent complexity with Chinese since it was made up of a finite number of sounds.

When I got home I picked up my pocket Chinese-English dictionary and found no fewer than twenty-eight entries under *shi*. And these only included *shi* as a single word, not *shi*-compounds. Starting with high level tone (first tone), the exact same tone and pronunciation as "poem," different characters with the same pronunciation of *shī* could also mean "wet," "master," "lion," "lose," "carry out," or "corpse." *Shí* said with a rising tone (second tone) also had a variety of meanings, including "ten," "real," "to know," "stone," "time," and "food." Then there was *shǐ* with rising falling tone (third tone), which had a plethora of meanings, such as "feces" or "shit," "history," "to cause," and "to begin." Finally *shì* pronounced with a falling tone (fourth tone) could mean "room," "city," "type," "to try," "to show," "to see," "to vow," or "power," or it could also be a family name.

This was bull*shǐ*!

Orally, context had elevated importance in Chinese. Back to my poem, Zhang taught me the best way to recognize *shi* as a poem was to look for its accompaniment, the special measure word for poems, *shou*. Therefore "one poem" was *yi* (one) *shou shi*. Still, in moments of frustration, I consoled myself by noting that this language, which allowed me to view the world from the eyes of a Tang Dynasty poet, called a poem by the same name as shit.

Chapter 6

高考
THE EXAM

The philosophy of the school room in one generation will be
the philosophy of government in the next.
—ABRAHAM LINCOLN

❊

BEFORE DEPARTING FOR CHINA WE ATTENDED A TWO-WEEK ORIENTATION
in Oakland, California, provided by our organization. We attended sessions on teaching pedagogy and listened to a variety of speakers on Chinese
culture. One speaker mentioned that the Chinese tended simply to accept
matters and not to question them. I thought about this. At that moment our
three children were upstairs with a babysitter while Chris and I attended
the sessions. Grace was three years old and in the Asking Why stage of her
development. Whenever we told her anything, her response was invariably
"Why?" For example:

"Grace, time to wake up." (sweetly)

"Why?"

"Because it's morning." (playfully)

"Why?"

"Well . . . because the sun came up." (matter-of-factly)

"Why?"

"It comes up every morning." (crisply)

"Why?"

"Because that's just how God made it. Now get out of bed." (crossly)

Then I would hand her some clothes before she could squeeze in another Why.

I looked at the presenter and raised my hand. "Do Chinese children ask Why?"

She thought for a moment. "Yes, they do," she answered. "But when they do, their parents say, 'Oh, quit worrying about such things,' and that ends the conversation. After a while, the children stop asking Why. But American parents actually try to answer their children when they ask Why."

I thought about that. Yes, it was true for me and my family. When Grace (and Katherine before her) had asked Why, I had done my best to answer, until I reached the point where there was no answer. I had no idea that in so doing I was acting according to my own culture. Not only that, but without realizing it, I was making my three-year-old daughter born in China into an American. Simply by answering her questions.

❀

When I first started teaching in China, I would often read a passage to my students that was quite difficult. Then I would pause.

"Are there any questions?"

Silence.

"Does anyone have a question?"

No raised hands. I would move on. But after a few weeks, I was no longer satisfied with this.

"No questions?" I would ask incredulously. "So all of you understand what *fits like a second skin* means?"

At this point they would shake their heads and smile sheepishly. After I explained the idiom they would nod, happy to finally comprehend the meaning.

"See, you must ask questions if you want to understand. No one in this class knew the meaning, but not a single person raised their hand and asked a question."

❀

In our life here we were immersed in Chinese culture; but more specifically, we were immersed in the Chinese education system. With our children, we experienced the entry level; in our jobs, we helped shape the finished product. We were intimately involved in the bookend levels of Chinese education. If asking questions and seeking answers was not part of the Chinese tradition, then what was the point of Chinese education?

Many students were curious about our children and asked me to describe their personalities. Katherine, I would tell them, was a precocious deep thinker, a born philosopher. She often posed questions whose answers I found difficult to articulate, and would answer them herself while I was still mentally fumbling around with the response.

Grace was naturally gifted socially. She had a way, no matter whether in the East or the West, to make herself the favorite in whatever classroom she entered. Her world revolved around people: teachers, grandparents, children, neighbors, aunts and uncles, cousins—all were potential playmates. While her siblings stared uncomfortably at the ground when meeting new people, Grace never shied away from eye contact. She made connections with people at amazing speed. She was also greatly agile; we were sure she would be a gifted athlete someday.

What people were to Grace, books were to Andrew. He taught himself to read and often slept with a book on his pillow or carried a book around as a security blanket. Even as a baby, when we read to him he would stare at the letters and words, not the pictures. When I took the children outside to play, Katherine and Grace would quickly find neighborhood friends, but Andrew played happily by himself or stayed close to me. The Chinese language presented him with new words to learn, and he embraced it, surprising his teachers with his affinity for the Chinese characters.

My students would nod their heads. "Andrew will be praised by Chinese teachers. They will say he is a good student."

"But what about my daughters?" I would ask.

"These kinds of things are not praised in China," they said. "Reading and memorizing are more important, because you must do well on the exam."

高

TALL

考

TEST

THE EXAM

The Exam. Discussion of education never strayed far from it. Discussion of life never strayed far from it. In Chinese the college entrance exam is known as the 高考, the "tall test." The first character, 高, meaning "tall," looks like a rather tall, elongated pagoda. Its use here is fitting, for The Exam indeed looms over Chinese students, even young children, as they are exhorted to study and urged to practice their calligraphy.

The second character, 考, meaning "test," is also instructive. The top half of the character signifies age or respect, suitable for a scholar. The bottom half has the meaning "obstructed breath." I wondered why, and what this had to do with "test." When I asked my students, they chuckled.

"It's probably because we are so nervous when we take the exam that we are hyperventilating," they told me.

I'm not sure if that's what the calligrapher had in mind. But certainly in today's China, The Exam stirred up a great amount of anxiety. Students' performances during the three-day exam determined if they would go to a famous university or none at all, if they would move to the big city or remain in the village forever, if they could be dubbed a filial child by proud parents or struggle to support their family with meager prospects.

With so many people competing and taking this tall test, there is little room for such superfluous luxuries during the student years as reading novels for fun, learning something just because it is interesting, or even—I read once in *China Daily*—choosing your own subject on which to write a research paper.

One of my students, who chose the English name Echo, wrote about this in her journal:

> First and foremost, I think the most important thing we should do is develop our education system. That's because I think our Chinese students learn too many things that we needn't, and most of them are what we do not like; it feels like we are compelled to learn these things. So we can't have enough time to learn some subjects we are really interested in. I think this way destroys our true genius; even some students have no time to think about what they *are* interested in. It cannot help our country's development. . . . All of us college students have been learning English for more than ten years, but most of us still cannot speak a long sentence in English fluently! They cannot open their mouth because speaking does not belong to the test.

Once behind them, The Exam never truly fades away, as a major life turning point rarely does. Soon, the student is married with a child of his own, and The Exam once more looms on the horizon.

On my commute aboard the bus from old campus to new I once sat next to one of my Chinese colleagues, Zhao. Since Zhao's daughter, Tian Tian, had just entered the kindergarten our children attended, she had begun to think more about China's education system and the implications it would have for her own daughter. She told me that in an effort to reduce the pressure on students, schools were no longer allowed to schedule classes on weekends or in the evenings. However, the students themselves were still finding ways to study during these times, perhaps recruiting a teacher to teach them anyway. The pressure had transferred from without to within.

Zhao remarked offhandedly: "They want to pass the college entrance examination. They want to change their lives."

I pondered that. Grammar might split this into two sentences, but it was uttered in one breath, a single coherent thought. In a culture where one's destiny was quite fixed, The Exam was the one event that could dramatically change one's fate. In the China of old, an ordinary townsman might pass the imperial examinations and be summoned to the capital to serve the emperor. In today's China, the fable runs like this: a child from the countryside studies hard and scores high enough to attend the prestigious Peking University. He is plucked from his hardscrabble village, has to contend with life in the big, cosmopolitan city, but eventually is successful and perhaps even goes abroad.

All my students knew these stories. But the truth was, although a few each year had a lucky star, the vast majority spent their entire youth preparing for The Exam only to achieve an average result, or even fail. Taishan Medical College was a minor university, so my students, bright as they were, were all a bit disappointed their score wasn't high enough to land them at a more prestigious university. I even had a few students with whom I was particularly impressed—confident, studious, nearly fluent in English—whom I later learned had failed the college entrance exam the first time. They then went through a year of independent study, falling behind their peers, reviewing and memorizing all the material from their last year of high school, before taking The Exam again and finally passing.

Our students were raised on stories from Chinese history as exhortations to diligence in their studies. They were told the story of Su Qin (pronounced Soo Chin) from the Warring States period (475–221 BC), who stuck a pin in his leg so the pain would keep him awake, allowing him to continue to study instead of falling asleep. Another bookish hero, Sun Jing, tied a string from his hair to the rafters. Should he fall asleep and bob his head, he would be jerked back awake, allowing him to study further. These two men had gone down in history as the protagonists in the couplet:

头悬梁, 锥刺股

"head hang crossbeam, pin prick leg"

Exams, rote memorization, endless mind-numbing drills, and ritualistic learning had been a pattern in China for centuries. The imperial examination system, a means to secure the best and brightest to serve in the imperial bureaucracy, began in the Tang Dynasty (AD 618–907) and continued, with breaks for dynastic upheaval and warfare, right up to the last emperor. Though dynasties would fall, the examination system always survived. A new dynasty would reinstate it as a sign that order was emerging from the chaos (and to co-opt the intelligentsia they would need to run their regime). The Qing Dynasty (1644–1911) continued the exam used by the Ming Dynasty (1368–1644). It was based on memorization and analysis of ancient Confucian texts, written not in the vernacular, but in classical Chinese.

Mao suspended The Exams during the anarchy of the Cultural Revolution, choosing to use political background and work performance to allocate university slots. Finally he closed the universities altogether. Signaling a return to normalcy, Deng Xiao Ping reinstated the exam in 1977 after Mao's death. That year, 5 million Chinese, aged thirteen to forty, took the exam to compete for 270,000 university spots. In 2006, the year we started teaching, 10 million students took the exam trying to get one of 5.67 million openings.

In ancient times, the Confucian classics were the subject covered on the imperial exam; thus, Confucian thought became the curriculum in schools, or a Confucian scholar was hired to teach the boys of a family. The Exam no longer covers Confucius. Rather, it includes Chinese, English, math, and a smattering of other subjects. But it is unmistakably the successor to the imperial examinations of old.

The Exam reduces everything to points: to correct answers; to multiple-choice; to true or false. My tutor Zhang told me that students in Chinese schools were asked to find the reasons for an event, for example, World War II. Their teachers told them, "Now list the reasons for the start of World War II. Name them . . . 1, 2, 3, 4." Real history is not this precise and cannot be broken down so easily into well-defined lists. But history needs to be reduced this way to accommodate The Exam. Even extracurricular activities are quantified. Achievement with piano or ability with sports is tested and assigned a level. If the threshold is passed, a student will earn an extra ten to twenty points on The Exam.

The objective in a child's education is singular: pass The Exam. This requires memorizing The Facts. There is no room for asking questions, no time for deliberation, no space for debate—and no tolerance for asking Why. Memorization has taken the place of thinking.

But not asking Why wasn't just a matter of curbing curiosity; it was also a matter of instructing compliance and conformity. Chris and I both enjoyed teaching our bright freshmen students double majoring in English and clinical medicine. However, after teaching them for only a few weeks, I was called by a professor in the English Department who told me that at the end of the week, those classes would be canceled.

"But why?" I asked.

"I don't know why. I was simply notified," he replied.

I was confused, but still prepared one last class for these students. When I walked in, I asked them why the class had been canceled.

"They just informed us. We thought you would know the reason."

"But I don't know why either. I'm just a foreign teacher."

"We want to continue learning English with you," they said. "They canceled both of our classes with foreign teachers. We don't understand."

"That doesn't make any sense," I told them. "Have you raised this issue with the administration? Have you asked them why?"

They hadn't.

"Have you complained to your adviser? Does he know why?"

"No."

"Well, can you get the student government involved in some way?" I asked.

"What is student government?"

"Well, never mind. Is there anyone you can talk to, any way that you can express your views?"

They just threw up their hands.

"What will you be doing instead of going to my class?" I asked.

"I guess we'll just sit in the dormitory," they told me.

After much questioning of the English Department, I found that the university was preparing for an evaluation, and the clinical medicine professors thought the course load for freshmen double majors was too heavy. They decided to rectify this by cutting out their English classes taught by foreign teachers. My class, Oral English, generally had no homework, so it wasn't a great burden to the students. The administration was robbing their students of the opportunity to spend two hours practicing their spoken English with a native speaker, which they desperately needed, so that their program could look better on paper to evaluators.

The students were upset. They actually got together as a class during that time to converse in English on their own. But that was as far as the protest went.

In class students rarely disagreed with me, even though I tried to ask difficult questions or take extreme positions to force them to. Even in routine matters like scheduling they toed the line. They were not told their class schedules until the last minute, and they had no say in what classes they took, apart from one elective each term. The sophomores told me they were informed that they would start taking Japanese the next semester as their second foreign language. They didn't choose it. They weren't asked their opinion. They just accepted it.

I wondered where this left our children. They were attending Chinese kindergarten full-time, albeit a high-quality one with kind teachers, but nonetheless, one that was fully in line with the Chinese educational model. Art classes consisted of copying the teacher's drawing from the board, and even recess time was carefully regulated with specific exercises and games, and little free play. They had to line up, copy, and recite, along with the unspoken rules of not drawing attention to themselves and of conforming to the group. And of course, they were not encouraged to ask questions or to ask Why.

Then we took them home and educated them. Home schooling is focused on the individual. I read them stories snuggled up in their beds. Katherine loved *The Story of Doctor Dolittle*, so we continued with his adventures, reading *The Voyages of Doctor Dolittle*. Grace was a kinesthetic learner. Chris affectionately called her his "hands-on girl," so in her math curriculum we used blocks to teach addition and subtraction. Andrew loved language; he sat and read. That adaptation to the individual was the very nature of home schooling. But beyond that, in our little home school we wanted to encourage their creativity, their powers of observation, their critical thinking, their elucidation of their own ideas, and their questions.

But in so doing, we were creating children who would be at odds with the education system in which we had placed them. Our children did not have the chance to read about cultural differences like us; they lived these differences every single day. Our aspiration was that they would emerge with the best of the East: the ability to speak Chinese and a solid grounding in mathematics; and the West: a critical, inquisitive, and innovative turn of mind. But sometimes I feared that the absence of cultural rules that applied across the board would completely confuse them.

One day I had lunch with Christina, who had become a regular visitor to my office. I was quite surprised to find a student of Christina's caliber at our university, since it was not a "famous university." Her English was extremely articulate. She had obviously spent hours in self-study, which caused her to ask provocative questions.

There were some students at our university who were intelligent, but didn't have the foresight (or maturity) to buckle down during their high school years and accept the necessary pain. Others were just not good test takers, a lethal disability in China. Then there were those like Christina, with tendencies to think for themselves in a society that rewarded regurgitators.

Christina's exam scores only merited entrance to a three-year college. She had now come to our university for an additional two years to upgrade her degree to a full bachelor's degree. After ordering several dishes, we began to talk.

"Darwin, for example," she said. "I have a hard time believing this. If we came from monkeys, why aren't there others in a more in-between stage of evolution to a monkey than we are? But the textbook says this is a fact."

"At last, I've found a student who asks Why!" I told her.

"But this has always hindered my studies," she countered. Instead of accepting what she had learned as fact, memorizing it, and moving on to the next required piece of knowledge, Christina had the habit of considering it, thinking critically about it, even doubting it. As a result, she had fared poorly on The Exam.

"A thinker in China has no prospect," she said, "and I must have a good prospect if I am to support my parents."

Chapter 7

WINTER

❀

ALTHOUGH TAI'AN HAD SEEMED LIKE A FURNACE WHEN WE ARRIVED, NO sooner had we started getting used to it then the weather changed. Behind our campus the entire mountain transformed from the greens of summer to the oranges and yellows of autumn, and finally to the browns of winter. We could smell the chill in the air, and wondered how we would fare during our first Chinese winter—with no heated vehicle to drive us to and fro, when walking everywhere with children would remain a necessary part of our routine. We worried about our children in frosty classrooms and wondered if we would shiver in our tiny apartment.

"We're a little bit nervous," I once confided to Sally in the university's foreign affairs office. "I'm not sure how we'll manage it."

She looked at me strangely. "It's easy. You just put on more clothes."

We noticed the arrival of the layers. First came the long underwear, which our students began to wear even when we thought it was still quite pleasant outside. This was eventually followed by gloves, hats, scarves, and long down coats lined with fur.

The neighborhood children began to wear more clothes as well, their bodies gradually losing their shape entirely, submerged under layers of garments.

"They look like the Michelin tire man," Chris said.

Our children resisted such constriction and preferred to simply wear a long-sleeved shirt with a windbreaker. This was one of many cultural changes their daily lives presented them with. But their greatest challenge remained managing a school day in a foreign tongue.

When we discussed moving to China with our children people would often remark about how quickly our children would pick up the language. They made it sound like it would happen almost by magic, that the language would just seep into their pores, effortlessly absorbed, and that at three months tops, they would be speaking fluent Chinese.

Not so. It was a hard-fought battle, and at least from the perspective of a parent outside looking into their world, it did not seem easy at all. I remember well the first time Chris said "Qiu Hua" and Andrew turned around smiling, recognizing that this was his name. I remember also the first time the kids sang a Chinese nursery rhyme, replete with motions, and how happy we were. Soon, the children began to pepper their home speech with various bits of Chinese here and there.

First there was milk. "Mommy, can I please have some *niunai*?" Andrew often asked.

The next language progression wasn't exactly a happy one. Instead of hearing "mine" or "that's mine" or some other version of that oft-repeated preschool phrase, we were subjected to the Chinese version, a high-pitched *"wo de!"* with all the tones overemphasized.

Grace added another phrase to her repertoire. I would usually ask if she had cleaned her plate. Now she answered *"mei you le"* (roughly meaning "there isn't anything there," with the *le* particle on the end noting that this was a change from a previous condition).

One day I arrived to pick up Katherine from school while she was playing with the teacher's son, a little boy probably two years old. Katherine loved babies and little children and would make a great babysitter someday. She enjoyed her big-sister role and was very protective of her own little sister and brother. Katherine wanted the small child to come, and said, *"Guo lai."* This was the first time she said something I couldn't understand. The teacher told me it meant, "Come here." So we were making progress, gradually. The children now understood much more than they could speak, and they spoke more at school than we heard at home.

One afternoon, tired from their endless whining and Katherine's difficulties at school, I returned home with the children. In the courtyard, Mr. Jia greeted us with a basin filled with tiny crabs for the children to play with. Once Mr. Jia taught them the word, they excitedly talked about the *pangxie* (pronounced pong-she-ay) as they played in the courtyard. Other Chinese children came by to see the crabs and play with our children. A modicum of Chinese was spoken among them.

Another afternoon Mr. Jia had some *jian bing*, a flat papery pastry that is common in these parts, often filled with a tofu mixture. Katherine had fun giving some to me, her siblings, and Mr. Jia. As she handed it out she said, *"Hao chi"* (literally, "eat good"—actually meaning something like "take some . . . it's good to eat").

"Where did you learn to say *hao chi*?" I asked her.

"It's what my teachers say when they pass out our lunch," she replied.

This was exactly how we wanted her to pick up the language: in its natural context. There's a difference between inserting a word because the dictionary tells you it's the correct word, and using a word because experience tells you that it's correct. For Katherine *hao chi* was inseparable from its lunchtime context. This phrase, for her, got its meaning not from the dictionary, but from the hot pork dumplings and sticky rice that invariably surrounded its utterance.

Early November brought Katherine's fifth birthday. We made a deliberate decision to have her party at school with her class. When we first made this plan she was against it, saying she would prefer to have her party with some of our university students. But slowly the idea grew on her. When I walked into the classroom on her birthday, the students were already seated in a semicircle around a table that had been cleared for the cake. Each student had made Katherine a birthday card, and they sang "Happy Birthday" to her several times in English and Chinese. They had decorated the chalkboard, and her teachers had bought her a present. We cut the cake and Katherine, wearing a new dress, brought a piece to each classmate (saying *"Hao chi"* as she gave it to them). We took pictures, played with balloons, and sang and danced. Katherine had a great time, enjoying the attention. But, more important, this was an event connecting her with her classmates, her teachers, and this new culture and language.

A few days later when I picked up the kids, Katherine didn't want to leave. She was busy cutting and pasting. When at last we departed, unprompted, she yelled *"Zaijian!"* to her classmates and even went back into the classroom to say good-bye to a few others.

❀

As winter temperatures plunged in early December, months into our assignment, we had the opportunity to take our first trip out of Tai'an. Martha Chan, the president of our organization, was going to be in Qufu, the hometown of Confucius, and asked the Tai'an teachers to join her there. We were excited to see something new, even if it was only an hour down the road.

With the home of the great sage so close, I wondered about his effect today. Driving down the highway, every vehicle license plate was embossed with *lu*, 鲁, the one-character abbreviation for Shandong province. This character stood for the ancient state of Lu, the home state of Confucius before China was unified, and reminded Shandong people, even those modern enough to possess a car and driver's license, of where their origins lay.

I'd kept Confucius, who lived from 551 to 479 BC (roughly at the same time as the Buddha and the biblical Daniel), in mind since arriving in China, wondering if I could discern his imprint upon this culture. Of course, it was hard to tell exactly what was Confucianism and what were other strains of Chinese culture, for at this point they were all mixed in together. The emphasis on the orderliness of human relationships and submission to authority certainly were Confucian in origin, but I wondered if there were any other aspects.

Confucianism is a religion without a deity. As Lin Yutang said, "It solved the problems of human nature, but left out of consideration the riddle of the universe." Rather than consider God, Confucianism took humans as the start and end points. If they lived according to the codes Confucius set forward, and ordered their relationships accordingly, they could achieve "perfection."

Today's China is officially atheistic. Relationships are still a priority, and government authority remains paramount. Harmony, peace, and stability are still the cravings of this culture. Through a right ordering and hard work, so they believe, China can achieve higher development, better living conditions for its people, and pride as a nation. But the source is entirely from within itself. I think Confucius would have approved.

❀

Most of our time in Qufu was spent chasing the children around temple complexes the various emperors had built to honor Confucius. We also had an interesting "Confucius-style" lunch with a centerpiece of boiled scorpions. But in Qufu, we were once again our own traveling tourist attraction. Soon we were drawing crowds. We had not realized how comfortable we had become walking the streets in Tai'an, where we were now such a normal sight people hardly glanced our way. We found ourselves comparing Qufu's temple complex (unfavorably) to our own Dai Temple in Tai'an, a place we enjoyed taking the children on a Sunday afternoon. On the drive back to Tai'an, we were so happy to see our mountain, our street, our university. In Qufu we felt like strangers and tourists. In Tai'an, we were at home.

Now nearly Christmas time, we were in the thick of winter. Chris came in after a day of teaching, feeling his beard.

"My winter coat is coming in nicely," he said proudly. "Kiss me!"

I pulled away. "It's beginning to smell," I said. "Do you shampoo it?"

"No, should I?"

"Unless you want something to start growing in there."

"Pretty soon I'll be able to braid it," he said. "Won't that look cool? I'll tie little red strings on the end of each braid."

"I'll pick up some red string next time I'm at the market," I said. I refused to give him the satisfaction of letting him know how much I despised that mass of hair.

"By spring I'll have birds nesting in it," he said, pulling on his long strands.

I too was looking forward to spring, though not for that reason. I was simply ready for the oppressive cold to disappear, and to feel the warmth again. The Chinese language also expresses such a desire. One book I read said the character for winter, 冬, shows two drops of melting water dripping from the roof, meaning that although it is winter, spring is coming. I liked that sense of hopefulness, for I too was hoping spring would come soon.

Since the onset of winter, more Chinese grandmothers than I could count told me my children were not wearing enough clothes. The Chinese children I saw all looked like their limbs were sausage links. I thought they would be hard-pressed to touch their toes or put their hands on their hips. Our children had no use for this. They would rather have been cold than to have their freedom of movement restricted; but frankly, they weren't that cold.

Still, I heard about it all the time. At first I got annoyed, for I took it personally, feeling that people were commenting on my parenting abilities. I also was frustrated because it was a no-win situation for me. On the days when I demanded the children put on an extra layer to please the clothing police I was sure to provoke a round of whining. On the days I felt weary, and let them make their own clothing decisions, I would certainly be pulled aside on the way to school by a well-meaning grandmother informing me my children were not wearing enough clothes. *"Leng, bu leng?"* was a phrase I became quite familiar with, literally meaning "Cold, not cold?" but actually translating to "Are you cold?"

I expressed my frustration to Zhang, my Chinese tutor. She told me Chinese people believed clothes were very important. Starting as babies, children were always layered up. I remembered this when we first received Grace. We had to take off layer after layer before we could get to our baby. The Chinese had to start this practice as babies, for early conditioning was necessary for active preschoolers to accept these limitations on their movement. It was much too late for mine.

"Our children aren't even cold," I told Zhang, "but still I hear this!"

She taught me a smart Chinese phrase to say: "Chinese children wear way too many clothes." There were many times I thought about using it, but decided I was supposed to come to China to love and learn from Chinese people, and I didn't need some smart-aleck expression in my vocabulary of useful phrases.

We had been nervous at the prospect of winter, but were managing quite well. Having a warm and toasty apartment was a great help. Not only did we have radiators, but also a wall unit in each bedroom. Our students were not so lucky; their rooms were quite cold. Still, putting on long underwear first thing in the morning became my habit along with eating breakfast and brushing my teeth. The children now had a wardrobe full of fur-lined boots, flannel- and fleece-lined jeans and corduroys, and lots of smocks for added layers.

As a mother, there were many things I could do for three children just as easily as I could do for one. Cooking dinner, for example, took the same amount of time no matter how many children. Walking to school was fifteen minutes each way whether one walked one child or three. When it was time for showers, I piled all three children in at once, and had one lathering up her hair while the others rinsed off. It was simply economies of scale. However, getting three children ready for school in the dead of winter held no such advantages; it was just three times the work of having one, if not more, considering their interaction during the process.

First, each child times three needed to be stuffed into long underwear, then slid into quilted pants. Three pairs of socks, three sweaters, six boots, three coats, three hats, and then sweating and impatient, my personal vexation: coaxing thirty individual fingers into gloves. I often turned them over to their dad for this stage. Topping off with three scarves, we were ready to head out the door. I started this process while the children were eating breakfast, pulling on long john shirts in between their bites of cereal. Thankfully their classrooms were not too cold; the children never complained about being cold at school. In fact, they only complained about having to wear so many layers of clothes.

Another consequence of the cold winter was that we spent more time in our apartment and less time outside. Our Chinese neighbors did the same, retreating inside to the warmth of their homes. I felt more isolated than before. Walking home, shivering, along the gray streets after an errand, I'd look at their lit-up windows, wondering what was cooking, what people were talking about, what was on the TV, and how they were passing the long winter nights.

❖

Zhang, though she heard so many stories about our children during our tutoring sessions, had never met them. She finally got a chance at the Foreign Languages Department New Year's party in December. We climbed aboard the bus arranged specially to take the teachers to the venue. Zhang was already on the bus and excitedly came to sit with us to meet the children and talk with them.

After a few minutes, she said to me, "Aminta, I really do think your children are *not* wearing enough clothes!"

"No, Zhang! Not you too! It never ends!" I slumped down into my seat.

At the kindergarten, Katherine's class also had a New Year's performance for all the parents and grandparents. Katherine's teacher told me about
it in advance, asking if I would sing "Jingle Bells" with Katherine since
she didn't want to participate in the dance with the other children. She
wanted to make sure Katherine was involved in the program in some way.
My heart sank when I heard this—Katherine didn't even want to participate
in a dance? I talked to her. She said she didn't like everyone looking at her,
but maybe she would try. The next day I asked her about it. She just mum-
bled a reply.

So on the day of the performance I trudged to the school wondering
what sort of event this would be, and what behavior from my child I would
have to contend with. I walked in. One parent, a chemistry professor at our
university, motioned for me to sit next to her, which cheered me.

Then it was time for the children to come in, all dressed up. Katherine
wore the flowing robes of some kind of Turkish whirling dervish, and wore
a big smile as well. She had a red spot on her forehead and wore lipstick,
like the other children. The first group began their dance. Katherine sat off
to the side with some other children, happily watching. As the children finished she helped them get offstage. Then it was her group's turn. To my
surprise, Katherine danced with the other children. She didn't know the
dance very well, as she hadn't practiced, but she followed along with a
smile on her face the whole time. During the remaining activities Katherine
alternated between sitting on my lap or with a group of classmates. The
whole event was a huge success. I was thrilled.

❁

Soon final exams were over and grades turned in. We now had about
eight weeks' vacation before the spring term started in March. We fled winter and headed to fairer weather down south. Our first stop was Chiang Mai,
Thailand, for a conference. We weren't that excited about going to Thailand, honestly. It cost a lot of money, and we would need to take three
flights to get there. It just seemed like too much trouble.

But from the moment we arrived at the Bangkok airport we felt as if
a cultural burden we didn't even know we were carrying was suddenly
lifted. For five days we did not have to speak Chinese, did not have to eat

Chinese food, did not have to bring toilet paper with us for use in a public toilet, did not have to put up with squatties—whatever it was, we did not have to do it. As we boarded the flight from Bangkok to Chiang Mai the flight attendants gave us newspapers, not only in English, but the same day's paper! In Tai'an we could only buy the government *China Daily*, and it was never more recent than two days old.

Northern Thailand was pulsating with color. China in winter is gray. The buildings are gray; the skies are gray with pollution. Even though we lived at the foot of a beautiful mountain, because of the poor air quality it was often gray too. In contrast, the bright colors of Thailand almost hurt my eyes. The trees were so green, the skies so blue. The clothing, jewelry, scarves, and lanterns of the night market in Chiang Mai turned the street into a blur of bright reds and oranges, greens and blues. And I saw wood again. There is not much wood to be found in China: plastic rules the inner realm and cheap bathroom tile, the outer. The markets of Chiang Mai were filled with wood carvings bringing so much warmth—I never realized how much I missed wood.

Chiang Mai, although relatively small, is a very cosmopolitan city. I had always been a bit peeved at Americans who visited other countries and expected to be spoken to in English. But in Chiang Mai, I arrived without even one word of Thai, and found it comforting that I could speak my native language everywhere I went. In China I had grown so accustomed to being stared at that I no longer noticed it. But in Chiang Mai, lost among tourists from all over the planet, I reveled in retrieving my anonymity.

After such a high point, it was only natural we should have a let-down upon returning to China, but we crashed down hard when we arrived in Sanya, the beach city on Hainan Island, located in the South China Sea. We were there for a second conference, this one with our sponsoring organization, ERRC. All the Chinese cultural pressures we had escaped in Thailand came right back even more than at home in Tai'an. My heart sank when I saw we had no built-in shower. We're back in China, I thought. Actually this shower was a step above ours at home, because at least it had a curtain separating it from the toilet. But in Thailand we had a bathtub/ shower combination, and the kids loved being in the bathtub together after so many months without one.

Additionally, the hotel had no breakfast. Chris went out to try to scrounge something for our family.

"Well, I found a small supermarket," he said when he returned, "but all I saw that the kids would eat were these cookies." I always tried to prepare a healthy breakfast for our children, but here I was, feeding them cookies.

"By the way, I don't want you walking around Sanya with the kids. This place doesn't feel safe to me."

We were there for a conference, but there was no child care available, so only one of us could attend the meetings. The first two days in Sanya I sank into a depression. As a family I felt we were barely holding it together. Chris attended the meetings and enjoyed the camaraderie with the other teachers, but I felt stuck in a hotel room with three children, completely isolated.

"You go to the meetings today. I'll watch the kids," he offered. But I was gripping my anger tightly, and refused.

We tried to enjoy the beach, but since Sanya was not used to Western tourists, we were immediate targets for persistent and annoying vendors. One lady told me she would not leave until I bought something, and sat in front of me for fifteen minutes, subjecting me to a constant stream of vendor talk the whole time. By the time she left, I was almost in tears.

After an hour at the beach, we felt we had exhausted Sanya's possibilities. Other than the beach, it seemed to offer only China's frustrations, but none of its joys. Having just had a taste of freedom, I now felt unable to venture out. I began to isolate myself from the ERRC group, and felt angry at the hotel, at the traffic, at the whole country.

The subliminal anger made me feel terrible, for how could I be angry at China, when I had come here to learn and appreciate the Chinese language and culture, to serve the Chinese people; and I was a Chinese mother after all. How could I feel this way? Now I was angry at myself too.

A few weeks later, after returning home to Tai'an, I exchanged a series of e-mails with Martha, the president of ERRC. Martha had been sending teachers to China for twenty years by that point. She told me that what happened in Sanya was a second culture shock, caused by coming back to China after Thailand.

When I read her e-mail, I was flooded with relief. Suddenly I understood, for the first time, my feelings. This second culture shock was more severe than when I first arrived because it was unexpected; throughout the experience I never even knew I had it. I was returning to China, my "home." Why should I have culture shock? But coming from Thailand, where we had enjoyed the international scene, speaking English, the food, the shopping, and then going to the loud traffic and seedy underdevelopment of Sanya, caused me to lose my bearings.

Martha's e-mail was instructive. She said culture shock was completely unrelated to the "love" we think we should have for the Chinese people. In fact, this love was a completely romantic notion; we shouldn't expect this of ourselves. Going through culture shock did not mean we did not love the Chinese people, or respect them, or like them, or whatever it was we were supposed to do. I felt released from the burden of my feelings, but more important, I understood them. I was grateful we had this agency behind us when we, especially I, faced our own barren winters.

Chapter 8

山水
MOUNTAINS, WATER

The river forms a green gauze belt; the mountains are like blue jade hairpins.
—HAN YU, Tang Dynasty poet, about Guilin

❀

WITH EAGER ANTICIPATION WE LEFT HAINAN ISLAND AND LANDED IN the southern Chinese city of Guilin (pronounced Gway-leen). I recognize now that my interest in China started with Guilin. More specifically, it started when I watched the movie *The Joy Luck Club*, based on the novel by Amy Tan. The year was 1994. I drove from North Carolina, where I was living after graduation from college, to Atlanta to meet some old college friends. I walked into a movie theater with my girlfriends having no idea what I was about to watch. I sat spellbound. This tale of Chinese-born mothers, their American-born daughters, and their mutual frustration at not being able to relate to one another at times, completely captured me.

The movie went back in time to when the mothers were young, living in China, and suffering as only Chinese who lived through the war and upheaval of the early twentieth century know suffering. In one flashback, a Chinese woman trudged along in a long line of refugees fleeing war. She struggled to put one foot in front of the other as she pushed a wheelbarrow with two bundled-up babies, her twin daughters. Afflicted by dysentery and other maladies, she was certain she was about to die. To save her daughters from the bad luck of being found with their dead mother, she abandoned them by the side of the road, leaving a note as well as jewelry and anything else valuable she had remaining.

Aside from the poignancy of this scene, I was equally moved by the scenery. Particularly, the mountains. They speared straight up out of the ground like teeth poking out of gums. Was this scenery real or just a Hollywood invention? I had no idea that such landscape even existed.

I harbored this image in my mind for years. When I was a student at Waseda University in Tokyo, I described this scenery to my Chinese classmates. "Ah yes," they nodded knowingly, "Guilin."

At last the image had a name. Guilin.

Guilin was the only place that fascinated me simply for its landscape. I am just not that much into scenery. I get more excited about culture and people. That's why I like to go places. But Guilin was all about the scenery. I just had to see those mountains. No other scenery has had such a hold on me as Guilin, and for so many years.

When we were in the process of adopting Grace, I would daydream that she was from Guilin, thinking this would be quite a poetic ending if the daughter of my dreams were from the landscape of my dreams. But in fact she was from Jiangxi, a province I had never heard of and could only find on the most detailed of maps. As we planned our adoption trip I thought about trying to add a side trip to Guilin, but finances precluded that, as they had on my earlier trip to China.

This time, since we were already down south with our travels to Thailand and Hainan Island, Chris mentioned we should make a side trip to Guilin. As I made the flight arrangements I could see it would be more convenient to fly through Kunming, and I suggested to him that instead we see Kunming since we had to go through that airport anyway. But he insisted we see Guilin.

"You've been talking about this for so long, as long as we've been together. We just need to go to Guilin to fulfill your dream. And to get you to shut up about it!"

With that kind of personal history, Guilin had a lot to live up to. We flew in after nightfall. I strained my eyes looking for their forms, but the mountains were invisible, cloaked in darkness. I awoke in the hotel room the next morning, opened my eyes, and quickly drew the drapes. I was not disappointed. The mountains jutted upward right from the street, vertically, like pencils with worn-down erasers. The hazy forms of my memory turned into solid bedrock right outside my window.

On the agenda for that day was the Li River cruise, a must on any tourist trip to Guilin. The mountains seemed to form a crowd at the river-bank—standing room only. One was so perfectly cylindrical it looked like a prehistoric giant had made it using a prehistoric oversize soup can. Another looked like a camel with seven or eight humps. I enjoyed the scenery immensely. But there were a lot of distractions. The river was saturated with tourist vessels, and we were never free from vendors.

While cruising, a man in one of the Phoenix Tail Bamboo rafts Guilin was known for pulled up to the side of the ferry. The raft was a single layer of bamboo poles, tied together and rising at one end. I watched the man curiously, wondering what he was doing. I decided he must be attaching himself to the boat as a means of hitching a ride downstream. Grabbing on near the bow, he gradually made his way back until he reached the first window, ours. I pointed him out to the kids, showing them the raft and pointing out the bamboo. As if on cue, he smiled and waved. We smiled and waved back. He then opened the crate in the center of his raft, withdrew some items, and with a flick of his wrist displayed a fan painted with Guilin scenery. He was a vendor. And I, innocently, had allowed my guard to drop.

The raft vendors accompanied us the rest of the way downstream. Passengers, if interested, would open their windows and the bargaining would begin over carved frogs, crystals, various stones, and other trinkets.

After the cruise, we headed to Yangshuo. I added Yangshuo to the itinerary after hearing a snippet of conversation in which one of our ERRC colleagues mentioned that Yangshuo was a nicer place to visit than Guilin. That turned out to be great advice, for we thoroughly enjoyed this small town. One guidebook we read aptly described Yangshuo as having an "international, bohemian atmosphere."

"This place is great," Chris said. "I could just hang out here." We loved it from the first moment, walking from our hotel to West Street, a pedestrian walkway filled with sidewalk cafés, clothing stores, local gift stores, and art galleries containing scroll after scroll painted with Guilin's famous scenery.

In Chinese, this scenery is dubbed 山水, literally "mountains, water." This is a typical Chinese linguistic pattern: choosing two characters to denote the boundaries of a concept. Here it refers to landscape containing both mountains and water, and everything in between.

We spent the next morning in a private calligraphy lesson arranged by our guide. The girls and I had great fun practicing the strokes, numbers, and a few basic characters. Grace was still a bit too young to truly enjoy calligraphy, but Katherine loved all of it—the ink, the brushes, the paper—she loved anything having to do with art. Chris videotaped and took pictures, while Andrew sat at his own desk immersed in a book.

For the afternoon, we were scheduled to take a bicycle tour of the countryside. The kids couldn't ride yet, but Chris offered to take care of them in the room so I could go.

"Are you sure?" I asked him.

"It's no problem. I'm just riding along anyway, facilitating your dream."

So Cherry, our guide, and John, a fellow ERRC teacher who was accompanying us, and I rented bikes on West Street, then headed out of town. Our first stop was a farmer's house. At last I would have a peek inside my first Chinese home. The seventy-one-year-old woman of the house was our hostess. Her husband also peeked in briefly. She served us a pomelo, similar to a gigantic grapefruit, grown herself. As we peeled the thick membranes from each segment of pomelo to reveal the delicious interior, a large portrait of Chairman Mao looked down at us from the living room wall. To his left and right were red paper couplets with large Chinese characters, though the woman explained that she could not read them because she was illiterate.

After eating she led us into the courtyard, the centerpiece of her 340-year-old home, where we washed our hands using water from the hand pump. The kitchen—an outbuilding next to the courtyard—consisted of a low cement counter with two holes for woks and charcoal fires underneath.

We returned to the living area via a side room. There she presented two wooden rectangular boxes: coffins. Her children had purchased them about eight months previously, she informed us. She lifted the lid of one and proudly showed us the inside.

Our guide explained that this was a Chinese custom. In fact, it was the duty of children to buy their parents coffins, and for the parents to approve. This was a way of expressing care and fidelity.

"In this way, they know everything is taken care of," she explained to us. I immediately wondered what my parents would think if I suggested such a coffin-buying shopping trip. I wondered what it must be like to live in my house with my own coffin, which I would inevitably inhabit one day; to walk by it day in and day out. How would this affect my life? Would it make the menial tasks of the day, still important to this elderly couple who made their living by farming, seem trivial? My Western mind had a hard time grasping how the presence of these coffins could be comforting to the elderly couple, as our guide explained that it was.

I had finally had the chance to visit a Chinese home. However, I was a paying customer, not a welcomed guest. Still it had left my mind whirling with questions, and had opened up the mysteries of this culture at least a crack further.

From the farmhouse we bicycled to a small tributary of the Li River, where we boarded a two-seater bamboo raft, our bikes tied to the back. The karst mountains—geologic formations carved when water wore away the limestone millennia before—seemed even more fantastic and distinct than the day before, and there was nothing to do on the raft but take them in. The mountains were visible in layers, the ranges behind visible between and gradually fading into lighter shades of blue, like rows of hunched animals. The raft master, perched on the back, steered us along with the help of a long bamboo pole, along the way navigating three or four small dams. He pointed out key scenery, exhorting us at times to lift our legs to avoid getting our feet soaked.

On the Li River cruise the day before, I was too distracted by kids, as well as other tourists, vendors, and passing boats, to really take in the scenery. But this time only a layer of bamboo separated me from the water, only fresh air between me and the mountains. I finally felt I had truly breathed in the 山水.

Following the raft trip we bicycled back to our hotel in Yangshuo. We were staying on the fifth floor. Actually it was the fourth floor; however, our hotel did not have a fourth floor. The number four is considered unlucky in China, because its pronunciation, *si*, has the same pronunciation as "death," though the tone is different.

This seemed a contradiction. Coffins brought comfort to an elderly couple. But the fourth floor was conspicuously missing because of its association with death.

❀

The next day we departed the abrupt mountains of Yangshuo and headed toward the more sloping inclines of Longshen. Long ago poets had dubbed Longshen "the dragon's back rice terraces," for in the ancients' effort to produce rice even amid steep gradients, it looked like they had actually cultivated the back of a dragon itself. Longshen was also home to a few of China's ethnic minorities, the Yao and the Zhuang peoples.

My students spouted that China had fifty-six ethnic groups, of which the Han were the majority, comprising 92 percent of China's population. Although the remaining minorities constituted only 8 percent, they seemed in a remarkable way to have preserved their distinctive cultures. Our guide, Cherry, gave us a further education about the minorities in her province, describing their adeptness at handicrafts, embroidery, and construction.

After lunch served by Zhuang women, we hiked the dragon's back itself. The kids did great, and the terraces were stunning. Their beauty was their symmetry. Each terrace seemed exactly the same width, each vertical drop exactly the same height. And since the rice fields required flooding, the result was a perfect leveling of the horizontal part of the terrace. When the fields were flooded, later in the spring, the terraces would look like mountains of mirrors. We had seen pictures of this, but unfortunately had arrived before the spring watering.

On the way we walked through the village of Ping An (meaning "peace"). When we entered the village we were greeted by three Yao women. They were dressed in traditional costumes, homemade, with hair down to the ground. At the cue of our guide, they undid their hair from the wraps around their head and combed it. They then rewrapped their hair in its traditional wrap with a bun in the front, signifying they were married.

We were entranced by these women, mainly for their ready smiles. They were very photogenic. However, the tourist/vendor relationship soon set in. They started putting their trademark silver bracelets on my daughters as a sales ploy, and we had to walk away, politely but firmly declining to purchase their wares. Although aggressive, they were easier to take than most vendors in China simply because they were so charming.

But what was most interesting was that although China—with its appetite for cars, its choking pollution, its manic desire for development—was obsessed with catching up with the rest of the world, these mountain people lived not even on the fringes of globalization. Cherry mentioned that if a Yao woman went into the outside world, and later wanted to rejoin the community, she had to grow her hair long again. Living quietly in the mountains, the minorities had that which they wanted most: the opportunity to keep their customs alive. They had certainly been impacted by tourism, but tourism also served to promote their cultural identity, creating a market for their handiwork, keeping their crafts alive. Yet whether the tourists were many or few, the work in the rice fields remained, a line of work that had not been eased by modern technology, but still was done as it had been for centuries: by plowing with water buffalos, transplanting seedlings into knee-deep water, and laboring with backs bent.

The Chinese government seems to have a pact with the minorities: don't seek power, and we'll give you autonomy and allowance to live traditional lives. The government does not force them to become acculturated into the majority. The minorities, having no aspirations for power, pose no threat to the government. On the whole, the relationship works out quite well. There are exceptions, of course, such as the Tibetans and the Uighurs who are unwilling to consent to such a pact, but on the whole I was surprised to find such a positive relationship between the Han majority and the numerous minority peoples.

Not everything was "roses and flowers," as Katherine would say. Achievement in education was not as high, and as a result, minority students had trouble competing with Han students. Cherry told us minority students did not have to score as high on the college entrance examination. This caused some amount of consternation, but it appeared most Chinese students understood and agreed with this policy.

Minorities were given other concessions as well: special schools, exceptions to the one-child policy, and official encouragement of their culture. But there was something else they had. These traditional peoples with their heads bent over their needlework, with their wooden villages nestled in the mountains, these people had something that had eluded other minorities, from Australia's Aborigines to America's Native Americans to Europe's Gypsies: respect, the respect of the majority among whom they lived.

As we left Longshen and Ping An village, we again crossed paths with the Yao women. They capitalized on the opportunity to ply their wares once more. I wondered how much of what we had seen was just for show, for the tourist's benefit, and how much of the Yao life we saw was authentic. As we drove away I looked up at the rice terraces and saw the profile of a Yao woman, easily recognizable by the wrap of hair on her head and the trademark knee-length flared skirt. She was bent over, hoeing her rice field, accompanied only by a water buffalo. I felt somewhat reassured.

Chapter 9

外

FOREIGN

> Throughout the ages Chinese have had only one way of look-
> ing at foreigners. We either look up to them as gods or down
> on them as wild animals.
>
> —Lu Xun

❀

ARLIER THAT AUTUMN, I HAD ARRIVED FOR MY CHINESE LESSON WITH
Zhang feeling frustrated. I had taken the children to the Tai'an city
square the previous weekend. They had run around the fountains and played
on granite statues of Chinese zodiac animals. One man walked up to my
children, pointed at them, and said to the child in his arms: *waiguohaizi*,
"foreign children." How early to train children to recognize someone as
different, I thought.

Walking down the street people would point to me and say: *laowai*, "foreigner," as if my tall blond head needed this statement of the obvious. The
character 外, pronounced *wai*, and meaning "foreign" or "outside," was necessarily prefixed to my job, my address, my children, even my very person.

Perhaps this bothered me because it was so different from how I defined myself. I had come to China because I felt a strong connection with
this country. Having adopted a daughter from China, I further defined myself as not just a mother, but a Chinese mother. I had the responsibility to
teach Grace to celebrate her Chinese birth and for Katherine and Andrew
to take pride in the Chinese heritage her adoption had given our family. But
this irremovable scarlet *wai*, 外, seemed bent on separating me, isolating
me, keeping me at arm's length.

Our building, the *wai-jiao lou*, the foreign teachers' building, housed
only us foreigners, no Chinese. There were even minders, certainly there

to help us, but also to keep track of us. I asked Zhang why we were given the special moniker, *wai-jiao*, "foreign teacher," and not simply called teacher, *laoshi*, like everyone else. And while Zhang had a cubicle with all the other teachers of the English Department on the seventh floor, our foreign teachers' offices were located on the lonely third floor.

I wondered about China's longtime penchant for separating foreigners from the Chinese people. Then I found while reading a book on *chengyu*—Chinese proverbs—that they even separated foreign vegetables.

The *chengyu* in my book were wise sayings that specifically mentioned plants. But not just any plants, only indigenous Chinese plants. This made sense as most *chengyu* date from the Spring and Autumn (770–476 BC) or Warring States (475–221 BC) periods (roughly the same time frame as Plato and Socrates in the Western tradition), which were long before the Silk Road or trade had begun in any kind of earnestness.

But the book went on. It said it was easy to tell which vegetables were not indigenous to China, for they were prefixed by one of the following:

Xi, 西, meaning West, as in *xi-gua*, 西瓜 (watermelon).

Yang, 洋, meaning overseas, as in *yang-cong*, 洋葱 (onion).

Fan, 番, meaning foreign, as in *fan-qiejiang*, 番茄酱 (ketchup).

Or *Hu*, 胡, referring to the northwest part of China, as in *hu-jiao*, 胡椒 (pepper).

Zhang told me her grandparents referred to a bicycle as a *yang-che*, "foreign vehicle." She also told me oil used to be called *yang-you*. And *yang-hui* was the old term for cement. Zhang didn't know why the names had changed. But Ji Li Jiang, in her memoir *Red Scarf Girl*, explained the reason. She reported that *yang*-compounds, such as *yang-huo* (literally "foreign fire," referring to matches), were deemed "old thinking" during the Cultural Revolution, and their *yang*s were chopped off and replaced by more revolution-friendly terms. In her memoir, Ji Li Jiang recalls a lecture by a zealous classmate:

> *Yang* means foreign. *Yang-san* means foreign umbrella. They were called that because before Liberation we had to import them. Now we make them in China. So why do you still call it a *yang-san*? Doesn't that show that you're a xenophile who worships anything foreign?

Yang not only carried the idea of "imported," but had the additional burden: "imported, because China isn't advanced enough to make its own, so it has to borrow from foreign countries." My colleague Teacher Hu told me that dolls used to be called *yang-wawa*, for "Chinese children were too poor to have dolls."

Today's Chinese words, for the most part, have been severed from their original *yang*s. But the dictionary still lists a few *yang*-compounds. A round head of cabbage is called *yang-baicai*, to distinguish it from the indigenous variety of cabbage, which is oblong. And showing the Chinese ambivalence toward those foreign things, *yang-qi*, literally "foreign style," means fashionable, a very positive meaning. I also found this interesting phrase: *yang wei Zhong yong*—"Make foreign things serve China."

Under the character *fan* I found *fan-shu*, meaning sweet potato. Another dictionary gave *fan* the meaning of "barbarian." But *hu* was the most interesting of all. I found words prefixed with *hu* fell into three categories. The first had to do with recklessness. There were many such entries:

hu-hua, 胡话, ravings, wild talk

hu-lai, 胡来, bungle

hu-luan, 胡乱, carelessly; casually

hu-nao, 胡闹, act willfully and make a scene

hu-shuo, 胡说, nonsense, drivel

hu-zhou, 胡诌, tall story, fabrication

hu-zuofeiwei, 胡作非为, act in defiance of the law or public opinion

All of these had a negative connotation to their meaning.

The second category of *hu*-compounds had to do with music, such as *hu-qin*, meaning a bowed string instrument like the *er-hu*. Finally, there were *hu* words having to do with beards or mustaches, like *hu-xu*.

I did a little research. It turns out that all these various meanings of *hu* are related. The term *hu* originally referred to non-Han nationalities living in northwest China in ancient times. Unlike the stereotypically calm and patient Han people, these facial hair–sporting nomads were viewed as having a more rowdy, wild character. Still, in modern China, respectable men holding stable jobs are usually clean-shaven; bearded men are either artists or homeless. Finally, all *hu-qin* family of instruments, including the *er-hu,* are believed to have descended from instruments played by the Xi, a nomadic people of Central Asia.

These words taught me that my status as a foreigner was not that simple. Initially, I thought it only meant separate, different, unable to ever truly understand Chinese culture or literature. Even barbarian.

But it is more complicated than that. Sadly, it also has overtones of "better." It also means "from the most advanced country of the world, the one we compare ourselves to, and feel we come up short." Or, "a member of the West, who humiliated our country for one hundred years."

It can also mean coming from a culture with dangerous ideas. Or conversely, coming from a country that truly has freedom. Or, coming from a culture that looks down on us. It means "foreign devil." It means "missionary." Seeing the baggage these words carried showed me some of the baggage I unknowingly carried as a foreigner in this foreign-phobic -loving -fearing -loathing country. And I wondered how I would ever find my place here.

But it isn't just the Chinese who are ambivalent about foreigners. If we are honest, we know that if we dig deep enough, we'll find similar thinking. I remember our first days with Grace. I held this crying, red-faced child who wanted nothing to do with me and thought: I did paperwork for eight months for this? I spent thousands of dollars for this? I've spent the better part of the last year and a half longing for this? I held her and looked at her. She looked so alien, I thought.

Perhaps it was all the more evident because Andrew, at the time four months old, accompanied us to China to adopt the nearly twelve-month-old Grace. From his fair skin to his reddish blond hair to the dimple on his chin, he resembled me exactly. At that point in his life he slept with me, fed from me, and, carried snugly in a sling, accompanied me almost everywhere. He was so familiar to me that he felt like one of my own appendages rather than his own separate person. In contrast, this brown-skinned dark-eyed baby seemed completely different from me. Even a little bit strange. Ultimately, she just seemed foreign.

Our first weeks together were difficult. Many of our issues had to do with sleep—our mutual lack of it. It seemed Grace's every instinct and natural schedule were different from those of my other two. They barely tolerated naps; Grace needed two per day or her entire bald head turned red and her open mouth screamed with rage. At times I resented her for disrupting our happy routine. In retrospect I know that we were just getting to know each other and understanding how she was wired. Additionally, it took her months to become fully healthy.

The first few weeks, until we figured her out her schedule, Grace woke me up every morning at three. She played with toys while I lay groggily on the couch. The good news was that she was ready for her first nap around nine. I would carry her upstairs, feeling guilty that I had been counting down the minutes until her naptime, grateful for the few hours of freedom her sleep gave me.

"I love you," I started saying in a matter-of-fact tone as I laid her down. But even as I said it, I wondered if it was true. It should be true, I knew that. But was it?

We gradually got used to being a family of three kids, all under age three. I took daily walks around our neighborhood, Andrew and Katherine in a double stroller and Grace in a carrier on my back. She loved it. From her perch she laughed and giggled, something she rarely did in those days, playing with my hair and looking at the world around her. She also grew to enjoy bath time. It was a happy ritual we looked forward to every night—Katherine and Grace splashing and playing, Andrew in my arms, his favorite place, me happy knowing everyone was at peace and bedtime approached. Every night after bath time Chris and both girls sang "Ring Around the Rosie" while I nursed Andrew. Grace loved this, expectantly holding up both hands to be made part of the circle, then falling down with gusto.

I discovered Grace adored wearing hats, and I took out all the hats I had bought for Katherine, who never tolerated wearing them, and dressed up my Asian beauty. And while Katherine and Andrew were picky eaters, Grace ate anything I put in front of her. She had been sick when she came to us. Thick yellow snot ran constantly from her nose, and her skin was dry and flaking. It was satisfying to feed her flaxseeds and sweet potatoes, yogurt and tofu, and watch her grow and become healthy. She became more comfortable in our home, scooting along the couch and cruising along the walls, until, three weeks after we got her, she proudly walked on her own.

One day I carried her upstairs for her morning nap and laid her down.

"I love you," I cooed, spontaneously. Then I stopped with a start. I wasn't just saying it anymore, I realized. I really did love her! I smiled and tucked her in. She no longer seemed foreign at all.

❖

When we returned from our winter travels China was celebrating the lunar New Year or Spring Festival, as it is called in China. This is the most important holiday of the year, a time of family togetherness and long-held traditions. Everyone returns to their hometown for the celebration. We stayed put, wanting to avoid this mad transportation rush. Having no extended family here, we were necessarily left out of all this revelry. So for us, Spring Festival was a forlorn time. Stores and restaurants were closed. Even the buses stopped running. Our routine was quiet. It felt like everyone had happily left for a party, except us. We felt our foreign-ness keenly, and it was lonely.

But then I received a text message from Jessica, who had been in my British and American newspaper reading class, inviting us to her home to share a meal with her family. Jessica's family lived in Tai'an where they made and sold *shaobing*, a flaky pastry I had grown to love. Since I frequented a *shaobing* seller on our street, I could picture the work they did behind a hot iron stove, true physical work with sweaty brows and aching backs.

Excitedly, I got the kids ready, putting on their layers of clothes and helping them with mittens and boots.

"You know, with you and the kids out of the house, I could really get a lot of class prep done for next semester," Chris said. I looked at him, his straggly beard now reaching nearly to his collar, his mustache covering his lips completely. He was choosing to miss out on a great cultural opportunity. But I understood. Holing himself up in our apartment was one of his coping mechanisms for dealing with life in this foreign culture.

Regardless, I had been invited to a Chinese home, and even Chris's absence couldn't dampen my enthusiasm. The kids and I got in a taxi and headed south, across the railroad tracks, further south in Tai'an than I had ever been before. We finally approached a dilapidated apartment complex. Jessica was standing at the gate, waving. She brought us into her family's first-floor home, where her parents and a few other relatives warmly greeted us.

My eyes immediately scanned the bare cement floors throughout the tiny apartment and noted the posters of Mao Zedong and Zhou En-lai, the centerpieces of the living-room wall. As I peered around the corner into the combination kitchen/master bedroom, I saw several dishes of food laid out. Jessica's mother must have been chopping meat and vegetables for hours. I felt privileged to be her invited guest.

I was initially nervous about bringing the children, warning them there would be no toys. But they were easily entertained by the chicken strutting around the back porch and the large fish kept in a basin. The Chinese love fresh food, and when I thought about it, it made sense to just keep the animal alive until one was ready to eat it. Jessica's mother spent most of her time on the back porch as well, cooking dish after delicious dish outside on a wok over a charcoal burner. Jessica's father insisted on toasting every five minutes or so, and poured me a teacup full of beer, which he placed in a bowl of hot water. I can't stand the taste of beer, so I switched to a can of Pepsi and toasted with that, which he found quite humorous. Jessica's mother never joined us around the coffee table in the living room. After serving each dish, she started in on the next one in her wok on the back porch.

Once we had finished the main courses, it was time for dumplings, making me feel I was at last celebrating Spring Festival the traditional way. For dessert we were served glutinous rice dumplings called *zongzi*—a ball of sweet, sticky rice with a date stuck in the middle. Each ball was wrapped in large bamboo leaves, tied with string, then steamed. They were traditionally served for Dragon Boat Festival in June, but Jessica and her mother had made some as a special treat for us. We took several photos as we departed. Jessica's mother wore a navy blue blazer a few sizes too big, and her father smiled as he smoked his cigarette.

When we returned home, our small apartment, one of my greatest complaints about living here, felt more cheerful, bright, and airy than it ever had. And I no longer felt as lonely, nor as left out. For I had finally spent the afternoon in a Chinese home. I had experienced the hospitality that is the pride of Shandong people. I had been invited in from the cold to experience the warmth within, to chat, to drink, and ultimately to eat, for food is the mainstay of any Chinese gathering. During Spring Festival, a time traditionally reserved for family, I had not been on the outside, but on the inside.

❀

A few weeks later it was March, time for the spring semester to begin. The winter holiday was coming to a close; life was returning to our campus. Laundry and bedding hung out the window of the students' dorms. Fruit and vegetable sellers were sweeping out their stalls. People hustled and bustled about, something that had been missing for weeks.

On Monday the kids went off to school for the first time in over a month. Katherine woke up to announce that she didn't want to go to school, didn't want to be in class without Grace and Andrew, didn't like her teachers, didn't have any friends, and on and on. She pulled out every line she had ever used.

But when we reached the kindergarten she excitedly ran to see her teachers, presenting them with scarves from Thailand, with her well-rehearsed *"yi diar xiao yisi"* (just a little something).

Chris and I enjoyed our walk home, arms laden with groceries. The sky was unusually blue and clear, thanks to the recent wind and rain. A puffy white cloud even dangled in the air, something we rarely saw. The cobbler was at his post outside the supermarket. He pointed to a stool and gestured for us to sit down and chat. *"Mei banfa,"* we said, laughing. "We can't stop, there's no way." We passed some of our neighbors, a grandmother with her grandson. The toddler, still wearing his layers and padding despite the onset of spring, recognized us and pointed up at Chris. Chris patted the boy's head and said, *"Xiao pengyou, ni hao."* Hello little friend.

"This really is our street," Chris said.

After dinner that night I filled our washbasin with hot water from the bathroom and starting washing dishes. The girls were all in the bedroom with Chris, "helping" him play Solitaire on the computer.

Later, Chris put in a tape of their school songs, and all three kids happily jumped on the bed. It was a great first day of school.

❀

It was good to be back teaching. I felt more comfortable at the podium because I had a semester under my belt. Our class introduction was a lot more polished. Instead of taping a weathered map of the United States onto the chalkboard and passing around a creased 8 x 10 family photo, we had several slide shows Chris had put together with family photos and pictures of our hometown in Washington State. We also had a PowerPoint presentation about our trips that winter, as well as slides on classroom policies and procedures. On Wednesday I got my sophomores back. I was so happy to see them, like a classroom of old friends.

"It's been a great first week so far," I told Chris. The two of us were hanging out in our small kitchen while I tossed vegetables into the wok and kept an eye on the rice cooker. The kids were playing in their room. Katherine and Grace were wearing their ballet leotards and tutus and dancing about. Andrew had no interest in dancing, but hung out with them nonetheless, providing them an audience of one.

"It has been a good week," Chris replied. "It was good to get away from China, to get some perspective. But it was good to come back too. When you compare this week with our first weeks here, you realize how far we've come, how far the kids have come."

I reached into the cupboard and pulled out some plates.

"You know, we really do have a great life here," Chris said. "I know I carp a lot and let little things bother me. But I think we're exactly where we're supposed to be."

Once the kids were in bed, Chris and I sat engrossed in a game of Scrabble on the computer, our nightly habit during the three weeks we'd been home waiting for the semester to begin. Chris beat me nine games out of ten, but for some reason I kept coming back for more.

H-I-R-S-U-T-E, he spelled on the board.

"What is a hirsute?" I asked.

"Look it up," he said. "But I'll give you a hint. It's not a noun."

I gazed at my letters, hoping I could answer his hirsute with something equally erudite. We chatted while I shuffled my letters around.

"I think I'm starting to grow tired of this beard," Chris said.

"Oh?" I said, trying to act nonchalant. I continued to stare at my letters.

"It's just been itching all day as I sat here working on my classes. Maybe I'll just shave it off."

"Whatever you want to do," I said.

"What would you prefer?"

E-X-H-U-M-E, I spelled. "And on a triple word score." Then I turned around and looked at him. "I have no preference. It's your beard. Whatever you want is fine."

"I'll need you to help me. It's too thick for a razor. Can you help me trim it with a pair of scissors first?"

"Right now?"

"Yes, now."

"Let me get the scissors." I forgot all about Scrabble.

We cut and snipped, got a basin of hot water from the bathroom, searched for and found his shaving cream, and after nearly nine months, I got back the man I married. He still needed a haircut, and his face was rather pasty—the impenetrable beard had not allowed a ray of sunlight. I grabbed his face with both hands and kissed him all over. Finally.

At the end of the week the children and I walked home slowly from school, reveling in both the sunshine that took some of the chill out of the air and in having such a good first week. The fruit seller we frequented on our campus had just purchased an ice cream freezer, so we celebrated by buying some ice cream to eat the rest of the way home.

"Everybody, lick your fingers," said Katherine, telling her siblings to get the melted ice cream off their hands before they sat down on the furniture.

I felt obligated to make a cultural point. "But remember, sweetie, Chinese people don't lick their fingers."

"Yes," admitted Katherine. "But we are American children, so it's okay for us to lick our fingers."

I didn't argue with her, but wondered about how inside that five-year-old brain, she was constructing her identity. She knew she was a foreigner, a term that sometimes meant being left out, at other times meant privilege. Or at least a free pass now and then.

I continued to pester Zhang about being a foreigner during our twice-weekly lessons. She didn't have any good answers for me; she just laughed at my frustration and shrugged her shoulders. But once, as she left my office and began to walk back upstairs to her office, she said, "Well, I no longer think of you as a foreign teacher. I think of you as a friend."

Chapter 10

独立
INDEPENDENCE

❀

A NECESSARY PART OF OUR ROUTINE WAS COMMUTING BY BUS BACK AND forth from the old campus, where we lived, to the new campus, where we taught. Bicycles and cars may have once vied for preeminence on the city's streets, but it was clear that the cars were now winning, although bicycles still demanded their rightful place. Along with the traditional two-wheeled variety, there were also three-wheeled variants with carts attached, electric bicycles, and the popular motor scooter, all darting in and out among the cars, using rules of the road completely unfamiliar to us. En route to the new campus, we would pass restaurants and hotels where uniformed employees lined up in formation to be inspected or to hear announcements. Then we would cross the railroad tracks and head out of the city into the countryside.

Staring out the bus windows, we would see buses, three-wheeled trucks, three-wheeled taxis (called baby taxis), as well as the occasional donkey cart with a sunburned farmer and his wife perched on top of a load of firewood. My favorite vehicle was a small truck whose open bed billowed over with its load, like a man whose ample girth spilled out over his belted trousers.

Driving under the Beijing-Shanghai expressway, we would continue along Great Wall Road into the countryside, where stone and mortar village homes with chickens in the yard gave way to industrial complexes, finally leading to our university's new campus.

One morning as we cruised along Ying Sheng Road on the way to class, I looked through the bus windows with a feeling of detachment at the various scenes of buying and selling playing out below me. There was room for all manner of entrepreneurs in the post-Mao China. One woman laid out a canvas in front of the kindergarten to sell children's clothing; another pulled up a three-wheeled cart filled with tomatoes, peanuts, cabbage, and whatever else was in season. Pull the cart up to a stop, set up the scale, and one was in business. Anyone with a front door opening to the street could open up a *bing* shop, a noodle restaurant, or any sort of repair shop—scooter, bicycle, mobile phone. I frequented a *bing* shop that decided to change to a noodle restaurant after Spring Festival. The owners assiduously cleaned, set out some tables and stools, and hung up a fresh red and white sign. It lasted for a few months, then they were back to *bing* again. The tables and stools disappeared, but the sign stayed.

Near our children's kindergarten was a small gravel parking lot. Every morning a woman pulled up in her cart, set out portable tables and stools, and began cooking breakfast over a charcoal stove. After lunch, she folded up and the site was only a parking lot again. Fresh tofu was sold every morning from the back of a cart. Our cobbler set out his tools and a few pairs of shoes in front of the supermarket for a few weeks. Then we wouldn't see him for a while. A few weeks later, he would be back. Boxes of fresh fruit were laid out on the sidewalk. At various times farmers came from the countryside bringing cherries, peaches, tomatoes, or other produce in baskets or just in the flatbed of a truck. They pulled up on the sidewalk and began selling.

During winter a lady with a cart-borne homemade oven would roast sweet potatoes whole, a popular snack. The proprietor was a round woman in a blue-plaid apron and red cheeks. She could be seen trudging up and down our street. Oil barrels were turned into steamers for *mantou* (pronounced mahn-toe), steamed rolls whose pale color reminded me of the pallid skin of someone who hadn't been out in the sun for a while, or a brown 'n serve roll yet to be browned. Once, in the alley near our house, a butcher pulled up in his three-wheeled motor cart. The meat counter was the flatbed of his truck; his chopping block, a tree stump. All cuts of meat could be bought. Periodically a man would tie a string between trees and hang up some clothing and underwear. The next day, he was gone, likely to a new location. In early autumn a man on a bicycle rode around with a large cylindrical cork on the back of his bicycle. Stuck into the cork were skewers of candied hawthorns. After passing him by several times on the way home from the kindergarten, we finally tried his treats. Everything just mentioned could be found in one block of Ying Sheng Road between our university gate and the kindergarten.

I had long been lost in thought as we rumbled along, considering the lively entrepreneurial spirit I had observed since moving here, but now the bus pulled into the main gate of the new campus, and I began to mentally prepare for the more immediate task of teaching. On my schedule that day was an Extensive Reading class.

For English majors, the university had divided the subject of English into various classes by component. Thus, the students took classes in listening, speaking, grammar, and reading. Reading was further divided into Intensive Reading, reading passages in depth, and Extensive Reading, where each unit had a variety of passages centered on a theme. This semester the English Department had assigned me several classes of Extensive Reading.

The first time I taught this class, I told the students to read the first passage. All at once, thirty students immediately proceeded to read the passage *out loud*, not at all in unison. I almost jumped out of my skin at this sudden cacophonous Tower of Babel. I had seen individual Chinese students reading aloud from their textbooks all over campus, but to hear them all in a classroom echoing together produced such dissonance, I wondered how they could even think or consider any of the ideas in the passage. They were obviously used to it, conditioned since childhood. It made sense to a certain extent, for saying something out loud did help internalize it. I quickly became used to it, for all my classes used this method, except one. Only during Extensive Reading on Thursday afternoons did the students read silently. Now I found them a little disconcerting. "Why are they so quiet?" I wondered.

The Extensive Reading class for sophomores had a section in each unit on idioms. That week I had to teach the idiom "to be on one's own." Try as I might, however I explained the meaning, my students just gave me blank stares.

It was our second semester together and I knew their English was advanced enough to understand this simple idiom. But still they could not grasp it.

Up until then, most of the idioms had fit nicely with Chinese culture. For example, I had taught several idioms related to harmony, such as "to hold one's tongue" or "to go with the flow." Another lesson contained idioms related to compromise. My students could easily comprehend the notions of "give-and-take" and "meet someone halfway." But this week, the category was independence. Now we were treading on unfamiliar ground.

For although many big cities in China were rapidly Westernizing, Shandong was an agricultural province where the traditional ways lingered. Children still had their heads shaved. New mothers observed a one-month "lying-in period." When eating in a restaurant people took great care to order an even number of dishes—four, six, or eight—but never an unlucky odd number. While my students expected to marry for love, their parents had met through the services of the village matchmaker. The Kitchen God was still given a send-off before Spring Festival. And my students had often been raised by their grandparents, and grandparents naturally brewed a stronger cup of tradition than parents.

Tradition meant that my students, from birth until death, were deeply (and happily) entangled in a web of dependent relationships. My students knew they could lean on their relationships; they need not "stand alone," which is the literal meaning of "independence." Independence is written 独立. The first character means "alone," and the second is "stand."

As one goes from child to adult there is a natural shift from being dependent on to being depended on, but there is always some level of dependence. What there rarely is, however, is independence. Or, as Lin Yutang put it: "Society is built on the principle that a man is not an individual but attains his full being only in having harmonious relationships."

Finally I realized why my students could not understand this particular idiom. In our part of China, one was never really "on one's own."

To make this idiom more clear I gave some personal examples. My brother had recently graduated from college, I told them. As a college graduate, my parents expected him to now be completely responsible for himself financially. A collective gasp arose from the students. Buoyed by this drama, I continued.

"Not only that . . . they told him it was time for him to move out of the house." The students gasped in shock. Many of my students would never "move out of the house" but would continue to live with their parents even after marriage.

I went on. "When he didn't want to move out of the house, my parents agreed to let him remain. But they charged him rent." At this point my students just stared at me silently, somewhat incredulous, completely unable to comprehend such a thing. In our province, many parents still purchased a home for their son. I told them my parents were not an aberration; rather, this was completely in line with American culture, where parents viewed part of their responsibilities as raising their children to be able to function in life independently, to enable them to stand on their own two feet.

A while later I e-mailed my Chinese friend Ruby, still living in Tokyo, and asked her about this. She responded in her e-mail:

> We understand that family and social networks are the only reliable insurance system protecting us. In return, we have all sorts of duties from various directions. We have to live our lives caring how other people consider us. Sometimes we have to bend our own desire to meet other people's expectations. We cannot live in the country by ourselves, left alone.

Dependence, while providing security, also entailed duties: duties to classmates, duties to coworkers, and, most important, duties to one's parents. I had kept in touch with many of the seniors I taught last term, and sympathized with them as they now tried to find jobs with a 30 percent unemployment rate for new college graduates. Some would tell me matter-of-factly that they had received a job offer, but turned it down because their parents didn't approve. Perhaps the job was in Beijing and they wanted their child closer, or it was a job that involved a lot of travel and they didn't think this was a good idea. What surprised me, besides the fact that the parents had that much say, was the manner in which the students accepted this. There was no anger or resentment, simply acceptance. Often, children were expected to submit to their parents into adulthood on most matters— marriage, job, residence.

I found this difficult to comprehend, so I questioned Reese, one of my students. She explained it this way. When it came time for her to enter high school, her father had moved with her to a bigger city nearby, leaving her mother and sister behind, so she could attend a better high school. While she was at school or studying, he prepared all her meals, washed her clothes (by hand), and did all the necessary shopping and cleaning. Recently, her father had forbidden her from seeing a boy from her hometown. She was upset, but accepting. After recounting to me all her father had done for her, she then asked rhetorically, "How could I not honor my father by obeying him in something he thinks is important, even if I disagree?"

❀

I pondered all that I had learned as I packed up my books and walked back to the bus stop. Throughout the day, a haze had gathered over the sky, rendering everything a brownish-gray color. As the bus headed back home, I stared out the window at the sun. Pollution had snuffed out the sun's brilliance, allowing one to gaze at it at length. It sat in the sky as an orange circle with a clearly defined border, like a happy face sticker affixed to brown construction paper. As the bus weaved its way through countryside and city, I thought about my students, their duties, and their dependence.

And I thought about my own Chinese daughter. I had learned today a little of what she had lost, and what she had gained, to become who she is. Perhaps this dichotomy—dependence and independence—was where Grace would be changed the most. Chris and I would raise her the only way we knew how: to think for herself, to stand up for herself, and ultimately to go out on her own and care for herself. This was the American way, a requirement to survive in our culture. Yes, she would be freed of the burden of duty, but she would also grow up without the security those duties provided. She would learn to stand alone, and would gain the pride, and sometimes the loneliness, that that entailed.

Chapter 11

泰山
MOUNT TAI

To die for the people is weightier than Mount Tai, but to work
for the fascists and die for the exploiters and oppressors is
lighter than a feather.

—MAO ZEDONG

❁

ACCORDING TO CHINESE LEGEND, WHEN PANGU, THE ANCESTOR OF ALL
things, hatched from his primeval egg, the top half of the egg became
the sky and the bottom half, the earth. Pangu stood up to separate these
two, earth and sky, yin and yang. When he died, his hair became the trees;
his blood became the rivers; his left eye, the sun; and his right, the moon.
Wind was formed from his breath, rain from his sweat, and from the fleas
on his body, human beings. Finally, his head became Mount Tai, and his
remaining limbs, the four other sacred mountains of China.

Mount Tai (called Taishan in Chinese, as *shan* means mountain) provided the geographical backdrop for our time in China. We lived at the foot
of this icon, in its gradient, even having to walk uphill to our small apartment. We often took our children to play at the Dai Temple, a large courtyard complex downtown that served as the traditional starting point for the
trek up the mountain. One block behind our old campus is Tianwaicun
Square, where one can take a bus to the cable car station and ascend the
mountain without actually climbing it. Between our campus and the square
are small gift shops whose chief wares are small oval-shaped pieces of Taishan rock carved with Chinese characters and mounted on wooden stands.
The rocks are clustered outside the entrances, looking like each shop is
guarded by a congregation of petrified ghosts. Shortly after we arrived, we

bought a rock inscribed with 福, our Chinese family name, and placed our own overlooking ghost in our bedroom bookcase.

As with all mountains, the different peaks and crests of Mount Tai change shape depending on one's viewpoint. Behind our home is one particular peak. As we ride from the new campus outside of town toward the old campus, it has a long gentle slope like a cat's arched back. At various times, the feline-shaped peak disappears behind less significant foothills, then reappears at turns, always with a slightly changed shape. Upon finally reaching the old campus at the foot of the great mountain, the long arch vanishes behind the peak and assumes a perfectly round shape, like a crusty old man wearing a stocking cap standing head and shoulders above the crowd. Seeing that crusty old man came to mean I was home.

In the morning when we awakened, one look at the mountain would tell us if our air was clear and fresh or gray and polluted. On clear days it seemed every leaf had definition, every rock stood out in relief. But on hazy days when the pollution hung in the air, the entire mountain retreated into a dull monochromatic figure of gray.

❀

In the spring semester one of our colleagues returned to the United States, so Chris and I decided to use her office. It was a little brighter than our old office, and we wouldn't have to share it with anyone except each other. She also left a huge stack of *National Geographic* magazines. We had no idea what a treasure this would turn out to be. The magazines were quite old, many from the 1970s, a few from the 1960s, and one even dating back to 1958. On our lunch breaks we enjoyed relaxing in our office reading old articles. I naturally gravitated to the articles about China. Reading articles from the 1970s, when China was just opening to the world, provided a fun comparison with the China of our everyday experience.

I glanced through one article dating from December 1970, looking primarily at the photos. One photo showed an adult tricycle with several children in the back, a common type we still saw on the streets of Tai'an. But it was the caption I found the most interesting:

> Everywhere workers, peasants, and officials travel by bike in a China that counts the private auto an extreme luxury. But they enjoy the blessing: an

almost complete absence of pollution from car exhausts. Premier Chou En-
lai believes that by starting late to industrialize, China may avoid the pollution
now plaguing other nations.

How ironic, for despite China's late-bloomer status in industrializa-
tion, it is plagued with systemic pollution far surpassing that seen in the
West. I remember my first trip to China in 2001, when I strained to look
out the airplane windows to see some lights in the dark night—my first
glimpses of China—but saw nothing, only blackness. It wasn't until I arrived at the Beijing airport, and saw the haze hanging along the long corri-
dors leading us to customs and baggage claim, that I knew the lights had
been invisible because of the blanket of pollution covering the area. We
were lucky on that visit: the next day a strong wind blew out the smog and
left us with a clean-aired city to enjoy.

Now living in China, wind always excited us for this very reason.
Wind meant the next day would have clear skies, with beautiful views of
this mountain right behind us. But those winds were few and far between.
Most days our standard mountain view was a gray one, with much haze
between us and her. There were days when I was downtown and despite
being only two or three miles away, I could not even tell there was a mountain at all. Other days we could see only a dim outline.

❧

In late spring the entire university was mobilized for the annual sports
meet and the kids were in school. That left Chris and me with a day off together, something we rarely had. This was our chance to climb Mount Tai.
For me, it was the first time. Chris had climbed it once on his own in the fall.

The 5,000-foot high Mount Tai, though largely unknown in the West,
was known by every Chinese as the foremost of the five sacred mountains
in China as well as its most climbed mountain, a national holy altar. From
its heights, Mao, watching the sunrise but not missing a propaganda opportunity, had famously declared, "The East is Red," and Confucius, who
hailed from the city of Qufu (pronounced Choo-foo) just down the road,
had contemplated how the world seemed small. It is a unique combination
of nature and culture. Temples, steles, inscribed poems, stairways, and
pavilions had transformed the natural crags and peaks of the mountain into

a cultural relic, representing the three major religions of China: Buddhism, Daoism, and Confucianism. Seventy-two Chinese rulers had made a pilgrimage to Mount Tai, seeking heaven's favor for an auspicious reign.

The *Tai* of Taishan, written 泰, means "grand," "tranquil," or "peaceful." But many locals also told me this character has a feeling of stability, of steadiness, of immovability—as firm and fixed as Mount Tai itself. The character is immortalized in a *chengyu*: 国泰民安, "country . . . stable . . . people . . . peace"—when the country is stable, the people will have peace.

Sacrifices, rites, and ceremonies have been held on Mount Tai perhaps as far back as recorded history. China's first emperor, Qin Shihuang, traveled to Mount Tai in 219 BC to offer sacrifices to thank heaven after unifying China, the first in a long line of imperial visits. The capital at the time was in Chang'an, today's Xi'an, several hundred miles away. Thus, the emperor's journey from his western capital to climb this eastern mountain symbolically marked the unification of the two parts of China: the western portion overlooking Central Asia and the interior, and the eastern portion facing the sea.

For succeeding "preeminent" emperors, performing such rites (called *fengshan*) on Mount Tai served to let friend and foe alike know that the emperor had received the Mandate of Heaven. It was also a handsome opportunity for a show of force. Not just any emperor could perform *fengshan*. In 110 BC, Emperor Wu of the Western Han Dynasty, just before departing with a procession of 180,000 people to perform *fengshan*, formulated three preconditions for performing the rites. I found these instructive, for they identified their qualities of an ideal reign and also foreshadowed the expectations that current Chinese had for their government: first, unification of the country with no rebellions; second, a long period of order, peace, and tranquility; and third, auspicious signs.

Li Shimin, known as Emperor Taizong of the Tang Dynasty (AD 618–907), aspired to perform *fengshan* since peace and prosperity had returned to China after the dynastic turnover from the Sui Dynasty (AD 589–618). Taizong, regarded by many as the greatest Chinese emperor, well-known even at the time for his statesmanship and military exploits, thought himself qualified to perform the rites. However, one of his counselors, Wei Zheng, still celebrated in China as a straight-talking adviser, persuaded the emperor to abandon the idea. He reasoned that although the country was at peace, the road from Chang'an to Mount Tai led through Henan, at that time a dilapidated area with little to commend it. Envoys from neighboring states would certainly join the procession, and this weak underbelly would be exposed to their eyes. Taizong was disappointed but had to agree, and never performed *fengshan* during his reign.

His son, Emperor Gaozong, accompanied by his ambitious consort Wu Zetian, fulfilled his father's ambitions. In 665 a procession of the leading officials, generals, and concubines; ministers from neighboring states in what is now Xinjiang; minority chieftains from southern China; as well as envoys from Korea, Persia, India, and Japan, set out eastward from Chang'an. The procession, several hundred miles long, took two months to reach the base of Mount Tai. Once there, in an unprecedented move, Wu Zetian offered her own sacrifices after the emperor, prefiguring her later ambitions to seize the imperial reins and form her own short-lived dynasty, the Zhou Dynasty.

When my parents were here, the first question the students asked them was if they had climbed Mount Tai yet, assuming that its fame was what brought them to Tai'an (as opposed to wanting to see their daughter, son-in-law, and grandchildren!). My students were always surprised, and a little crestfallen, to find that most Westerners had never heard of their beloved Taishan. So climbing Mount Tai was honoring not only their mountain, but also their culture and traditions. I was happy to have the chance.

Chris and I took a ten-minute taxi ride east from the old campus to the Red Gate, arriving around 9:30 a.m. to begin our climb. Chris carried a backpack with several bottles of water, and I had packed boiled eggs and a few other snacks.

"Well, only 6,666 steps to go. We better get started," Chris said.

Climbing Mount Tai is unlike any idea of mountain climbing we have in the United States. There are no ropes required or even any skill. Instead, a broad path leads through the woods, punctuated by stone steps and bridges. Meter after meter of the climb we found Chinese characters carved into the rock and painted red, or temples of various kinds—Buddhist, Daoist, and Confucian. We passed the tree where Qin Shihuang, the first emperor of China, sought cover from the rain when he made his climb. And we gazed at the poems of Mao—easily recognizable by his signature flowing calligraphy—inscribed upon the mountain.

Also along the way were many refreshment stands offering pineapple, melons, tomatoes, and drinks, along with a crepe-like pastry filled with a stalk of green onion. Other vendors sold pieces of rock, statues, herbs, ice cream, or Coca-Cola.

"The prices are rising just as we are," Chris said. He was pleased to be carrying our own water, thereby not subjecting us to this price gouging. "I suppose at the top the prices will also reach their pinnacle."

One of my more cynical students told me that Mount Tai has always been closely bound with Chinese culture; now Mount Tai was only about money, she said, thus keeping current its representation of China.

We enjoyed a lunch stop just before the Path of Eighteen Bends. Eating our boiled eggs, chips, and bananas, we viewed the sixteen-hundred-some steps we still had to climb. That final leg was brutal. What had been a moderate incline thus far turned into a vertical wall of steps, with the South Heavenly Gate gazing down at us from the top. We could understand why so many emperors thought this the stairway to heaven. It reminded me of Jacob's ladder, although in my childish perception Jacob's ladder seemed more an effortless escalator; this required a great deal more exertion. Along this arduous portion we made our ascent with the same group of people. Our fellow pilgrims encouraged us by saying *jia you*, which literally means "add oil (to the engine)," but could be better translated as "Come on!"

When we had first arrived in Tai'an, another teacher at a university in town remarked that climbing Mount Tai was symbolic of the sweat and toil many people exerted to try to reach heaven on their own merits. I thought of this a lot during my climb, as I tried to imagine a Chinese emperor making this arduous climb for the purpose of seeking the benevolence of heaven.

Once through the South Heavenly Gate we found ourselves in a mountaintop city. Restaurants, hotels, and gift shops lined the streets. Climbers grabbed snacks and souvenirs and visited the various temples. Chris and I made our way to the Jade Emperor Temple, whose inner courtyard, filled with the smoke of incense, contained a stone block inscribed: 1545m. We had reached the highest point. We entered the hall housing the Jade Emperor himself, who, to my surprise, was not made out of jade at all, but rather burnished brass.

After relaxing for a few hours, we started our trek down. Now I had this milestone behind me. I could tell my students that I had climbed Taishan.

Chapter 12

WORDS

A man hath joy by the answer of his mouth: and a word spoken in due season, how good it is!
—Proverbs 15:23, King James Bible

Water and words are easy to pour but impossible to recover.
—Chinese proverb

THERE IS SOMETHING ABOUT THE MOUTH THAT SEEMS TO INVITE IMAGERY and metaphor. Rivers and caves have mouths. Bottles and cannons have mouths. The Bible often invokes imagery of mouths. When God punished some Israelites for rebelling against Moses, the Bible tells us that "the earth opened its mouth and swallowed them up." In the Psalms, God says, "I am the Lord your God, who brought you up out of Egypt. Open your mouth wide and I shall fill it." And in the children's favorite, Daniel in the Lion's Den, Daniel tells us, "My God sent his angel, and he shut the mouths of the lions."

Mouths are used in numerous idiomatic expressions in the English language. We describe one with a legacy of wealth as "born with a silver spoon in his mouth." Someone who utters embarrassing words is "putting his foot in his mouth." When surprised by someone of like mind, we exclaim, "You took the words right out of my mouth!" The Chinese language also acknowledges this relationship between a mouth and words. The Chinese character meaning "words" truly looks like words emanating upward from an open mouth.

言

WORDS

I thought of the character for "words" as I kept an eye on my daughter at the playground. We were thawing out from winter and anxious to spend time outdoors again. When I picked up the children from school, we usually stayed awhile so they could play on the school grounds. That particular afternoon I watched Katherine as she played with one of her classmates. Unlike the open mouth the venerable Calligrapher had drawn, my daughter's mouth was pursed tightly shut, demonstrating physically the sense of muteness she felt. She waved wildly with her arms or pointed to where she wanted her friend to go. But no words accompanied her frenzied gestures.

It was a poignant scene, for Katherine's nature was never to be without words. If she was feeling something, it came out of her mouth. If she had an idea, she shared it immediately. Thoughts made only momentary pit stops on her brain before they continued to their final destination out in the world. Yet I had placed her in a situation that rendered her wordless, so contrary to her very persona.

Chris and I discussed Katherine's frustration at her inability to communicate. We thought about trying to get a tutor for her, but wondered how that would fit into our busy family routine. At my next tutoring session with Zhang I sought her advice. I asked what she thought about our paying one of the kindergarten teachers to spend some time one-on-one with Katherine during the course of the day, deliberately teaching her the words she needed to know, instead of Katherine trying to pluck out word meanings as they rushed by in a torrent of classroom instruction.

But Zhang shook her head. "The teachers are all so busy," she said. "Since there are only two teachers in each classroom and usually more than forty students, they just don't have time to focus on only one. It would be very difficult."

I knew she was right. And even requesting such would be to ask for special privileges as foreigners, something we tried not to do. So we were left with no remedy.

Later that week we were finishing up dinner, usually a disjointed affair in our apartment. Our living room was so small that the table was wedged against the wall and an easy chair. There were spaces for the three kids to eat, but that was it. Usually Chris ate in the bedroom by the computer, and I in the kitchen. I felt guilty about our lack of family dinners, but the combination of our small living space and the fry-it-then-serve-it nature of Chinese cuisine made a family meal difficult to pull off for one of questionable homemaking skills like me. But that night was different. We didn't all sit around the table, but Chris took his plate and sat on the living-room couch, and I joined him.

It was a noisy affair with all five of us together in such a small space, each child more interested in talking than eating. As I watched the kids at the table I noticed Andrew had a bruise on his forehead.

"Grace, did Andrew fall down at school?" I asked.

She reported back in an authoritative manner: "Yes, Andrew fell down. Then a *Chinese* boy tried to jump on him, but I put up my hands and blocked him."

I looked at Chris. We chuckled at her rancor, for it seemed incongruous to hear Grace tell of how she had protected Andrew from the *Chinese* boy. "Doesn't she realize she's Chinese too?" we thought.

But quickly the reality of this little comment settled in. When Grace said the "Chinese" boy, she was saying this in a negative fashion. Where had she heard this? From her parents. We realized that quite often, in the course of telling each other about our day, words about the "Chinese people" figured into our stories somehow, usually when recounting our little frustrations.

Earlier that week Chris had said: "I was standing in line at the supermarket and a Chinese man cut right in front of me."

I recalled an earlier trip to the park, and later telling Chris about it: "A whole group of Chinese people gathered around and stared at us, and some older Chinese ladies kept trying to grab Andrew's hair."

Or, "These Chinese plastic bags (or insert another item that had just torn, or broken, or fallen apart) aren't worth anything. This one just got a hole in it."

In every case, our choice of words had created a negative image of people or things Chinese.

Had Grace gotten the idea that when we talked about a "Chinese" person we were downgrading that person with our speech? Her comment gave us insight into something we were doing, albeit unconsciously.

"Why did I even add the word 'Chinese'?" Chris asked himself out loud. "Of course the man who cut in front of me was Chinese. We're in China."

We felt ashamed. In the frustration we sometimes experienced living here, we had resorted to labeling. And we realized that by adding the word "Chinese" we were automatically dividing people into "them" and "us." We were making a distinction.

This eye opening was particularly painful because one of the main reasons we came to China was to give Grace pride in being Chinese. We wanted her to enjoy a firmly implanted identity and to know where she came from. This incident showed us that our careless remarks were doing the opposite of what we intended. I hoped we could rectify it before this idea seeped deeper into her consciousness.

How I wished I could take those words back. But like the black marks used above the mouth by the Calligrapher in his interpretation of "words," 言, once uttered, they remained.

❀

The Chinese took 言 and used it as a radical to form many other characters that have words as an integral part of their meaning, such as "language," 語, "speech," 話, "poem," 詩, and "thanks," 謝謝. But in the classroom, I learned a few more terms that the Calligrapher visibly viewed as rooted in words: "mistake," depicted as 誤, and "taboo," shown as 諱.*

The word "taboo" leapt into the English language from the journals of Captain Cook, who in the 1770s visited the Friendly Islands east of Fiji (now Tonga). It was originally used to describe in an anthropological sense forbidden customs, or sacred items consecrated for special use. The Chinese word, with its 言 radical, foreshadowed what the English term would gradually come to mean: sensitive topics that we tried to avoid talking about.

ERRC, our sponsoring organization, advised us to stay clear of contentious issues, particularly the issue of Taiwan. I felt I understood the

---

*In the course of simplification 言 remained unchanged, but characters that used 言 as a radical shifted to a simplified version; for example, 語 became 语. For this chapter, I used the traditional characters, for they kept the image of the words much more than the simplified version. 諱 is the traditional version, still used in Taiwan and Hong Kong. When China simplified its characters, 諱 became 讳.

Chinese point of view that Taiwan was an integral part of "one China," so I was completely taken aback when my Extensive Reading sophomores and I had an incident over Taiwan. I read the following sentence out of their textbook: "Since the mid-1980s, Japan, South Korea, Taiwan and Thailand have all succumbed to pressure from Washington and allowed the sale of foreign-brand cigarettes."

At this point I paused.

"Do you know all these countries?" I asked, just to make sure they were aware of the English names.

There was immediate commotion.

"Which country don't you know?" I asked.

"They are not all *countries*!" they indignantly replied.

Then I realized my error. Lumping Taiwan together with the other three and labeling them all as "countries" was taboo, 諱, a blasphemy they had caught immediately. I rolled my eyes and said, "Oh, I'm sorry. What I meant to say was, 'Do you know these three countries and one Chinese renegade province?'"

They nodded approvingly.

Later in the course, we had a unit on diplomacy, and as part of the lesson I showed them a map of Asia so we could review the English names for all the countries. As I was speaking, I noticed that while mainland China was the color yellow, on this map the island of Taiwan stood out in pink. I pointed this out to the students, making a passing remark that in the West we had a different view of Taiwan: while it may not be its own country, it was somehow separate from the PRC.

This was a mistake, a 誤, as the Calligrapher styled it. To so offhand-edly make such a remark to my students, wound up after years of indoctri-nation over the Taiwan issue, only inflamed them. As the Calligrapher wisely knew, most mistakes have a great amount to do with opening our mouths; in this case, he added a second mouth to the character just to underline the point.

I began to go on from the map exercise, but one of the students, Roy, raised his hand. Roy, like most of the boys, had never been particularly vocal in class. But at that moment he felt compelled to stand up and give me a for-mal speech demarcating the history of Taiwan and its relationship to the mainland, concluding of course: Taiwan was intrinsically part of China.

He was immediately followed by another student, who wished to elaborate on points Roy had made. Altogether four students, three of them male students—normally quiet in class and usually speaking only to inform me they had to miss class for soccer matches—stood up to give speeches. This was not a political issue; it was a deeply felt personal issue.

They were resentful at U.S. "interference" when they felt there was a chance to regain Taiwan some decades ago, and felt the continued separation had reinforced China's "weak" status; that this label would not be removed until Taiwan was back in the fold. It was an open wound not just on the country, but on themselves. Except perhaps the 9/11 attacks, in my lifetime I had never known Americans to be so personally affected by international relations. China's history, particularly its recent history involving weakness, capitulation, and embarrassment at the hands of the West, was completely intertwined with the personal self-esteem of my students.

On the break, Lois, who had been to my house and taught me to make hot and sour potatoes, came over to chat.

"In my mind, the issue of Taiwan is the biggest international relations issue facing the Chinese government today. Only when this issue is put to rest, in a satisfactory manner, of course, will we Chinese finally be able to restore our national pride."

"But Taiwan has achieved economic prosperity and rather enjoys being separate," I told her.

"But for the mainland, the family can never truly be happy until the wayward son has returned home," she replied.

On a Saturday a few weeks later I took the children to the kindergarten playground. Again, a classmate was there. This time Katherine, to my complete surprise, chatted away happily with her friend.

The other parents around us chuckled and looked at me with surprise. "She speaks Chinese!" I nodded in astonished agreement.

At one point her friend fell down and Katherine's words tumbled out as she comforted her with a long complex Chinese sentence, which she then roughly translated for me as, "Don't worry about it, you'll be fine."

Grace and Andrew picked up the cue from their older sister and the three of them began using more and more Chinese with one another at home, including the occasional insult, thinking their parents couldn't understand them.

"*Wo zui hao, ni chao hao,*" Katherine would say to Grace. I'm the best. You're the worst.

"I understand you," I'd say sternly, whether I did or not. No matter what language they used, the surly tone translated easily.

Our children's language range remained limited, as they were only exposed to schoolchild Chinese. They would continue to learn as their context expanded. But I was thrilled with their progress, particularly Katherine's. This had been a long road for her, and for us, but we now felt that all three children had a strong foothold in this language that would serve as a foundation for the years to come. From that beginning, when the mouth finally opened, the words flowed faster and faster, every day and every week, freely and naturally, just as the Calligrapher imagined.

Chapter 13

上帝
GOD

Mao used to be god. Now there is no god for the Chinese people.

—ZHANG, my tutor

❦

WE ATTENDED CHURCH OUR FIRST WEEK IN TAI'AN, RIDING THE NO. 3 BUS across town. From the outside it looked like a typical Methodist church on Main Street of small-town America—arched windows, high ceilings, even a steeple with a cross on top. I was so happy that at least it "looked" like a church. When everything around us seemed so strange and foreign, at least church looked "churchy." We later found out the church was built by American missionaries in the late nineteenth century, which explained its Western appearance.

We found seats, no small feat. Although the service had not started, it was already crowded. After some hymns came prayer, but a prayer unlike any congregational prayer we were used to. Everyone prayed out loud, sounding as if three hundred conversations were going on at once, which I suppose is exactly what it was. It was a cacophonous surprise. Later I became used to it, but never became comfortable praying that way myself. I would sometimes look around and see earnest facial expressions or perhaps a tear running down a face as each person fervently prayed.

We had brought the kids to the pseudo-nursery. All the children were together in a courtyard next to the church, somewhat supervised by a few grandmothers. I left the girls there and took Andrew into the service with me. But a few times during the service they came looking for me because Grace was crying, so I had to make my way out. This was not a simple matter. The church was packed. The wooden benches on bare cement floors were stacked so closely together that when we stood up to sing we couldn't quite stand up straight. The aisles themselves were crammed with stools. We were seated near the back so while carrying Andrew, I had to step and hop over people and around stools just to get to the door. After doing this twice, I just stayed in the courtyard with the kids. They were still uncomfortable and as yet spoke no Chinese.

In the courtyard nursery a grandmother held her split-pants-wearing grandchild facing me, who let out a stream of pee right there on the cement. No one was the least bit perturbed, or even tried to clean anything up. I later became completely inured to this, but at the time I was stunned. The grandmother got a little pee on her hand. She wiped it off on her pants, leaving a wet smudge.

Since the service was piped into the courtyard on loudspeakers, I could hear the church members say something in unison that had a vaguely familiar cadence to it. The caregivers around me said it along with the loudspeakers, somewhat absentmindedly. Then two short words pierced my incomprehension: *san tian*, "three days." I suddenly realized they were saying the Apostles' Creed. My mind, brought into unison with them, began to chant along, "The third day he rose again from the dead. He ascended into heaven ..." I realized this was in fact church, a real church, and these women on stools next to me with pee-smudged pants speaking an alien language were connected to me, for we believed in the same God.

From that beginning we tried several combinations to figure out the best way for our family to attend church. We continued to try to attend the morning service as a family, but the children went from being uncomfortable in their nursery to being too comfortable; they would look into the windows of the sanctuary to tell us this or that or say they needed help using the bathroom. The bathroom was outside of the courtyard, and assisting the children with this was not part of the caregivers' job description. Once the children were comfortable walking to the bathroom, I worried they could just as easily walk right out into the street.

During the cold winter months we didn't want to leave the children in the freezing courtyard, so we stopped going altogether for several weeks. Finally, Chris and I left the children home with a babysitter while we attended the morning service.

We had grown happily accustomed to the order of worship. In the beginning, before the official 8:30 start, was hymn practice. People showed up early, often more than an hour before, to practice singing the hymns that would be sung during the actual service. So we walked in and found a seat during singing practice. Once we got our own hymnals this part was much better, for we could sing along and study the characters. Some of the hymns were translated from Western hymns so the music was familiar, a comforting old presence.

The bench in front of us had a small shelf, so upon arrival, we would pull out our two bilingual Bibles, our two hymnals, dictionary, journal, pen, and Chris's coffee mug and set them on the shelf in front of us. Now situated, we would turn to the hymnal to sing whichever hymn they were practicing, or just chat quietly to ourselves.

In the beginning of the service the Lord's Prayer was said in unison, and at the end, the Apostles' Creed. Chris and I liked being able to count on these bookends. The Lord's Prayer was followed by a few hymns sung by the choir. The piano was always out of tune, which enabled the entire choir to sing off-key.

"Well, they are making a joyful noise unto the Lord," said my husband, the musician in the family. "Emphasis on noise."

Scripture reading was our favorite part of the service, and it became somewhat a self-created contest that we looked forward to. As they flashed the reference in Chinese on the overhead screen, we immediately turned to our bilingual Bible's table of contents to try to match the characters of the book of the Bible with their English equivalent, for example, 创世纪 with Genesis. Once found, we raced to find the passage, hoping to beat the pastor and be ready before the church began reading in unison. If so, we tried our best to read along; afterward, we'd read it to ourselves in English.

❦

The Chinese have had a word for God since the origin of their language, possibly even before Moses wrote the first word of the Old Testament. The characters 上帝, literally meaning "the emperor above," and pronounced *Shangdi*, are found on Shang Dynasty (1600–1046 BC) oracle bones. *Shangdi* is also referenced thirty-two times in the *Shujing*

(Book of History), one of the five classics and possibly the earliest narrative of China.

The church in Tai'an had three pastors, one woman, one older gentleman, and one younger man, Ma Xiao Wen, a recent graduate of the Three-Self seminary in Nanjing. The open church in China was called the Three-Self Patriotic Movement, short for self-governing, self-financing, self-propagating, which itself was a rephrasing of "absolutely no foreign involvement whatsoever." One of the three pastors usually preached, though we never could follow along with the sermon. The Chinese language of the preachers was a droning sound in the background of our own thoughts, though it occasionally recalled us with a familiar word or phrase.

The church is located in an older part of town, and its street, Qingnian Lu, is particularly beautiful in spring and summer, as the trees branches on each side meet in the middle, providing an arch of leafy branches that we passed under as we approached church in a taxi. After church Chris and I would walk along Qingnian Lu to McDonald's, about half a block away, and order our customary double cheeseburgers and fries.

❁

One Sunday morning we sat with a student of ours, Miriam. The older male preacher got up and made an announcement. Then a man positioned by the main entrance raised his hand and motioned for people to follow him. There was a commotion as several people left the church and followed him out of the building. Normally the church did not deviate from its set schedule. We had never seen anything like this before.

Miriam explained that a few blocks away there was another old church building originally constructed by the Church of England. The building used to belong to this church, but now the government had possession. The church wanted to take it back, so they were sending people to go and hold a church service there; to occupy it, so to speak. Chris and I looked at each other. We were quite interested in the history of the church.

"Should we go?"

Then she added, "I don't think the government wants them to do this."

Reason prevailed. We settled back into our seats. As interested as we were to know where this old church was and to see the outcome of their service, having two foreigners attend would only draw attention to the event. And we certainly didn't want to lose our right to teach on account of this. After church we went outside where they had photos displayed of a dilapidated building with the roof falling in, along with about six or seven pages of typed text. I asked Ma Xiao Wen, the younger preacher, what it was.

"It's a call to the brothers and sisters of the church to take back this building," he replied. I asked if I could have a copy, but he smiled uncomfortably and shook his head. Then he left to lead another group from the church to walk to this outlying building.

I discussed the event with Chris after church at McDonald's. "It seems so strange to hear Miriam say the church wants to take the building back from the government, because the church itself belongs to the government," I said, completely confused.

The next week I saw Miriam in class. At the break, I jumped at the chance to find out more about the church and its buildings.

"The church wants to fight," she told me. "They want to get more people involved so they can get their building back. It's a big building, bigger than the present church, in a good location in the center of the city. But the government doesn't want to give it back because they want the church to stay small." She mused for a moment. "Right now the church has so little power, so they must fight in this way."

"But will there be any repercussions?" I asked.

"No," she answered.

During my nine months thus far in China, I'd seen English classes capriciously canceled by uninformed administrators. Quiet acceptance.

The cafeteria went back to the normal tired old food with dirty bowls and old chopsticks after a week "as it could be" during an important outside evaluation. Not a whimper.

I asked the students to come up with ideas to change China's exam system for gaining entrance to college. They told me they just trusted their government to do the right thing. No suggestions. No ideas.

I asked my tour guide in Guilin, who attended a university for minorities in the provincial capital, if she ever felt it was unfair that ethnic minorities received special treatment on the college entrance examination. She simply stated the government thought this was the best policy.

I'd been wondering how on earth this country could produce some-thing on the scale of Tiananmen Square, a nationwide movement where the students were on the brink of changing their entire country. I certainly hadn't seen any such determination or questioning in my students. Where were the rebels? Where were the fighters? Why was everybody willing to accept the status quo? The China I had seen this far, if it wanted something, would follow the established rules and procedures, wait patiently, and then accept whatever the outcome might be. The first time I notice any kind of mass movement, any sort of disagreement, any sign of protest, and it is at church! The church, a powerless institution, a branch of the government it-self, was declaring it would "fight" the government and march to take back their building. I was stunned.

A few weeks later Miriam sat with us again on Sunday morning. Afterward, she walked us over to the site of the old building. It was just about half a block past McDonald's, on the other side of the street, down a narrow alley.

A church service was going on when we arrived. Many people were seated on stools in a half-torn-down building. Ma Xiao Wen was leading the service. A fresh red banner with large white characters hung above the entrance.

The building had a British colonial style. It belonged to an earlier time period, its beautiful brick and stonework standing out amid the cheap white tile and cement of the neighborhood. It was surrounded by open space, a rarity in Tai'an, particularly in the older section of town. If rebuilt, this would be a huge asset to the church.

"The government has started to tear the building down," Miriam said, pointing to the piles of broken bricks scattered about. We walked around and took pictures.

Miriam took us around the corner and showed us two other church buildings in this same British style. These buildings weren't as dilapidated as the first, and we went inside. In their heyday they must have been fine, beautiful structures, but today they were worn from seeing too much of the darker side of China's history. I arranged to meet Miriam for lunch later that week. I asked her again about the church's decision to fight for the old building.

"Aren't you afraid there will be repercussions?" I asked her again. I'd asked her this question at least three times by now, but had yet to be satisfied with her answer.

She wrinkled her nose and looked at me. "Well, I guess it's because we are God's children that we feel we don't have to be afraid."

I was flabbergasted. I had never considered this angle. I had simply not considered that their faith made a difference, made *the* difference. I felt humbled because I should have known. My preoccupation with a cultural answer had blinded me. She gave me a universal answer, one I should have seen.

While searching for an explanation of the Chinese mind-set, what was revealed instead was my own Western mind-set: I didn't consider that faith made one brave. In America, being religious was easy; it was culturally accepted; it rarely meant sacrifice.

Miriam said she was also a member of a house church.

"The house churches don't really like the Three-Self church, for they feel it is submitting to government control. The Three-Self church also doesn't want to be a part of the government, but it has no choice." She mentioned the lack of freedom at the Three-Self, and said there were spies at the seminaries, that spies attended the Christmas Eve service here in Tai'an.

I had always wondered why the government feared religion. Pious people were usually law-abiding citizens, didn't they know that? But Miriam's answer explained it to me. The devout weren't afraid of the government. They were willing to fight, if need be. They, whether Buddhists in Tibet, Muslims in Xinjiang, or Christians scattered around the country, acknowledged a source of power outside of, even above, government control, and that made the government afraid. For the Chinese government is a jealous government.

❀

When my parents, brother, and sister-in-law came to visit us, we arrived at church late since they wanted to stop at McDonald's first for morning coffee. All seats on the benches were taken. We ended up sitting on foot-high stools, one in front of the other, in the crowded aisle. I turned around and looked at my parents, their knees awkwardly about chest level. My mother shot me a surprised look at the start of the dissonant out-loud prayer. She looked ill at ease. I passed them hymnals and they did their best to sing along, then sat patiently through a sermon they could not comprehend. I assured them the service was almost finished.

But as it turned out it was Communion Sunday. Several ushers came forward delivering round crusty pastries, *bing*, 饼, that would serve as the bread. The pastor blessed the *bing* and then proceeded to crush them, making a terribly loud crinkling noise into the microphone. The ushers were all garbed in white, bearing for us an unfortunate likeness to the lab-coated medical students we saw on a daily basis carrying in the cages of rabbits for dissection.

We sang the same hymn over and over while the lab-coated ushers distributed the crackers throughout the congregation, a difficult task since every aisle or walking space was crowded with humanity. They finally got to us in the rear, where we received one flake each of *bing*. As the man next to me took his flake, he spit onto the ground, then rubbed the spittle into the bare cement floor with his foot. After the bread came the wine, although in this case it was apple cider on the verge of becoming rancid, leaving an aftertaste of fermentation. The color was light brown, giving no visual relationship with the blood of Christ, but the small cups, although plastic, were the exact same shape and size I was used to.

As I listened to the pastor, I figured out from his words that communion in Chinese was *bingbei*, 饼杯, literally "bread, cup." It was different from any communion my parents had ever experienced, yet also familiar. For me growing up, communion was a sign of relationship between Christ and me, for I was symbolically taking part in his body and blood. It was an individual act of devotion. But in such a crowd of humanity, communion felt more like a community event. Hands touched as the plate passed, eyes made contact, concern was shown to make sure everyone had enough. It was a group effort just to get the elements to each far-flung corner of the church.

My family and I, sitting on our little stools, were swept along with this process. My parents left the church with the feeling, completely unexpected, that they were one and the same with these people who had seemed so foreign when they walked in. Though separated by history and culture, by ethnicity and language, they were bound together in this ceremony of bread and wine.

Chapter 14

农村
COUNTRYSIDE

The Chinese ideal of happiness . . . [is] the enjoyment of
this simple rural life, together with the harmony of social
relationships.

—LIN YUTANG

❊

CHINA, LIKE MANY SOCIETIES, HAS A LONG HISTORY OF CLASSIFYING ITS
people into groups. In the early Communist period "capitalist roaders"
or "landlords" were despised classes. During this time peasants were the
ideal, and landowners—or their children or grandchildren—suffered for
their ancestors' good fortune one hundred years back. During the Cultural
Revolution, as all education and learning came under attack, it was the in-
tellectuals who were the despised class. China doesn't have such radical
classifications today, but the society still has some great divisions, most of
which are apparent by a quick glance at one's national identification card.

One distinction is between north and south. The dividing line is the
Yangtze River. Under central planning no heaters were installed south of
the river, though the Yangtze was an arbitrary line and it could still get quite
cold, as the winter storms of 2008 proved. Southern people were known as
rice eaters; northerners as noodle or *mantou* (steamed bread) eaters. This
is natural as rice needs hotter weather to thrive while wheat is more preva-
lent in northern climes. The language is different as well. For the most part,
the north speaks Mandarin Chinese or a minor, yet still understood, varia-
tion. In the south there are numerous dialects including the nine-plus-tone
Cantonese of Hong Kong and Guangdong province, which is completely
unintelligible to those in the north. Even their personalities are supposedly
different. Northerners are known as *haoshuang*: straightforward and out-

spoken, concerned with government affairs. Southern people are described as *siwen*: refined and gentle, concerned with business matters.

Yet perhaps the greatest divide in China is between rural and urban. There is a direct relationship between the size of the city and its level of development as well as the quality of education it offers. Going from city to village means going from tree-lined boulevards to cracked, dusty roads and finally to footpaths. It requires leaving behind state-of-the-art computer labs for dirt-floored schoolrooms, where students are required to bring a stool from home each day to have a place to sit. It means trading dishwashers and shiny porcelain toilets for straw-filled outhouses and no running water.

The countryside is written in Chinese as 农村, *nongcun*. *Nong*, the first character, means "agriculture." In its traditional form, 農, the lower part, 辰, shows a plow. Above the plow is 曲, which, as a stand-alone character, means a song, a melody, or an opera. Why is there a song in the character for agriculture? Perhaps I hold a slightly romantic view, as I grew up in an agricultural community and come from a long line of farmers, but I can easily imagine a Chinese farmer singing a song to the water buffalo as he plows his fields.

辰

AGRICULTURE
(traditional)

村

VILLAGE

COUNTRYSIDE

The second part of the word is *cun*, 村. This character is formed as the majority of Chinese characters are, one part signifying the meaning and the other part the sound. In this case, 木 gives the meaning of "trees." The second part, 寸, lends the word its pronunciation. But more interesting to me is the dictionary definition of *cun*: "a village, the countryside, a hamlet, vulgar, coarse, naïve, simple-minded."

An article in *China Daily* said that the countryside lagged behind the cities about twenty years in terms of major home appliances. In an effort

to shrink this divide, the central government was offering 13 percent sub-
sidies to give farmers incentive to buy household appliances in three categories: refrigerators, color televisions, and mobile phones. The pilot
program would be launched in the three major agricultural provinces of
Henan, Sichuan, and our own Shandong province.

My student Amy told me that when visiting a fellow student's home
in the countryside around Tai'an, she was surprised to find they only had a
black-and-white television. It was hard to imagine in booming China that
in the countryside there might be homes with no color TVs, refrigerators,
or phones. Another article in *China Daily* declared that annual per capita
net income for farmers increased to 4,000 yuan ($540) in 2007. My own
salary was 3,600 yuan per month, which my Chinese neighbors were not
very impressed with; even so, I made nearly as much in one month as a
farmer made in a year.

My paternal grandfather raised almonds in California, and my maternal grandfather milked cows on his dairy farm in Washington State. My
father also farmed for a time, so I felt a strong connection with and respect
for China's farmers. Most of our students grew up in the countryside, where
their parents were still farmers, small shopkeepers, or workers at a local
factory. Now by virtue of their attendance at university, our students were
in effect excluding themselves from ever living in their hometown. The
countryside, apart from a few teachers, could not absorb educated college
graduates. So our students knew they were now choosing an urban life. But
they were happily making that choice. Each step up the ladder, from village
to small town to small city, medium city, and finally large metropolis, meant
a rise in the standard of living. But it was more than just trading in hardship
and privation for material prosperity, it involved changing in traditional
thinking for modern ideas.

Rural thinking, as may be expected, is more traditional than urban
thinking. But this leads to a paradox. For the educated city dweller, the
rural countryside is backward and undeveloped. But at the same time, the
countryside is the fount of truly authentic Chinese culture. As Zhang told
me, it was best to spend Spring Festival in the countryside. It was just not
that festive in the city; there weren't as many traditions. The countryside
is looked down upon, yet at the same time, sentimentally longed for by

the Westernized cosmopolitans of the city. To live a simple rural life is an ideal, yet simultaneously, most Chinese have the ambition to escape the countryside.

❀

Several weeks into the spring semester our student Reese suggested we come and visit her family during the upcoming Labor Week holiday in the beginning of May.

"Mrs. Arrington, during the May holiday everyone will be going to the bigger cities, so that is not a good place to go. It will be too crowded. But to stay home and do nothing is boring. Why not go to my hometown, Dongping, since no one will be traveling there?"

I had to admit her logic was compelling. I broached the idea with Chris, and to my surprise, he liked the idea as well. So we began to make our plans.

We were supposed to leave on Wednesday. On Tuesday Chris and I panicked. "We are going to spend three days with a Chinese family we don't know," Chris said. "Are we sure we want to do this? We're taking our children into a completely unfamiliar situation."

"My main concern is different," I told him. "It's that we might mess up culturally in some way."

"What's the name of her hometown? Dongping?" he asked. "I'm going to Google it." He found nothing. Google came up with absolutely nothing.

"So we don't know these people, we don't know where we are going, we don't know anything."

"Right," I sighed. "But we know Reese. And we've agreed already. We can't back out now. We're going."

On Wednesday we set off as planned. Reese met us with her brother-in-law, who had a car. We had insisted on taking the bus; Reese had countered that the car was much more convenient. She finally consented and we agreed on the bus. But when she showed up at our door, there was the car. As it turned out, she was right. The car had plenty of room for everyone, and it was much more convenient than trying to manage a long-distance bus, especially on a heavy travel weekend.

But we soon figured out that Reese was not from Dongping at all.

The entire time we had discussed this trip she had said Dongping. I had told everyone we were going to Dongping. I had a mental picture of Dongping, a smaller city one class below Tai'an. As my tutor had explained to me, in China the bigger cities govern the smaller cities surrounding them, and the smaller cities govern the towns, and on down. It goes like this, first country, 国 (*guo*), then province, 省 (*sheng*), city, 市 (*shi*), smaller city, 县 (*xian*), town, 镇 (*zhen*), and finally the bottom rung, village, 村 (*cun*).

Tai'an is a city, a 市, albeit a second-tier city of Shandong province compared with other cities such as the capital, Jinan. Dongping is a smaller city, a *xian*, one step below a city, and in this case, actually belonging to and governed by Tai'an.

It was not until we drove up that Reese told us her hometown: Yinshan belonging to Dongping. Dongping itself was about an hour away. Yinshan (meaning "silver mountain") was not a *xian*, as I had thought, but a *zhen*, or town, one step above a village. The entire mental picture I had created was incorrect. But I was excited. I had viewed this trip as a baby step toward getting to an actual village. I knew our Grace's first year had been spent in a village, and I wanted to experience the traditional village life. But I was a little nervous. Just getting used to Tai'an had taken some time. I thought I would wade in gradually, first a *xian*, then down to a *zhen*; finally I hoped to experience actual village life. But as I was to find out, I was jumping in completely on this trip, leapfrogging the other levels and landing squarely in the village.

We started by having lunch with Reese's family. We ate at a small restaurant on Yinshan's main road, its only paved road. The restaurant was run by a friend of Reese's brother-in-law. Actually, wherever we went in Yinshan, we were greeted by friends of Reese's brother-in-law. He had good *guanxi* (relationships), which enabled him to get many of the things required for our stay, such as meals and hotels. We of course had no *guanxi* but thanks to Reese, we were able to ride his coattails. The lunch was delicious, and the setting one that we were accustomed to: a private room with a lazy Susan in the center of the table and many Chinese dishes. Reese took care to order items she knew we liked, such as *basi digua* (toffee sweet potatoes) and *yuxiang rousi* (pork with tree fungus and vegetables). After lunch we went to the hotel to rest for a bit.

The hotel would have been lucky to earn itself one star. Though Chris said he had stayed in worse, I certainly had not. It was dirty, with holes in the walls and decrepit furniture, and the bathroom, never a highlight of Chinese living, was grimy. The showerhead was poised just above the toilet. Later in the afternoon we met Reese and her brother-in-law and they took us on a drive to see the Yellow River. This was a real treat, as the Yellow River was known as the mother river, the cradle of Chinese civilization. The river was wide and fast-flowing, both of which surprised me since it had hardly rained since we had arrived in China, and Tai'an's bridges spanned large dry ditches that cut through the city, showing us where the waters used to run. On the other side of the river was Henan province. We spent a lot of time along the riverbank, visiting pavilions, watching women doing their laundry in the river, and walking along the shore.

After seeing the river we headed out. To my surprise, we went right past the small town of Yinshan. We continued on, driving through several miles of steep hills, until we finally arrived at a small village—a village of dirt roads leading to traditional courtyard homes, of weary peasants returning from a day in the fields, of old men with weathered faces smoking cigarettes and playing cards.

There are hardships as one travels from an urban city to a rural village. The hotels, if they exist, are substandard. Western amenities are unknown. Comfort and luxury are replaced by pothole-filled roads and reeking toilets. But at the same time, the level of authentic Chinese life rises. And that is what makes such a journey appealing.

This particular village was the home of Reese's brother-in-law, and his mother welcomed us at the courtyard gate, which opened to the south, in accordance with tradition. I stepped inside this simple village home where we would spend the evening as Reese's family showed her American teachers a traditional Chinese welcome.

The house was typical for this part of China. From the outside it looked like a windowless high-walled cement compound. Once inside we were standing in a courtyard. To our front we saw the doors of the main house. Off to the side were many outbuildings: the kitchen, the bathrooms stalls, separate for women and men, and, to the children's delight, animal pens housing rabbits, goats, and dogs. We entered the main house, consisting of a large, airy living area and a bedroom or two off to the side. Members of Reese's family were already in the process of making dumplings. They invited us to join in.

Making dumplings is labor-intensive work. In the Chinese tradition it is usually done for a festive occasion, such as Spring Festival, or to welcome someone home. Since it requires so many hands, it is a fun family activity. Reese's sister was rolling out the dough into small circles, and her mother and mother-in-law were placing a small amount of the meat mixture (pork, celery, spices) in the center, then folding the dough over it to form a puckered half-moon shape. This was my workstation as well. The two older ladies gave me a lot of instruction on proper dough folding. I made some progress, although later as we ate the dumplings, Reese held up a misshapen one and said, "This one was certainly made by Mrs. Arrington!" I agreed, but told her though it might not look as beautiful, it tasted just as delicious. In fact, the dumplings were incredibly delicious, the best we had had in China.

My girls, Katherine and Grace, took seats next to Reese's sister and rolled out the small pieces of dough into flat circles. They stood by their task for some time, until they could no longer stand not being outside with the animals, then ran outside. They jumped into a huge pile of leaves, then brought a few leaves to feed the hungry goats. I glanced at Chris. He had a small grin on his face, and a look of contentment as he watched the children play: American kids enraptured by the simplicity of a village home—animals, fresh air, and a big pile of leaves.

After we had made all the dumplings, it was time to cook them. Once again, this was a labor-intensive process. The kitchen was an outbuilding, off to the side of the main house. Inside this windowless cement structure was a traditional wood-fed stove. The mother-in-law seated herself between a pile of sticks and the stove, and began to stoke the fire. Reese's mother filled a huge iron bowl with water to boil the dumplings.

As I watched the two older ladies hover over the dumplings, I noticed the stove stretched out into a large rectangular shape. Then, with a start, I realized I was looking at a traditional *kang*, a Chinese bed attached to the stove. The *kang* was hollow underneath, allowing the heat from the fire to go under the cement bed, providing a toasty winter evening's slumber. In my reading of Chinese history I had often read about a *kang*, but had never even seen a picture. Now I was seeing one in person, and spending the evening with the people who slept there during winter.

Throughout the evening, many of the local villagers stopped by to catch a glimpse of the foreign family. In Extensive Reading class recently we had been discussing American individualism. I told the students about American farms, about how the home sits amid a parcel of acreage, usually near the center, with no one else around. This is completely different from the Chinese model. Chinese farmers live together in villages, separate from their land. They walk or bike to the land to tend it, but their home remains in the village. This is necessary, for they have to live in the village for daily necessities such as food and schooling. But it is not just about practicalities; it reveals a more communal mind-set as well.

Back at the hotel, the kids went right to sleep. The next day was spent exploring the sights around Yinshan: first the lake, then the mountain. Dongping Lake is the second-largest in Shandong province. The island at its center is celebrated as the site at which 108 men from a few dynasties back who were opposed to the government gathered to organize an uprising. The island was set up for tourists, with some temples and a traditional dancing lion show every two hours.

After visiting the island, we had lunch at a nearby hotel, said to be the best restaurant in town, featuring fish caught from the lake. Eating Chinese style in a private room was convenient, especially as the children could run around a bit when they were finished. They enjoyed playing with Reese's four-year-old nephew. After eating we climbed the local mountain (only a hill, really, as Reese said), Lashan, or Mount La. It was an enjoyable hike, not too strenuous, and all the children, even four-year-old Andrew, did it without complaint. From the top we were able to catch splendid views of the countryside as well as the lake. We marveled the entire trip at the beauty and "greenness" of the countryside. This area had taken great effort to plant a lot of trees (木), and the young wheat we saw in the fields was just above knee-high, giving a view of green fields (田) for miles and miles. This was in contrast to the way we often saw China, as a brown country, the color of dirt.

After climbing down the mountain we went to Reese's house. On the way, Reese's brother-in-law received a phone call from one of his friends saying he had procured a room for us at the hotel where we had lunch, a nicer hotel than where we stayed the first night. When we arrived at Reese's house, we found her father had gone to the first hotel and retrieved our bags for us, all on his electric bicycle.

We spent a few hours at Reese's home, also a traditional Chinese courtyard–style house, arranged much like the mother-in-law's house we visited the previous night, except smaller. It was a "duplex" of sorts, with two families splitting the main house, as well as the outbuildings on either half of the courtyard. Reese's sister, brother-in-law, and nephew slept together in one double bed in their small bedroom. Her nephew was fond of playing games on the state-of-the-art computer squeezed in a corner. Reese's parents occupied the second bedroom. A double bed in the living room served as a couch by day and Reese's bed at night when she was home from college. The floors were bare cement; there was no running water. For their water needs, they filled basins from a faucet located in the other family's kitchen outbuilding. I had to use the bathroom while there and so ventured to the outhouse, a cement shack with a hole in the bottom, some hay to absorb moisture, and plenty of flies.

They lived on the edge of town. Across the dirt road was a beautiful orchard of young trees. Reese said she liked to get up early and walk among the trees to read or practice English. That night they brought us back to the first restaurant for dinner. There we presented our final gifts: postcards, a magnetic notepad, and a plastic serving tray with scenes of Seattle. Then we went to our new hotel, which was, as they promised, much nicer. We finally realized, when told we could not have a key, that technically we were not "staying" there. The hotel rooms had been arranged for by the brother-in-law's friends, and Reese's family did not have to pay. We never checked in or out. It was all taken care of by *guanxi*.

We liked being far off the beaten path, and we did not feel stared at to the degree we had expected. Reese's family was pleasant and generous. They told us that while other foreigners had been to their town, we were the first Americans.

"The students seem more real now," Chris told me. "They are each individuals with their own stories, their own lives, and their own struggles."

It was quite easy to see them as row upon row of gingerbread boys and gingerbread girls, all with gingerbread ponytails. While they might have similar hairstyles, laugh at the same things, and have parallel interests, they all came from a unique somewhere, often from quite humble origins in the countryside.

When we returned home both girls asked when we could go back and see them again. China has so many big sights to see: the Great Wall, Tiananmen Square, the Forbidden City, the Terra Cotta Warriors. But more than 60 percent of the population live in the countryside, a place few foreigners get to see. But I did get to see it. Not only that, I got to spend an evening in a home, a traditional countryside home, making, cooking, and eating dumplings with Reese and her family—our friends.

Much later, in our second year, a student described her father to me: "My father is a farmer. But my mother told me that he is actually very intelligent, but chose to remain a farmer because he wanted to keep his freedom."

I often thought about her father, for it was the first time I had ever heard of a Chinese choosing to be a farmer. But this farmer was different. He willingly chose a life of working hard for little gain, a life held to the earth when the city beckoned, a life of low status though he had an agile mind, just for the independence one can only have in the midst of a field. In my imagination, he was singing as he plowed.

Chapter 15

囗

RETURN

❋

ONE STRIKING THING ABOUT LIVING IN CHINA IS THAT ONE CAN ONLY BUY fruit in season. We noticed this first in winter. All winter we loved the tangerines, buying eight or nine daily, each of us consuming two, sometimes three a day. This played a huge part in our healthy winter. But no sooner had February arrived than our tangerines were gone. We kept checking back for them, even going to other fruit sellers besides our usual one. But they had vanished.

We weren't too sad, for we still had pomelos, the giant grapefruit we had first discovered during our visit to Guilin. But soon pomelo season was over. In early spring suddenly every fruit seller could be seen carving pineapples. First the entire outer skin was cut away, in a patterned fashion that dug out all the notches; then, the pineapple was cut into sections, and the final flourish, a chopstick stuck into the fruit to turn it into a naturally sweet fruit popsicle.

A few months later, these disappeared from the markets as the heat of summer rolled in. No matter what season, we could always find apples. That is, until late May when even they disappeared. Earlier in the month we had enjoyed cherries, usually sold by the cartload on the street by the farmers themselves. By June we had peaches and a tricolor menagerie of oval-shaped cherry tomatoes in bright reds, oranges, and yellows.

One sunny June day I walked along the shopping street at lunch to get my *jidanbing* (similar to a pancake with an egg cracked atop while it was being fried), and was greeted with a new (albeit familiar) smell: corn. Corn, not yet shucked, was being sold on the street in giant pots of hot water for 1 yuan an ear (about 15 cents).

As the days steadily grew hotter our family grew beans, tended during outdoor home schooling. First, we sprouted the seeds in an old baby-food jar. About a week later we transplanted them into paper cups and kept them on our windowsill where the kids and I checked them before and after school. They were so excited to see the leaves sprout and to chart the progress. Then, with the help of Mr. Jia, four clay pots, an ample supply of dirt, and a trowel, we transplanted our beans into larger pots outside in our courtyard. Katherine was her usual take-charge self, but I was amazed as I listened to her. She would talk to me in English, then turn to Mr. Jia and talk to him in Chinese without missing a beat. The words seemed to flow effortlessly and naturally.

In contrast, I remembered an incident that had occurred when I picked the kids up from school earlier that week. They had played on the playground for a while, as I usually let them do. One of the teachers was also on the playground with her daughter. Since the gate was locked, I wanted to ask the teacher if we could leave with her when she decided to leave, as she had a key. I started to speak. But then I had to stop, do a mental translation, specifically choose the correct grammatical construct to communicate this particular thought; then finally, after a rather pregnant pause, present my request.

Katherine required no mental translation. She easily moved between languages. She had long been capable of quite sophisticated verbalizing, which initially hindered her learning Chinese. But now she had arrived. The floodgates were open and those backed-up waters were released.

That weekend, in anticipation of an announced power and water outage, I took the kids outside for several hours. Andrew sat in his favorite spot: snuggled up next to me with his head on my shoulder. My relationship with my daughters was complex. Although we enjoyed being together, hanging out, and doing "girl stuff," we also had contests of wills, emotional outbursts, and, even at this young age, mind games. They seemed to need me yet need to prove their independence from me all at the same time.

But no such contradictions existed with Andrew. Our relationship was delightfully simple, defined the night we brought him home from the hospital. When he fell asleep I laid him gently in Katherine's old crib. He jerked awake and opened his eyes in near panic as if to say, "You're going to leave me alone in here? By myself?"

I picked him up and he immediately calmed down, soothed by the warmth of my body, quieted by our closeness. He slept in my arms that night, and continued to do so for the next three months. If we were connected, whether by his head on my shoulder, his hand in mine, or our eyes locked as he told me about his books or his classmates or his toys, then all was ordered and happy in his little world.

As had been happening in recent weeks, the girls joined up with some of their classmates from school. When Grace and Katherine played outside with their friends, they usually spoke Chinese now. And when they spoke Chinese, they always called each other by their Chinese names.

"Fu Zhi Chun, guolai!" Grace, come here!

"Fu Rui Xue, ni zai nar?" Katherine, where are you?

Unlike the American custom where, once we are familiar with someone, we usually just use the individual name, in Chinese our family name of Fu was never dropped off.

I liked that. My children announced their familial affiliation, their bond, each time they said each other's names. As I listened to my long-legged light-haired daughter and her petite dark-eyed little sister playing together, I could hear something deeper in their words. *You are a Fu, just like me. We are one family. We are the same.*

I noticed something else as I watched them play happily. Things were a little different this time. There was one boy from Katherine's class, and two older girls plus Grace, but Katherine was clearly in charge. She was running the entire operation in rapid-fire Chinese, directing the group to run under the trees, around the bamboo grove, through the circle door, on and on.

So now she could be bossy in Chinese. I never thought I would be happy to see her so bossy, but to be honest, it is part of her personality. She could be at home in her own personality in the Chinese language. This cross-cultural struggle for her had always been one of expression, a need Katherine plainly possesses. To not be able to express herself had made her feel completely foreign here. Now, not only could she express herself, but she could "boss." So she had returned to who she was, in Chinese. She had come full circle.

The Chinese character for "return" shows two concentric squares: 回.

I used 回 a lot in my daily life. When I was coming home after a long day I would say 回家, "return home"; when I wanted to tell someone I would be right back I said 回来, "come back." When our neighbors talked about our impending return to the United States, they used the phrase 回国, meaning "return to your home country." I don't know the etymology of 回, but when I see its inner and outer squares, it simply reminds me of completeness, of returning back to one's starting point, of coming full circle. And so Katherine had returned to her own personality, her own self, here in China. 回.

As I put her to bed that evening, our buzzer rang. Mr. Jia came up with some *zongzi*, saying someone had brought them for Fu Rui Xue. Katherine as usual didn't miss anything. She insisted on getting up to see what I had. She was excited that one of her friends had brought these to her, and said, "Actually, Mom, I really like these. I've had them at school before." We could feel the *zongzi* were still warm, so I let her stay up and eat one, then two. Watching my notoriously picky eater adeptly pull aside the leaves and enjoy the sweet rice inside made me so thankful she was finding her place in this culture.

❀

We prepared for our last classes and final exams in the heat of June. When we had first arrived in China, we were amused by the concept of *xiuxi*, the afternoon rest period. Right after lunch, every bench on campus, any ledge, even steps were taken up by napping grounds workers. Professors took naps in their offices or at home; students in their dormitories. But after waiting so long for the cold winter to succumb to spring, spring was over in a heartbeat and the heat was upon us—heat in no way lessened by the comfort of air-conditioning, except in the foreign teachers' building. In our airless office on the new campus, we draped ourselves over chairs or couches, at that moment so thankful for the Chinese wisdom of *xiuxi*.

As we began to pack our suitcases and think about returning home for the summer, I realized that I was truly happy in this routine. I enjoyed teaching the students, reading to the children, having a place in the community, and everything else about our day-to-day life. I was even somewhat dreading this summer, eagerly awaiting our return to China in the fall. This was significant, for I had never been happy in routines. I had always looked for something to break them, had intently made plans for the future, but had never been happy in the present. This was the first time I was savoring the "now."

A few days before departing, I strolled up the hill to pick up the kids from kindergarten. I was late, and the sidewalk was lined with scooters and bicycles and pairs of mothers and children. As I walked by one pair, the little girl pointed at me and said to her mother, *"Laowai."*

That dreaded word: *Foreigner.*

But I didn't even have a chance to think about this culture that taught its children to point out foreigners like they might giraffes or zebras at the zoo, when I passed the next mother-daughter pair.

"Ayi!" the daughter shrieked happily to me. "Auntie!" She was one of Katherine's classmates. *"Ayi, hao."* She waved happily to me. I smiled, waved back, and nodded to her mother.

Foreigner . . . Auntie.

❁

Exams graded and bags packed, it was time for our return to the United States. We flew to Beijing without any problem, but one hour before our scheduled departure to San Francisco, the clouds gathered and day literally turned to night before our eyes. The rain, thunder, and lightning arrived with an awesome display. It was so dark we could no longer see the aircraft on the tarmac, but could certainly hear the intense drumming of the rain on the terminal roof. Beijing's Capital Airport shut down completely. We finally departed four and a half hours late.

We arrived in San Francisco to find that not only had we missed our connection, but the airline had canceled another flight to Seattle that day, meaning we were not the only ones trying to hitch a ride in that direction.

After forty-eight hours in the strange virtual world of air travel, being passively carried along by moving sidewalks, escalators, and 747s, surrounded by our fellow traveling zombies, we were ejected into the Pacific Northwest. Being united with our family and friends, seeing crystal-clear views of Mount Rainier and Mount Baker, and breathing in the fresh clean air made us feel alive once again.

After a year immersed in a completely different culture, our return to the United States was an adjustment—from no longer speaking Chinese, to being strapped into car seats and seat belts, to being able to drink tap water. We felt overwhelmed that everything was so big, so clean, so convenient, and that there were so many choices.

When we came back to the United States, I expected that, in contrast to the grays and browns of our China, the greens and blues of Washington State would seem especially vivid. This was true. The beautiful skies and magnificent mountains seemed painted in Technicolor.

Other reactions surprised me. Staying at our hotel room in Seattle, I gazed at the TV and watched a commercial filmed in a kitchen. I looked at the huge refrigerator, the center island, the general spaciousness, and thought, "What is wrong with you! Why do you need so much space! It's gluttonous!" I had similar reactions to the large homes and yards in my hometown. Truly, we were a society used to rampant materialism and excess luxury. As a friend told me in an e-mail, "We all feel the need to constantly upgrade, even when the upgrade isn't necessary." I'm not sure we even knew how to live a simple life in America, and if we wanted to, we would find it quite difficult. It would be countercultural.

We began to settle into a busy summer of family gatherings, weddings, and road trips. Chris declared a moratorium on rice for the month of July, and we indulged ourselves in all our favorite American food. To be quite honest, it wasn't as good as I remembered it. "But it's just nice to know you can get it if you want to," Chris said.

Katherine started Vacation Bible School the day after we returned. Looking crumpled and disheveled, I brought her to the church, my clothes creased from suitcases, my overgrown hair at least three months past its haircut due date. Jet-lagged, I scrutinized the fashionable clothing and perfect makeup and hair of everyone at church. "You're at *church*—it's not a fashion show!" I thought, self-conscious and grumpy.

But what disturbed me even more was that within about two or three days I ceased to be disturbed. Homes and interiors no longer seemed grossly disproportionate. I quickly got a stylish haircut and took great care with my makeup when I went to VBS to pick up Katherine. Within a week, I was one of "them" again. I had come full circle. 回.

Chapter 16

熟

FAMILIAR

To read a book for the first time is to make the acquaintance
of a new friend; to read it a second time is to meet an old one.
—SELWYN CHAMPION

❁

As WE PASSED THROUGH SECURITY IN THE VANCOUVER AIRPORT AN
attendant, after glancing at our passports and boarding passes, waved
us through. Katherine turned around and announced, "We are going to China!"

After an enjoyable summer of family, friends, and American food,
we arrived back home in Tai'an. Everything seemed easier this time. The
lines were short, the planes on time, the children obedient. The trip took
only about eighteen hours. This made it feel somewhat strange. After forty-
eight hours of travel on the way over, China had seemed far away and I felt
I had earned my right to sleep in a comfortable bed and wake up to vanilla
custard yogurt topped with freshly picked berries and granola for breakfast.
But returning to China after a mere eighteen hours, I just felt that I'd stayed
up rather late. My hometown still seemed close as I climbed onto my hard
mattress in our small apartment. The trip seemed too short to account for
such an exchange in worlds.

We noticed what a difference a year made already in the Beijing airport. Both Chris and I felt it. As we retraced our steps—retrieving luggage,
rechecking in for our domestic flight, finding restrooms—we had flash-
backs of going through those same motions the year before.

Upon landing a year ago I had expected to feel jubilant. Not only was
the twelve-hour monster flight behind us, but the months of waiting, planning, and placement ups and downs were behind us as well. We had arrived

in China. But instead, as we navigated through the airport a year ago with two luggage carts piled high and three tired children dragging along, we had felt more unsure than jubilant. We had moved tentatively, not knowing where to go or what lay ahead, a few days or months, even a few hours for that matter.

Then it had been strange and alien; now, we were greeted by a feeling of belonging and buoyed by the sense of familiarity. As we asked directions, Chinese that we hadn't spoken in a few months strangely came flowing from our mouths. When the children needed to use the restrooms, we knew right where to go. The previous year, I remembered three separate occasions when we were the eye treats for gawkers, and how self-conscious and uncomfortable I had felt. This year I was sure there were just as many gawkers, for I did recall seeing some in my peripheral vision, but with self-consciousness replaced by self-confidence, I was unfazed. As we waited to check in two men unabashedly stared at our children drawing in their travel notebooks. Normally such occurrences bothered my security-conscious husband, but he just smiled.

"It's good to be back, isn't it?" he said to me.

I nodded. It was good to be back in China—familiar China.

The Chinese character 熟, pronounced *shu*, has several meanings, such as "cooked," "ripe," "done," "skilled," or "prepared." Most of these meanings relate to food. A plum that is plump and juicy is 熟. Rice that has reached the perfect consistency is 熟. Stir-fried vegetables that are just tender without being overcooked are 熟. That food preparation is involved can be easily seen by the ⺗ at the bottom of the character: the fire underneath the wok.

But 熟 also means "familiar." What does familiarity have to do with fire or food preparation or fruit? The answer could be that 熟 refers to a desired end state. A ripe plum is the perfect plum; cooked rice and tender vegetables are ready to eat. 熟 means the process is finished and the food is ready to eat. Likewise, becoming familiar, especially for a family in a foreign land, is a process. Our entire first year had been consumed with this process, this often difficult and sometimes painful process. But now we were 熟, familiar. So let the feasting begin.

❁

At baggage claim in Beijing I sat with our kids on a bench with our carry-on luggage, as was our routine, while Chris stood by the carousel to claim our checked baggage. "He's got two bags," I told the kids. Then I continued. "We have a total of nine bags. Since we've already got two, how many are left?"

"Mom, I'm just too tired for story problems," said Katherine.

Then she suddenly perked up. "Mom, when will I start school?" she asked.

"Not until Friday or Monday," I told her.

"No," she said, "I want to go today."

When I told her it was already late afternoon, she said, "All right, I'll go tomorrow."

I had been cautiously optimistic that the children would be happy to be back once they saw familiar surroundings, but never did I think Katherine would be asking to go to school early.

We were met by Sally from the university's foreign affairs office at the airport in Jinan, and then happily by our minders at our apartment. Mr. Jia came by especially to see us, even though he wasn't on duty. Greeted by familiar and friendly faces, we felt we were home.

I had thought that Katherine's airport comments were a jet lag–induced fluke. But she, along with her siblings, awoke bright and early Thursday morning ready to go to school. I had lain awake since about 1:30 a.m., and the kids all awoke around four. I crawled into bed with Katherine.

"Katherine," I said, "all the kids are going to be so happy to see you. They are going to shout 'Fu Rui Xue! Fu Rui Xue!'"

"Oh, Mom," she replied after a moment, "I just can't help smiling."

Propelled by adrenaline, they skipped, hopped, bounced their way to school, with me running along behind. The morning was bustling with produce vendors opening their stalls, older women in the square doing Tai Chi, and the smells of *shaobing* baking for breakfast. Familiar sights greeted us; homey smells wafted over us. When we arrived at the kindergarten, we saw to our surprise that they had installed new playground equipment. Before they had a basic array: one slide, one small merry-go-round, a trampoline, and a few other pieces that simply had no American equivalent. Now there was a huge labyrinth of slides, tunnels, bridges, and monkey bars. In our world, this was a huge feast.

We walked in and the children were greeted warmly with hugs by their previous teachers as well as the school cook and janitor. Katherine was beginning her last year of kindergarten, considered a prep year for primary school. Upon arriving, we learned from the teacher that she needed a backpack to bring markers, pencils, and notebooks, which she would use to practice writing Chinese characters. So her father, despite his jet lag, dutifully took her shopping that evening. The next morning she proudly strode to school wearing her new pink Cinderella backpack. Does it get any better when you are five years old? Katherine declared that this year school was so much more fun than last year, and in fact she continued to wake up excited to go to school. Her drastic attitude shift amazed us.

We stayed in high spirits, feasting for about a week. After a summer of staying with friends and relatives, we had our own space back, sparse though it was. Scenes that were so much a part of our Tai'an life—men on the sidewalks playing cards, bikes and every other form of two-, three-, or four-wheeled conveyance, honking taxis—all brought smiles to our faces as we viewed them again, this time not as a new curiosity, but as a recognizable signpost that we were home.

But I suppose it was inevitable that we would have a settling period. By the second weekend we couldn't venture out. Chris's stomach had been upset for three days and he didn't want to chance being so far from a bathroom. Spending forty-eight hours in our apartment with the children reminded us of how small it was. Then there was the short in the bathroom light that caused it to go off at the most inopportune moments. And we returned to an ant problem, giving me the daily chore of squishing at least fifty ants with a paper towel in the children's bedroom. It soon felt like we had already exhausted our dinner options, and we didn't really feel like having hot and sour soup yet again.

I had some goals for this, our second year. Our first year had been about survival. We had plummeted down to the first rung on Maslow's hierarchy of needs—food, clothing, safety. During those early days, if I got my kids fed, it was a good day. If my husband wasn't purging himself from an accidental encounter with tap water, it was a good day. We worried about crossing the street, about riding in taxis devoid of seat belts, about communicating our basic needs. At the same time, we were undergoing a complete career change and had new jobs to learn.

But with that successfully behind us, I hoped this year to climb a few rungs on the Maslovian hierarchy. I wanted to make some friends. I wanted to truly be proud of the classes I taught. I hoped for an opportunity to be creative.

But I had one more goal. This year, I wanted to get in touch with Grace's foster mother. Grace's twenty-seven-bed orphanage in Fuzhou, Jiangxi province, usually had custody of more than three hundred babies, so it was forced early on to find local families who, for a small stipend, would care for these abandoned children. Our Grace, therefore, had never been institutionalized, but had spent her entire first year, until coming to us, living with a family.

I had inquired about her foster mother at the time of adoption. The orphanage director told me that the woman who handed her to us was the foster mother. I thought this odd, as she had seemed rather pleased to give her away, and parted with no display of sadness whatsoever. But I accepted what he said, and wrote a letter to this woman, sending it in care of the orphanage. I never heard anything back.

Later an adoption research service announced they were going to Fuzhou, and I asked them to include Grace in their inquiries. A few months later they sent us the name and picture of her foster mother, a different woman altogether.

Yet, I had seen this woman before. Before we traveled to China to pick up Grace, I had sent the orphanage a box of clothes and a disposable camera, asking them to take pictures of Grace for us so we would have some record of her daily life before she met us. When we picked her up, they gave us the camera. We developed it, and saw twenty-four pictures of Grace with a caregiver—a slight woman with prominent teeth and a weathered face—on the orphanage grounds. Grace was posed in the same outfit for all twenty-four pictures: at the top of the slide, at the bottom of the slide, on the bench, and so on. The pictures had obviously all been taken within the space of about ten minutes.

We put the pictures aside and didn't think about them again. But when I saw the picture of Grace's foster mother, I remembered her as the woman in the pictures. This, I knew, was really her foster mother.

Though the research service had given me her address, at the time I was busy caring for three small children while Chris was deployed to Iraq, so I didn't write. Then, our first year in China we were so overwhelmed with adjusting to our new life that I didn't write. But this year, I said to myself, now that I was more familiar with our new life, this year I would write a letter to Grace's foster mother.

Chapter 17

同

SAME

❀

IT WAS GREAT TO BE TEACHING AGAIN—MEETING OUR NEW STUDENTS, happily running into our former students. Two weeks after the semester began, the first-year students arrived, fresh from military training, ready to start classes.

Teaching the freshmen was a great joy, the same joy one gets upon surprising one's child with a new puppy, or bringing home a report card of straight "A"s to parents, or presenting a spouse with steak and eggs for breakfast. The freshmen were thrilled with the idea of a foreign teacher. One student was so excited he was barely able to contain himself, nearly hyperventilating as he talked to me during the break. I posed for numerous pictures. One class broke into applause many times during the question-and-answer session.

In their faces was a combination of innocence and excitement. I knew they would soon get a little jaded; they might not put their best into an assignment, perhaps even skip class. But for now, we could revel in the wholesomeness of the educational experience.

This first semester was formative for them, and I wanted to make the most of it. I reminded them that the college entrance exam was now behind them. I told them that when they graduated in four years they would have another exam, but of a different sort. In this exam they would, in their profession, be required to communicate in English and understand the English of their colleagues and contacts. They then would have to wake up the next day and take this test again. I told them that with this new kind of exam, they needed a new kind of study method, not the old kind they used in high school when they were memorizing and reciting in preparation for The Exam.

Because it was the first day we had another task: choosing an English name. I explained how important this was. A good name would make foreigners feel comfortable around them; a bad name would make foreigners laugh at them. The majority of our students chose good, standard names. But despite our best efforts, a dogged few insisted on clinging to their not-so-good names. One morning I taught double majors in clinical medicine and English, and went down the list of these names of future doctors: Drama, Anatola, Long, Linkin, Beliek, and an unfortunate boy named Sherry. As I called roll I came to Alan.

He stood up. "My name is change," he told me.

"Okay," I said. "What did you change it to?"

"My name is change," he said again.

"Yes, what is your new name?"

"C-H-A-N-G-E," he said.

Now I understood. "Okay, your new name is Change. Change, will you please see me during the break?"

❁

As I was walking to the supermarket I saw an old bus by the side of the road leaking oil profusely. Standing around was a crowd of people watching. Not helping (for there was nothing they could really do), just watching.

It made me recall a week earlier when a policeman was trying to convince a woman to remove her cart from the middle of the road. She was equally stubborn in her refusal, creating a heated confrontation. A crowd gathered to watch.

I was interested as well, but just couldn't shake my mother's voice echoing in my head: *Don't stare! It's not polite*. And isn't that the greater part of what gives us our culture: our mother's voices, ringing in our heads? I put my head down and just kept walking, as my mother would have admonished.

But the Chinese rarely keep walking.

In Chinese, "same" is written as 同. This character is used to make many compounds, such as classmate, 同学 ("same study"), or comrade, 同志 ("same will"). But the compound word I needed to use was 不同 — "*not* the same," or just plain different. For unlike me, the Chinese almost always stopped to enjoy the show.

To my consternation, watching a harried foreign mother discipline her sassy five-year-old daughter seemed to be a favorite diversion; it always drew a crowd. And a group of grandmothers never failed to gather and observe this same harried mother change the diaper of her little boy (who should have been potty-trained), pointing and murmuring their comments about this strange foreign practice.

The Chinese have learned that observing everyday life is infinitely more interesting that some made-up drama on television, making "Standing and Watching" a favorite pastime, be it simply watching the comings and goings of the street, gazing at children performing their morning exercises at school, or scrutinizing one's food being prepared at a roadside stall. (Watching deft fingers expertly flip pastries with chopsticks in one hand while cracking eggs with the other always holds the kids' and my rapt attention.) But that's not the only reason.

In our part of China, far from the more impersonal big cities like Beijing and Shanghai, one's private sphere is quite small. Everything is out in the open, like the laundry we all have fluttering outside the windows. Intrusive advice is often given, and a friend might point out her friend's recent weight gain as a means of expressing her concern. In this arena, personal privacy, Chinese and Americans were simply *not* the same. 不同.

Of course, living in a foreign culture, we were often confronted by difference. We taught with different teaching methods, we ate with different utensils, and we dressed differently. But what I found most fascinating was the difference in mind-set, the difference in worldview, the difference in that "inner voice." For without that shared experience of culture, our inner voices gave us completely different instructions.

As I watched the children play at the playground after school, Grace came up to tell me she was going inside to use the bathroom. I give her a hug and a kiss. The lady next to me said to the lady next to her: "That's a Chinese girl."

"No, she's an American," I corrected, interjecting myself into the conversation.

"Really!"

"Of course," I said. "She's my daughter. She's a *meijihuaren*, Chinese with American citizenship. She's adopted."

"Oh, adopted, I see. Are you a teacher here?"

"Yes, a foreign teacher."

The other lady then asked, "How much money do you earn?"

No matter how many times I was asked this question, it startled me. I would always fumble over the answer, for a voice inside my head would start screeching: "Excuse me! Uhhh, we just met. I don't know you. That's private! That's privileged information! How dare you ask me!"

Hardly able to think for the blaring in my head, I usually forgot my salary altogether, and certainly forgot how to say it in Chinese.

Finally, my mouth, completely contrary to the wishes of that voice in my head, uttered a quiet, "Each month, thirty-six hundred yuan."

Not the same. 不同.

❀

In our efforts to have a more well-rounded life, a life focused on more than necessities, we thought we would start by adding some music. In the spring a departing American teacher at a different university in town asked us if we wanted to buy her digital piano. Chris excitedly agreed. He was the musician in the family, with several years of piano under his belt, as well as a few adolescent experiences in garage bands. He always hoped we'd be able to provide Katherine, Grace, and Andrew with the musical education he had so enjoyed in his childhood.

That fall the kindergarten posted their offerings of extra Saturday classes: art, dancing, Chinese checkers, and *dianzi qin* (electric piano). I asked our foreign affairs office to call the kindergarten to get the details, because I wondered how piano would be taught in a group setting. They told me that the class would have six to ten students, and that our children could go the first time for free just to try it out. All three kids were excited, so we signed up and waited until our first lesson at 2:00 p.m. on Saturday.

At about twenty minutes before two, we left for our lesson. But our happiness was short-lived. As we reached the courtyard, Mr. Jia looked at us with surprise.

"Where is your *dianzi qin*?" he asked.

"We don't need one," I answered.

We continued our walk toward the kindergarten. But the seed of doubt was now planted in my mind.

"Were we really supposed to bring our own *dianzi qin*?" I thought. I had wondered how they were going to teach a group of children, when I had never seen a music room equipped with electric keyboards.

I called the school on my cell phone. They said, yes, I was supposed to bring an electric keyboard.

"I didn't know," I said weakly.

I felt my chest tighten. I was beginning to yield to my enemy in our life here: irritation. I had taken such great care to make sure I knew everything. I had even had our foreign affairs office call the kindergarten, although I preferred to take care of these matters myself. But despite this, a key piece of information had escaped me. It was like I had shown up at a ball grossly underdressed, or shown up for class with all the wrong books.

I still felt so frustrated at my perpetual handicap of being a foreigner. Limited by lack of language skills and required to decipher societal norms, so many things just went over my head. Last year we were the last parents to figure out that we were supposed to drop our children off with a daily yogurt drink, which they had with their snack when they awoke from their naps. Before we realized this, they just went without. The same occurred with felt-tip markers; each child was supposed to bring their own set from home. Our children had to borrow from others until we figured this out. Just the previous week as I brought Katherine to her class, we saw all the other mothers and children line up so the teacher could check off that their homework had been completed. We just looked at each other and shrugged our shoulders. Who needs homework when you are in kindergarten anyway? But this situation with the piano lessons smarted much more than any previous faux pas, for we really cared about it.

I called Chris, to vent my frustration and get advice. "Just go on to the lesson," he advised. "It's only the first day. You'll be able to see what it's all about."

"Okay," I said, and we continued down the hill.

But Katherine came to a standstill. "If we are supposed to have a *dianzi qin*, I am NOT going without a *dianzi qin*." She had a look of

absolute determination on her face. Her visceral reaction made me wonder
how often last year she had felt the same way I was feeling now, and if that
accounted for much of her acting out. Since she was immersed in Chinese
school, she was bound to have experienced this feeling earlier, more frequently, and in more concentrated form than I.

Then I remembered that a fellow teacher from last year had given Andrew a toy keyboard for his birthday. It was quite loud for our small apartment, so when its batteries ran low, we had put it up out of sight. It was
more of a toy than a full-size digital piano, but it was all we had. I called
Chris and told him we were coming back. We ran back up the hill and he
met us at the door with the keyboard, batteries replaced.

Flustered and late, we ran back down the hill and caught a taxi at the
gate of the university. Arriving at the kindergarten, we found the gate still
locked. A Chinese woman and her son were waiting as well. To my relief,
she did not have a *dianzi qin* either. Soon a teacher came and unlocked the
gate, but told us that piano lessons did not start until two thirty.

"No, it's two o'clock!" said the other mother.

I chimed in as well, "Yes, I'm sure it's two o'clock."

Entering the school playground, we both made our way directly to
the poster announcing Saturday classes. To my chagrin, the poster had been
changed. Piano lessons were now listed from two thirty to three thirty, and
there was a key sentence at the bottom: "Make sure to bring your own *dianzi qin*."

"I didn't know!" the other mother said. She threw up her arms, then,
somewhat disoriented, glanced quickly around the playground as if a *dianzi
qin* might suddenly appear behind the monkey bars.

My frustration, combined with relief at finding someone else in the
same situation, trumped my normally omnipresent self-consciousness. The
words flew out of my mouth with a fluency and smoothness I had never
yet achieved in Chinese: "I didn't know either!" I exclaimed to my new
friend. "I didn't know until I called them a few minutes ago and they told
me. They must have just changed the sign because it used to say the lessons
started at two p.m.!"

As we were talking, looking straight into each other's eyes, we were
not foreigner and Chinese. The niceties that normally surrounded foreigner

to Chinese communication were dispensed with. She did not tell me oblig-
ingly how good my Chinese was, and I did not respond with my equally
obligatory *"Nali nali, mamahuhu"* (literally meaning "horse horse tiger
tiger," but actually meaning "just so so"). Instead, we were two mothers
standing on the school playground dealing with the same situation.

When I look at the character meaning "same," 同, I see one 一,
mouth, 口, under a covering: people speaking with one voice. Shared experience and mutual understanding. And on that kindergarten playground,
although we spoke different languages and came from different cultures,
this fellow mother and I were speaking with one voice. We were equals.
We were the same.

At two thirty the other parents arrived not only with their children,
but with quite long and heavy *dianzi qins* in tow as well. We saw quite
quickly that this method would not work for our children, simply because
I could not buy and carry three full-size keyboards to school each Saturday.
Despite that, we were happy with the teacher, and she offered to come to
our house on Monday evenings to teach the children privately. (The other
mother, my compatriot, called her husband, who soon drove up with the
required *dianzi qin* perched on a scooter.)

Chapter 18

累
TIRED

❀

DURING MY CHINESE LESSONS I ASKED ZHANG ABOUT THE CHINESE character meaning "tired."

累
TIRED

It struck me as an interesting character because it was composed of two elements: 田, meaning "field," and 糸, meaning "silk," one on top of the other. Often Chinese characters are formed with two parts side by side. One element offers a clue to meaning and the other signifies the sound. But in this character, none of the elements offered the sound. This led me to believe that they both played a semantic role.

So I sat with Zhang thinking out loud. "I understand the field, because working in the fields makes you tired. But what about silk? Why is silk there? Is it tiring work to make silk?"

Zhang suddenly sat up straight and said, "Yes, that's exactly it. *Nan geng nu zhi.*"

"What? Write it down for me."

She wrote: 男耕女织, then explained the meaning of each character, "man . . . plows . . . woman . . . weaves." She continued: "Everyone in China knows this. Life was this way in China for thousands of years."

Apparently the Calligrapher knew it as well, using "field" and "silk" as symbols for what make men and women tired. Studying Chinese is like an archaeological dig, finding treasures in the language that illuminate life long ago.

I had been plodding away at Chinese, putting in four hours a week with Zhang. There were so many times when I didn't feel like it, when I just wanted to sleep in or read or do something else with my time, so many times when I was just plain *tired*.

But now I was being rewarded with a level of comfort in my own abilities, and with surprised compliments from those with whom I conversed. More often than not I could understand the words of those speaking to me. I even found myself picking up Chinese when I wasn't paying attention—snippets of conversations on the bus or banter in the grocery store. I didn't stumble over my words nearly as often as before; in fact, when I was speaking with someone using halting English, I found myself involuntarily switching to Chinese so the conversation would flow more easily.

In my schedule that fall, Tuesday was my long day. This particular Tuesday was no exception. I taught four two-hour classes with a short break for lunch. My day began at 5:30 a.m. As soon as I heard the water begin refilling the pipes after the nightly shutdown, I got up to shower. Normally at least one or two kids were up by six, so while I got ready, I also was feeding and dressing them. But this particular day they all slept in, which meant I had some spare time as I got ready. A little before seven, I grabbed my purse, my school bag, and the trash, and was out the door.

As I walked through our courtyard, I waved to Mr. Jia in the duty room. *"Shang ke?"* he asked. "Do you have class?"

"Shang ke," I confirmed.

I walked across the street and put the trash in the dumpster. At that moment an older woman walking in the park called out to me. I recognized her immediately. We called her The Trash Lady.

When we first arrived in Tai'an Chris had noticed The Trash Lady right away.

"I dropped off our garbage, and a lady came and started looking through it," he told me.

"Are you sure she was looking through *our* trash?" I asked.

"Yes, she went directly to the bag I had just dropped off."

"You are so paranoid! What could anybody possibly want from our trash?" I said.

Then one day we set out for a lunch date and dropped off garbage on the way. This time I saw the woman. Chris was right. She deliberately found *our* trash and set about going through it. Seeing it firsthand was a different experience than having him tell me about it. As we walked away, I kept turning around and observing her. It was the strangest feeling watching someone going through our trash.

What made it even stranger was that we lived on a small campus. This was not some stranger, a bag lady, as we would say in the United States, but a lady who was part of our community and who we greeted on the street. We thought about what exactly we had put in our trash—potato peelings, beer cans, soiled diapers—and why she found it so special. I also wondered what this woman had been through in her life to compel her to go through others' trash.

Things progressed to the point that when we took out our trash, we would see this woman, or sometimes others, make a beeline for the dumpster. This was not subtle trash digging; there was no effort to hide anything about this operation. Then a few weeks later I took out the trash and I heard someone yelling. It was The Trash Lady, calling for me. She had been walking in the park and was quickly making her way over. I stopped what I was doing and waited for her. She came up to me, I greeted her, handed my trash right into her arms, producer to consumer, dispensing completely with the middle step of placing the trash into the dumpster.

She smiled and said, *"Xie xie."* Thank you.

"Maybe we should get her phone number and call her when we are taking out the trash," Chris joked, "to make it more convenient for her."

I watched her walk away happily with my trash, and continued through the park to the bus stop. My first class was Oral English with freshmen at 8:00 a.m. It was our second class together since they had spent the first two weeks of the term in military training. In the first class our priority had been giving each of them English names. So I started off this morning by calling roll using their English names. As anticipated, this took some time, as they were not yet used to their new names.

I then had the students do an exercise where they got up and walked around the room interviewing their classmates. I gave them each a sheet of paper with a list of items, such as "climbed Mount Tai" or "own a bicycle." Once they found a classmate who matched—who had indeed climbed Mount Tai or who in fact owned a bicycle—they wrote their English name down on the blank. In this way, they were practicing their English by asking and answering questions, and also learning each other's English names.

One of the items was to find a student with more than two siblings. My first year in China, I had been surprised at the big families my students came from. One student was even the seventh in a family of nine girls. But in this class of freshmen there was not a single student with more than two siblings. I asked for a show of hands for only children, and fully one-third of the class raised their hands. I realized I was seeing a demographic shift reflecting stricter enforcement of China's one-child policy, beginning with these freshmen, who were born in 1988 and 1989.

At 10:00 a.m. I remained in the same room for my Extensive Reading class, also with freshmen. This class had more than sixty students, so the roll call took some time. At lunch I had an appointment to meet with two freshmen, Kevin and Ann. I left the classroom and joined the flow of students going from the teaching buildings to the part of campus containing dorms, shops, cafeterias, and restaurants. A lake separated these two sections of campus, so all the students were funneled through one bridge, creating a black river of spiky hair and ponytails flowing toward lunch establishments or the dorms for a quick nap. On rainy days or hot sunny days, the river became a bright panoply of multicolored umbrellas.

I met my two students in front of the walking street at noon.

"Where do you want to eat?" I asked them.

"We're unfamiliar with most of the restaurants on the shopping street," they told me. "Why don't you choose?"

By this time I had eaten in quite a few of these establishments, so I suggested a good one on the second level. It seemed strange to me to be the expert. Usually the students directed me to the eating place.

We ordered some of my favorites: cabbage and pork dumplings, hot and sour potatoes, and toffee sweet potatoes. My seat gave me an unobstructed view directly into the kitchen. I watched as an older woman squatted

down on her haunches to shred potatoes into a basin filled with water that
had long lost its translucency. This potato water had spilled and, combined
with the dirt from the cook's shoes, left wet mud streaks all over the floor.
The cook, a large man in a dirty white apron, stood over a huge iron wok,
periodically dousing it generously with peanut oil. Next to the wok were his
ingredients. Depending on the dish, he would grab various portions: spices,
peppers, tree fungus. Black charcoal dust from the stove had collected in a
ring underneath the wok. As I took all this in, our own potato dish arrived.

"This is delicious," Ann exclaimed. And it was, although it would
have been more enjoyable had I not seen where it was made.

When the toffee sweet potatoes arrived, the waiter brought the customary bowl of water used to cool the threads of liquid sugar. Once cooled,
the threads became brittle and broke, allowing one to eat the hot, sugary
chunk of sweet potato.

But when this bowl of water arrived, my students asked, "What is this?"

"It's a bowl of water," I replied, somewhat surprised by the question.

"What's it for?"

"It's for dipping the sweet potatoes in," I answered, even more puzzled. I thought for a moment. "Have you ever eaten toffee sweet potatoes
before?" I asked.

"No," they answered.

Kevin added, "I'm quite unfamiliar with most food served in
restaurants."

"So your foreign teacher is introducing you to Chinese dishes!" I said
playfully.

Kevin and Ann were from the countryside, and for both of them this
was their first experience outside of their home county. But I was truly flabbergasted that they had never had such experiences as eating in a restaurant
and didn't know how to approach a food common to their own province.

After lunch I walked over to buy several days' worth of *China Daily*,
then went to my office to peruse them for a few minutes before my next
class. A headline caught my eye: "Self-developed 'bullet' train to debut by
year end."

I read the opening sentence: "China's first self-designed and self-
manufactured passenger train with a designed speed of 300 km per hour,

equal to that of the famous Japanese bullet train, will roll off the production line by the end of this year, the manufacturer has announced." I chuckled to myself. This sentence with its ubiquitous "selfs" encapsulated so much Chinese-ness. China ached in its knowledge that Western science and technology were superior. This self-designed self-manufactured train was in direct contrast to the new third terminal at Beijing's Capital Airport, which had received a lot of press recently. Built to accommodate the visitors for the 2008 Olympics, the terminal was designed by a Brit while the baggage handling system was made by the German company Siemens. This Olympic welcoming showcase was foreign-designed and foreign-built, a fact that chafed Chinese, demonstrating their dependent relationship with Western technology.

I was most familiar with the "self" language used in the Three-Self church: self-governing, self-financing, self-propagating. China, including its churches, would not be controlled by foreigners. And now, as the headline proudly announced, China's trains would not be built by foreigners.

I put the newspaper away and reached for the phone to call Chris.

For the most part, we communicated throughout the day by text message. It was the communication means of choice for our students, and worked well for us, as one of us was often in the classroom. But at lunchtime or on breaks we were able to sneak in a phone call.

"Hey, how's your day off?" I asked.

"Not much of a day off. I have so much class prep to do. I'm working way too hard. I thought I was supposed to be retired."

"Come on. You're only forty-seven."

"I'm getting ready to take a break from the computer and read for a bit," he said. "I may pick up another Faulkner short story. Actually, I think I'll read a magazine. I need something a little more mindless." Teaching English had made Chris realize how little American literature he had in fact read. He was trying to rectify that.

"I just picked up several days' worth of newspapers. They even had yesterday's already."

"That's our *China Daily*: 'Yesterday's News Tomorrow,'" Chris quipped. "I didn't even see you this morning before you left."

"Nope. You were snoring so I didn't wake you."

"That was kind of you. But I barely got the kids to school on time."

"Speaking of on time, I need to head to class."

"Okay. See you at home."

I grabbed my bags and headed back to the teaching building for four more hours of class. Following another class of Extensive Reading, I taught Oral English again, this time to sophomore tourism majors. Since we were practicing the past tense, I gave the students the assignment to think about an important lesson they had learned in their youth, then talk about it for three minutes in English. I gave them five minutes to prepare and make a few notes. Then I lined them up around the room in pairs, facing each other. One member of the pair was the "talker," while the other was the "listener" who was to listen encouragingly, pay attention for mistakes in past-tense usage, and ask questions at the end. At the end of three minutes, the roles would switch and the line rotate. In this way, each student told his story several times, ideally becoming quite comfortable with it, and also listened to several different stories from his or her classmates.

I set everything up, but there was an odd number of students. To even it up, I put myself into the lineup. We went through several rotations, and then I found myself opposite a shy girl with a short ponytail.

"What I have learned is that girls are just as important as boys," she began.

I was intrigued and told her to continue.

"When I was fifteen years old I went shopping with my mother. However, I began to feel sick and dizzy, and I had to lie down. My mother became worried, and I overheard her talking to the salesgirls about how she needed to get help and how she was so worried about me. I knew at that moment that my mother loved me very much, and loved me just as much as my brother. It made me very happy. Now I know that girls are just as important and loved as boys are," she closed, with a smile on her face.

"But you were fifteen," I said. "Up until that time, did you really believe that your parents loved your brother more than you?"

She related that when she was a young girl, one of her relatives had made a joke about her parents loving her brother more because he was a boy. She had simply believed it.

At the end of class, I got on the five thirty bus and slumped into my seat. I called and ordered pizza to be delivered, as was our custom on Tuesday nights when I had to work so late. Chris sent me a text message that he and the children were home from the kindergarten.

As we entered the old campus gate, suddenly I saw Mount Tai rising behind our campus. There had been so much pollution it had been invisible the past few days, but there it was again, like an old friend.

I retraced my steps through the park and up to our courtyard, a thin coat of sweat covering my entire body. I was glad to be off the hot bus and even happier to be finished with my toughest day of the week.

Mr. Jia looked at me sympathetically.

"Ni hen lei," he said. "You are very tired."

Yes, I nodded.

"Keshi . . ." he continued. "But . . ." He said some more words in Chinese. I caught the word in the beginning and the word at the end, but the middle word was a muddle to me, and the meaning as a whole escaped me. He said it a few times, then reached for a small chip of cement.

He started to scratch some characters on the pavement but then stopped.

Holding the chip up above his head, he adopted an erect posture and pronounced: "Mao Zedong said," then repeated the phrase, while writing it on the pavement:

为人民服务

Wei Renmin Fuwu

(literally, "For People Serve")

As soon as he wrote it I saw the middle word I was missing, *renmin*, meaning people. I don't know how I missed it. Perhaps his dialect was too strong. Perhaps I was just too tired. But there it was, Mao's famous slogan: Serve the people.

Mr. Jia continued. "Yes, you are tired. But because you are serving the people, you do not get tired."

"A profound sentiment," I thought. But as I walked up the stairs with my stiff legs and thought about my long day of teaching and the people I'd had contact with throughout the day—a neighbor who went through my trash, a student who didn't know she was loved, new freshmen I'd shared toffee sweet potatoes with—I thought that really, serving or not serving, I was just tired.

Chapter 19

矛盾
CONTRADICTION

❀

I HAVE A DISTINCT MEMORY FROM OUR FIRST YEAR. I TOOK THE CHILDREN downstairs. When we reached the courtyard, Katherine threw a fit. This could have been any of a number of times, really. But this one I remember as being particularly frustrating because we were doing something she had asked to do, play at the park. But the minute we were at the park, Katherine changed her mind, angrily asserting that I was forcing her to go to the park.

Mr. Jia was standing by and asked what was the matter. In my elementary Chinese I explained the situation.

"Ah," he said, and then pronounced his appraisal of the situation in one word: *maodun*. After dealing with our circumstances, I went home and looked up the word in our pocket dictionary: "contradiction" or "paradox." I moved around some of the dusty furniture in my brain to make a place for *maodun*, deciding I needed a few words like this to pepper my Chinese.

❀

I had always dreamed of studying at Oxford University. The reason was not the classical architecture (although it did seem that knowledge would more easily seep into my brain if I was sitting in a quad surrounded by arches and porticos), nor the fact that it was the first university in the English-speaking world. It wasn't that Margaret Thatcher, Indira Gandhi, or Bill Clinton attended Oxford. It was the tutorial system.

I romanticized what I thought was the ideal education: to bring my thoughts and ideas, written in creative prose, to my tutor's office. There, surrounded by wall-to-wall books and seated on Victorian-era furniture, I would present my writings. My tutor and the two or three others participating in the tutorial session would then engage in a multifarious discussion, pulled along by the force of ideas. Ideas that I had researched would germinate into directions I hadn't considered; my mind would be broadened. Under the power of such stimuli, I would return to my research and my ideas, refining them, expanding them, bringing them farther than I ever thought they might go.

I'm not sure where I got such a romantic idea. Perhaps it came from reading C. S. Lewis and the Inklings—his group of writer friends like J. R. R. Tolkien and Owen Barfield—who gathered Tuesday nights at The Eagle and Child Pub to read their unfinished novels.

But I never went to Oxford.

And such moments have been fleeting for me. But in what seemed a complete paradox, a *maodun*, this university of immense size where students had completed at least twelve years of rote learning, memorization, and recitation; this exam-based education system that placed no value on critical thinking or creativity or analysis; this institution with classrooms of collectively minded students whose thinking rarely deviated from the group norm sitting in desks bolted to the floor like so many eggs in a carton, cleared out a space for me to have this model of intellectual collaboration I had long sought but never found. This university gave me a time and a place where my students and I could gather—a safe place—a forum where thinking could be freed from its normal regimented boundaries. It was called office hours.

That year the English Department cut our weekly teaching hours from sixteen to fourteen, with the two hours left over to be used as office hours. Each of us foreign teachers was assigned a time when the students could come and talk with us to practice their spoken English. My assigned time was Wednesday afternoons from one thirty to three thirty. I thought having office hours was a great idea, but half of me hoped no one would show up so I would gain a few quiet moments to myself to study Chinese.

But I had plenty of customers, about five the first week and ten the second. Many of them were not my own students, but other English majors whose schedule allowed them to come. As the weeks went on, the group began to self-select: these were students who, instead of finding a classroom to read and memorize their textbook, were choosing to come to my office to discuss ideas. A core group began to collect each week, allowing us to discuss issues in-depth and continue interesting topics from one week to the next. This group was confident in their speaking abilities and comfortable asking questions and exchanging opinions. We also had similar interests: Chinese history, cultural differences, and the Chinese education system. But more important, they were not shy or impassive. They liked to play with ideas just like I did.

Office hours became my own Oxford tutorial session. The office had only the barest of furniture; in fact we often had to borrow folding chairs. There were no bookcases, no carpets or classical paintings, only faded pictures cut out of *National Geographic* taped to the wall. But office hours became the highlight of my week, a time where, freed from the formality of the classroom, we could have varied and far-reaching conversations that stimulated my thoughts and challenged many of my assumptions.

I had recently read *Nixon and Mao* by Margaret MacMillan, which recalled Nixon's week in Beijing in 1972 and the events leading up to it. In her book MacMillan described Mao as typically Chinese in that he looked to history for lessons and for guidance. In fact, he fondly compared himself to the first emperor of the Qin Dynasty who united China in 221 BC for the first time (and who, as MacMillan wryly observed, ruled tyrannically, burning books and scholars alive). If history really shaped the Chinese mind, I wondered, which version of history was it? Which version of history had they been taught? Which version of history had they then memorized, recited, and been repeatedly tested on? I was anxious to mine my students to discover more of the nature of the Chinese mind and how Chinese history had shaped it.

The Opium Wars of the mid-1800s were a subject I knew little about, but often found referenced in my readings about China. So in office hours I asked my student Amy about the significance of the Opium Wars. Amy had stood out from my first days of teaching as bright and confident. She came to the podium nearly every break to ask questions from supplementary textbooks. She was self-assured, with a flawless accent, and was willing to ask the questions her classmates were too shy to voice. I was surprised to find out that she was born and raised in the countryside and that her parents did not even speak Mandarin, only their local dialect.

Amy and I often met for lunch. Once I took her to KFC, as she'd never been there before.

"I'll just eat whatever you eat," she told me.

I ordered my standby, the Mexican roll-up, a tortilla filled with chicken fingers and salsa, along with a corn salad, and some egg tarts for dessert. I ate my tortilla quickly, then started on the egg tarts. As I was doing so, I noticed she was eating her roll-up in an awkward fashion, holding it still wrapped in paper, and maneuvering it to her mouth for bites. I started to tell her she could just grab the tortilla with her hands. But suddenly, I remembered. Chinese people do not eat with their fingers.

"Is that why you are holding it that way?" I asked.

"Yes."

I realized I had already eaten my roll-up the old-fashioned American way, and probably licked my fingers when I was finished, the ultimate Chinese faux pas.

"Uh oh," I said. "I ate mine with my fingers."

"Yes, I noticed," she said. "I know you did that because you are American, but I still thought it looked strange. We Chinese think that since our hands touch everything, to eat with our hands is just disgusting."

I did not want to be bested, so I countered: "Oh yeah? Well I thought it looked strange when we had lunch together a few weeks ago and you spit out the chicken bones on the table."

"Well, what are we supposed to do with the bones?" she asked.

"Put them on your plate, I guess," I said, never having thought about it before.

"But that's where your food goes. Isn't it strange to put your bones with your food?"

I didn't have an answer and gave up. I was in her country, after all. Since I had one egg tart remaining, I asked her, "How am I supposed to eat this?" KFC did not provide chopsticks.

"Here," she said, "pick it up with your napkin, eating it so your fingers don't actually touch it."

I always enjoyed my lunches with Amy.

"What do you already know about the Opium Wars?" Amy asked me.

"Very little," I told her, and sketched for her what I knew: that the Western powers, particularly Britain, wanted to sell opium to the Chinese to help correct the trade imbalance, but the Chinese wouldn't allow it. Britain then forced open the country to trade, and many Chinese people became addicted to opium.

"All that is true," Amy replied, "but that is not the real significance of the Opium Wars. There were actually two Opium Wars, and they were important because this was the beginning of a foreign 'invasion' into China. After this, China was subjected to a series of illegal treaties, and lowered to semicolonial or semifeudal status."

She looked around at the other students in the room. "When we students read this history we become angry that China was treated this way. China was ruled by the Qing Dynasty then. They were weak and ineffective, and caved in to the demands of foreigners. At that time, China was a like a sleeping lion. But now, we like to say, the lion has awakened and is beginning to stand up."

I thought a lot about Amy's words, particularly "caving in to the demands of foreigners." I remembered when a U.S. Navy EP-3 reconnaissance aircraft crash-landed on China's Hainan Island in 2001, after a collision with a Chinese interceptor jet. The Chinese government immediately assumed an aggressive posture toward the United States, one that I couldn't understand at the time. Amy's comments helped me realize that the Chinese government must not be seen by their own people as ever acquiescing to the demands of the West.

Taiwan was a subject that came up again, and frequently. I was surprised to find that the students didn't despise Chiang Kai-shek. Chiang was the anti-Mao, the face of the Kuomintang, the president of Taiwan until his death in 1975. He was widely regarded by most historians as corrupt and inefficient. I was sure their history books would have painted a similar picture. But as I looked around the room, the students seemed to bear no malice toward him. One girl even mused that perhaps China would have been better off if Chiang Kai-shek had led them after 1949 instead of Mao Zedong.

"I can't believe you just said that," I said. "I thought that was heresy in China."

"Well," she said simply, "look how successful Taiwan is compared to mainland China."

She had a point. But the interesting thing was that Taiwan was no longer so enthralled with Chiang Kai-shek, and had even removed some of his statues.

Then Kevin, one of few male students in our circle, mentioned that he was trying to join the Student Union. Office hours were like that: sometimes we would talk about one issue in-depth, other times we'd flit from one completely unrelated topic to another. "They haven't decided if I'm good enough yet," he said.

"Is it like joining the Communist Party?" I asked.

There were some nervous glances at one another.

"Are any of you members of the party?" I asked.

"I am," answered a girl named Betty. She mentioned that she had worked as the College Union secretary at her junior college and had proved herself, so was offered admission to the party.

I asked the others if they wanted to join.

"Yes, of course!" said Cathy. "Who wouldn't want to join? It helps you get a job and get promoted."

Kevin demurred and said he had no intention of joining.

"But don't you have to say you believe in certain things to join the party?" I asked.

They looked at one another. "We understand what you are saying," they said. "No, you really don't have to."

"I wasn't trying to say anything. I didn't have any hidden meaning," I protested. "But this is the Communist Party. Doesn't it stand for something? Don't you have to say you believe in it? Isn't this why you join?"

"Really, we are college students. We are too young to know what we really believe. To join is an honor and is something that helps your future."

I directed my next question toward Betty. "Since you are a party member, do you have to attend any meetings or do anything?"

"No," she said.

"Does anyone know you are in the party?"

"No," she said.

"Then what is the point of being in the party?"

"Perhaps later when I am working I can get promoted faster."

Our discussion reminded me of a talk I had had with my Chinese tutor Zhang a few weeks earlier:

"Zhang, I've been reading a lot in *China Daily* about China as a 'Harmonious Society.' What does this mean?"

"Well, this is an idea of our president, Hu Jintao."

"Yes, but what does he actually mean by it?"

"Well, you know that harmony is important to the Chinese people."

"Yes, I understand that, but what about this 'Harmonious Society' campaign. What does it involve?"

"I'm really not sure."

"You're not sure?"

"No, I don't really know."

"But you are Chinese!"

"Yes, but we don't really concern ourselves so much with politics."

"But you are a party member!"

"Really, Aminta, I don't care about this. All I care about is teaching and . . . beautiful clothes."

❀

In our discussions of China during office hours I became completely sensitized to all usage of the word "development." It was commonly used in the form "developing," as in the half-apology I so often heard: "China is a developing country." There was a comparison implied here, if not outright stated.

I began to rant to my students on this seeming obsession with development.

"Why is development all that matters? What about culture? What about history? Why is development all you Chinese care about?"

"Of course development must be our first priority," said Kimberly, a plump freshman from the provincial capital, Jinan. "When people don't have enough to eat, when they live in the countryside and must work so hard and get paid so little, of course their children want to live in the city where there is development."

"But the truth is, Kimberly, most people in China are no longer starving, and the development we are talking about here is not development to get people basic needs, but development to get more conveniences."

"Yes," said Kimberly, "but we remember our history. Not long ago China was very poor. People did not have enough to eat. It is natural, coming from this experience, that development would be foremost in the people's minds."

She continued. "Another reason is that the Chinese people are a practical people. They just want to enjoy their life. For them, greater development means greater enjoyment of life. It's that simple.

"And we are not like you," she added. "Since you are already developed, you don't have to think about this. It is something you've always had. You've never had to yearn for it. China doesn't have it. It knows that compared to other countries, it is behind and it needs to catch up. So of course it is the priority."

"That's true," I told Kimberly. "Of course we don't talk so much about development in the United States—we are developed, so there's no need. But isn't this focus on development, this obsession really, at the expense of China's strengths—its history and its culture?"

"Your country is only two hundred years old. You don't have much history and your culture is young. You are insecure in these areas, so of course you think about them. In China, we know we have an old culture. We know we have five thousand years of civilization. We are secure in this, so we don't think about it or long for it."

I had never thought of it this way before. Perhaps I was enthralled with China's old culture precisely because I was an American, coming from a young culture. China, culturally secure, focused on what it didn't have— economic development.

And where Chinese culture once flowed in one direction out to cultures less advanced, now China had to borrow heavily from the advanced technology and education of the West, a fact that severely hurt its pride, much like a once prosperous uncle who was forced by poverty to borrow money from his young upstart (and slightly impertinent) nephew. The old civilization borrowing from the new one. There was some dignity, and some face, lost in the transaction. And some resentment gained.

I understood the Chinese thinking on development better after our conversations. But I still thought that development came at a price, and the traditional culture, the heartbeat of China, was necessarily challenged in the face of development. Calligraphy was replaced by computers, water buffalo were exchanged for tractors, donkey-driven carts swapped for any variety of motor vehicle. What, which was of undying value, would be thrown away because it was in the way of development? What precious things would be lost as China raced to catch up with the West?

When a child leaves the traditional life of his peasant village for the more developed city, he not only leaves behind his parents and grandparents, but a little of himself. And when a culture that has a unique word for second-oldest maternal aunt or for wife of one's paternal uncle; a culture whose literary classics, such as *Dream of the Red Chamber* or *The Family*, are tales of large extended families; when such a culture imposes the one-child policy because China's huge population is an impediment to economic development, then something also is lost.

Students frequently asked me during office hours about the American education system. I explained that while American students should study American history, schools and teachers have more leeway to choose the textbook, and to teach it in the way they find most effective. Since all my students knew Abraham Lincoln, I used him as an example.

"One teacher might emphasize recitation of the Gettysburg Address; another, the Lincoln-Douglas debates; still another, the battle of Vicksburg."

"But how will the students pass the exam if the teachers teach with this method?" they asked.

"We don't have a national exam like you have," I told them. "Teachers write their own exams on what they covered in class, but there isn't a required national exam on American history."

They told me that province wide, all schools had to use the same textbooks, because the information from the textbook was used for the college entrance exam. Teachers had no leeway to choose textbooks or even to choose certain parts of the textbook to emphasize and others to gloss over.

The Exam was still a favorite topic of mine. One week in office hours four students attended: three female students from the city of Qingdao and one young man from the countryside. When we talked about the college entrance examination, the city girls told me the countryside students always fared much better and had more advantages than they.

"But how is this possible?" I asked. "In the city you have better schools, you have foreign teachers to help you learn English, and additionally, you are even allowed a lower score than students from the countryside. So how do you not have the advantage?"

"Well, the countryside students know this is their only opportunity. If they don't pass, they will be farmers like their parents and grandparents for the rest of their lives. They may never leave their village. We city students should still be able to get a good job in the city even if we don't pass. But for them it's their only chance. They can memorize entire textbooks and sleep only two hours every night. We simply can't compete against motivation like that!"

❀

I always, when discussing the Chinese education system with my students, pointed out that the Chinese were much better at math than us Americans. Partly I wanted to compliment their system in some way because I found a lot to criticize, particularly the overreliance on memorization and the under-stimulation of creativity.

Katherine began doing math already in her four-year-old class at the kindergarten, and it became more formal when she moved into her last year of kindergarten. That spring, for several weeks, she had a certain kind of math homework: story problems. She didn't have to solve them; she had to write them.

I was amazed to see math taught in such a creative way. Her math homework, which she always enjoyed doing, had many varied problems that made her think about addition and subtraction in so many different ways.

Then in office hours a student told me that in high school she always liked to write stories, but her teachers discouraged her, telling her that writing stories had no use on The Exam. So she had stopped.

"You stopped writing your stories?" I asked, incredulous.

Lack of creativity was always the topic whenever the issue of Chinese education was raised. I remember one class where I put this sentence up on the board:

China is a superb nation when it comes to _____, but perhaps the worst at _____.

For the first blank, the students had several answers: inventing, civilization, large population, long history, and unity. I then asked them for their answers to the second blank and they had only one: creativity.

The Chinese knew their education system did little to encourage creativity, but they didn't know how to change it.

"Until you get rid of The Exam," I declared, "your education system will never allow Chinese to reach their full creative potential."

The room was quiet for a moment.

"But we do have a chance to use our creativity," countered a student named Edie. "We have a chance to use creativity with our math."

I looked at her and nodded, remembering Katherine's experience with the story problems. But creativity with math? Wasn't that a contradiction? A *maodun*?

I had lunch with two of my students later that week, Miriam and Seven, and the topic came up again. They told me that in all their subjects— language, history, politics, and science—they were subjected to the Memorize and Regurgitate method. Except math.

Math was the one subject in which they didn't have to memorize anything.

"But what about addition facts?" I asked them, thinking about the flash cards I kept next to Katherine's bed.

"No, we never memorized those."

"But what about multiplication tables? Didn't you at least have to memorize those?" I asked.

"Never," they replied. "In fact, our teachers said this wasn't a good method and that we should not memorize in math. Math is the one subject where we really can practice critical thinking."

The one area that I thought called for rote learning, the Chinese thought the opposite. The paradox was that I had finally found creativity in China, in a place my closed American mind told me had no potential for it.

I thought back to my own lackluster math career, which careened to a close during freshman calculus in college, a required course. I memorized the formulas with the sole intent of passing the final exam. Then, once I had received my C+, I forgot all I "learned" and never looked back.

Then I recalled those weeks Katherine and I sat together while she dictated story problems to me in Chinese:

In mother's pocket is 10 yuan.
In father's pocket is 4 yuan.
Mother has how much more money than Father? 6 yuan.
$10 - 4 = 6$

Afterward she would read it over, then smile in satisfaction. Of course she did. It was her own creation.

❁

It wasn't until months later that I read a book titled *The Chinese Language: Its History and Current Usage*, and was surprised to find that very word, *maodun*, listed as an illustration of the role classical Chinese stories still play in modern Chinese. According to the book, the term *maodun* originates in a classical story more than two thousand years old. In this story, a man tried to sell both his spear and his shield. In pitching the two items, he declared that his sword, *mao*, 矛, was so sharp that it could pierce any shield, and also that his shield, *dun*, 盾, was so strong that no sword could penetrate it. Thus, modern Chinese now has the term "spear-shield," meaning "mutually contradictory."

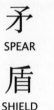

SPEAR

盾

SHIELD

CONTRADICTION

China gave us many moments of *maodun*: Volvos sharing the road with donkey-drawn carts, village huts along dirt roads whose residents owned the latest PCs and mobile phones, and yes, creative math. And in another paradox, China, in the midst of its regimented education system, gave me the Oxford tutorial experience my Western education never did.

Chapter 20

身份
IDENTITY

❁

IT WAS FINALLY NOVEMBER 15. THIS WAS THE DAY OUR RADIATORS WERE turned on. This is the day radiators have been turned on for decades, no matter if winter arrives unseasonably early or late. Despite the economic openness that describes today's China, some remnants of the old central planning system remain.

Recently, it had been colder inside the classrooms than outside in the elements. The floors, either bare cement or tile-covered cement, seemed to draw in the cold and hoard it. Only since coming to China had the bottoms of my feet ever felt so cold. Soon the quilts would arrive, heavy blankets encased in canvas, invariably army green in color, that covered the doorways to schools, supermarkets, and churches to keep the heat in and the cold out. When the green quilts arrived, we knew winter had as well.

One afternoon I left the apartment to pick up the kids and Mr. Jia was downstairs in the duty room. He motioned to his vehicle, a motorized three-wheeled scooter with a bench in the back. I eagerly nodded my assent. Since his grandson Feng Xin had started kindergarten, I had more chances to hitch a ride to or from the children's school, something I loved to take advantage of.

Mr. Jia knew almost everyone on the old campus, so the ride was punctuated by waving and nodding to his friends. During the day, Mr. Jia stood at the gate of our courtyard greeting and chatting with all who walked by; at night, the duty room became a hangout for the retired men of the old campus, who played cards or watched Peking Opera on television. In the old campus subculture, Mr. Jia was the ultimate insider; I, a foreigner, the ultimate outsider.

As we drove by, I watched his friends wave in acknowledgment when they saw him on his familiar scooter, then take a second look and smile in amusement when they saw me. When we arrived at the kindergarten, a huge crowd of parents was waiting for the gate to open. I felt I had arrived at the ball on the arm of Prince Charming. Our arrival together created quite a stir; everybody was grinning at us. By my association with him, I was less foreign, promoted to an approved neighbor.

Mr. Jia motioned for me to get off while he turned the scooter around, locked it, and went in to retrieve his grandson. I hurried to get the kids. All bundled up, we ran out the school gate to Mr. Jia's scooter. But there was no Feng Xin. I asked Mr. Jia, but he simply waved his hands impatiently for me to get in. The ride was fun as usual, with the kids bursting into fits of giggles every time we rode over a speed bump that sent them momentarily airborne. When he dropped us off, I again asked about Feng Xin.

"Ta gan mao le," he answered. "He has a cold and didn't go to school."

Mr. Jia had made this little excursion just for me.

❀

During office hours that week I hoped for a little peace and quiet, but soon after the appointed time Cathy arrived. Cathy had been a stalwart attendee, and an interesting personality.

I could tell from our first class together that she was more urbane that most of my students, usually wearing a fashionable headband or some jewelry, uncommon sights in this university. By her nature, she had difficulty concealing her feelings: if bored, it would be obvious from her facial expressions, slouched posture, or audible sighs. She told me in an earlier session that her mother was "a common worker, but still very fashionable." She seemed quite spoiled and usually regaled me with details about how her hometown, Qingdao (pronounced Cheeng-dow), was superior to Tai'an in so many ways. She talked about her hometown so much that Chris and I started referring to her as "Qingdao Cathy." She was having great difficulty adjusting to university life here. Complaining was her coping mechanism. During office hours she complained about the English accent of her classmates.

"Their accent is so terrible that I can hardly understand them! I actually want to laugh at them, but I'm worried that my accent will become worse from studying with them."

After some discussion I discovered that in her four-person room she was the only city girl; her three roommates were all from the countryside. While she found them kind and friendly, she often felt like a fish out of water. For starters, she was an only child. Her roommates all had siblings.

She told me, "At home, I offer to help my mother, but she says she can do it and asks me to just stay out of the way. Now I offer to help my roommates clean the room, but they tell me they can do it and to just stay out of the way." She threw up her hands in exasperation.

Her roommates preferred to speak in their local dialect rather than use Mandarin Chinese, for speaking in dialect made them feel closer. Qingdao Cathy didn't understand their dialect very well, so she felt left out.

She told me one of her roommates used a tissue, then threw it out the window.

"Why did you do that?" asked Qingdao Cathy. "There is a garbage can down the hall."

The girl answered, "We do this in my village all the time."

Qingdao Cathy said nothing. She felt she might hurt the girl's feelings if she pursued it.

"But there's no use trying to talk to a farmer," she informed me. "My mother has always told me this."

In another instance, Qingdao Cathy told one of her roommates that she had some coupons for KFC. To her surprise, her roommate had never heard of KFC.

"Cathy, there are no KFCs in the countryside. How would they have heard about it?" I asked her. "And besides, KFC is expensive."

"It's not that expensive," she countered.

"Well, not for you, a city girl, but for your roommates it would be very expensive."

"Now you are doing it too! My roommates keep telling me that I am rich, but I am not rich," she complained.

"Sure you are," I said. "You have lived a privileged life in Qingdao."

"But I am not rich. If I were rich my parents would have sent me abroad to study."

I laughed out loud. "Cathy," I scolded, knowing that the exchange rate made this nearly impossible, "how can you say such a ridiculous thing? Most of your classmates have never even left Shandong province. And you think this is the standard for a rich person in China?"

Shrugging her shoulders, Qingdao Cathy mentioned our lunch together a few weeks back.

"My mother told me to pay great attention to my manners, since I was having lunch with a foreigner," she told me.

"Well, did you think anything I did was strange?" I asked, sure she would comment on my lack of chopstick-handling skills.

"Not at all," she said. "In fact, I watched you carefully, so that I could try to emulate you."

This took me aback completely. "Why would you do that?"

"Don't you remember the story you told in class about how strange you thought it was that a Chinese student spit her chicken bones on the table?"

Yes, I did remember, horrified that she had taken my story in this way.

"But Cathy, I also said that the same student thought *I* was strange for eating with my hands. My point was that we have different manners and customs, certainly not that the Western way is better than the Chinese way."

She told me that since primary school, she and her classmates had been taught by their teachers how to act if they came across a foreigner. They had been told which habits foreigners found distasteful or impolite, and which manners foreigners were more comfortable with. They were given the idea that if they did not do this, foreigners would look down on them, and not only them as individuals, but as representatives for all Chinese.

The upcoming Olympics renewed this fear. The idea of having their culture on display for the whole world had made them suddenly aware of some "ugly habits"—not lining up, spitting, and so on. They weren't worried about such behavior before, but they were now.

❀

The following day I had lunch with Helen, one of my Chinese colleagues from the English Department. Helen taught medical English to undergraduates as well as coordinating English instruction for the graduate students. Last year we sat together on the bus a few times, and got along quite well. She was in her forties, married with a teenage son. Helen was always stylishly turned out, with beautiful clothes and long curly hair pulled back in a rhinestone barrette. Her English was excellent, allowing us to discuss issues in depth.

I met her as she was getting off the bus at the old campus after teaching all morning on the new campus. We walked to the street to catch a cab, and she suggested that we eat at Mao's House, the chain restaurant that boasted a little shrine to Mao. Chris and I had eaten there on one of our Friday lunch dates.

We started by talking about the food, as was Chinese custom. Helen ordered us stewed duck (which was quite delicious, although I had trouble figuring out how to eat it with my chopsticks); stir-fried mushrooms, also quite tasty; a soup containing dainty mushrooms and a long clear noodle made of beans; and for dessert some deep-fried pumpkin.

Since we were eating in Mao's House, it seemed appropriate to discuss Mao himself. Helen told me that the Chinese still revered him as the founder of China, but not as much as the older generation.

"My parents' generation worships him, and in fact, my parents will not tolerate a single bad thing said about him."

She thought for a moment. "But I am concerned about the younger generation in China, because they are growing up without any values. When I was young I was raised with the values of socialism and communism. Perhaps I did not believe everything about these values, but at least I had something to strive for and to teach me. Now my son is thirteen, and his generation doesn't even have what I had. This generation says, 'I only believe in myself.'"

I nodded. My students had often used that exact phrase with me.

She said, "If I try to talk to my son about the government or the party, he just points out the corruption."

We talked about some other things, such as teaching and the weather, but the topic soon returned to China's youth.

"You know China was closed for so long," she said, "and when we opened, we suddenly realized that other countries were more advanced than we were, and they were fascinating and interesting, perhaps more interesting than China. Our students nowadays are not very familiar with Confucius and don't know Tang poetry and the great Chinese literature. They think they need to spend all their spare time studying English and learning about Western ways and Western culture. They want to celebrate Christmas but don't celebrate Mid-Autumn Festival. They celebrate Valentine's Day but don't celebrate Spring Festival, the most important festival in China."

Helen stared down at her uneaten duck for a moment. "But they don't realize that if you don't know who you are, and where you come from, you have lost a part of yourself. They have willingly given up a part of their own culture, and so have lost themselves."

I told her about Qingdao Cathy, who was taught by parents and teachers not to offend foreign tourists. I relayed to her that when I asked Qingdao Cathy if I did anything strange, she answered that I could not do anything strange. That in fact she was hoping not to make a mistake and offend me, so she carefully watched me and did everything just as I did it.

Helen's eyes opened wide. "But you have come to *our* country."

"Yes," I agreed earnestly. "It's my responsibility to learn your ways, not the other way around!"

She nodded enthusiastically, then, staring into her duck again, said: "Yes, we look down upon ourselves. And we are teaching our children to look down upon themselves. This is the sad thing."

She mused. "Maybe all countries are like this. Do developed countries feel this way too?"

"No," I answered. "My country has the opposite problem. We think we are better than other countries, that we don't have to ask their opinion, that our way is the best way simply because we are American. We are too proud."

"Ah," she smiled, "so you should be more modest and humble like us, and we should be more proud and confident like you."

As I thought about Helen's words later, I reflected that we had brought Grace to China because we were proud that she was Chinese, and we wanted her to always be proud that she was Chinese. We wanted her to know the rich Chinese culture, to take pride in the five thousand years of unbroken civilization, to be acquainted with Tang Dynasty poetry and the four great Chinese novels.

But the China we had brought her to was not proud of itself. The current fascination with Western ways and economic development was teaching the younger generation, Grace's generation, that they were not as good as foreigners. How horribly ironic if instead of giving her pride in her heritage, her experience in China was teaching her to look down upon herself as Chinese.

Helen's cell phone rang. "I have to go back to the new campus for an afternoon meeting."

As she got up to go, she said, "There is a connection between us. In Chinese we call it *yuanfen*."

When I got home, I looked up *yuanfen* in the dictionary. It was translated as "destiny." I agreed.

❁

I thought a lot about the Chinese sense of identity. In Chinese identity was written 身份, pronounced *shenfen*. I understood the first character, 身, *shen*, for it meant "body." Of course one's body has a lot to do with their identity. The second character, *fen*, 份, was also a familiar one to me. It meant "portion." I used it frequently in restaurants, when I asked for one portion of hot and sour potatoes and two portions of *bing*. But why were these characters combined to form "identity"?

I asked my question to two Chinese professors. *"Bu neng fen kai,"* they told me. Can't separate.

"Many Chinese words are made of two characters. Some of them you can separate to understand the meaning; others you cannot. 身份 cannot be separated," they informed me.

But why were they brought together in the first place? I was still perplexed about this when I was chatting in Chinese with Mr. Jia on the courtyard steps one afternoon, while I watched the children play. I wrote the two characters on a piece of paper and showed him.

BODY

份

PORTION
IDENTITY

"In this word," he said, "*shen* has the greater meaning, and *fen* has the lesser meaning."

"I understand *shen*, and I know it means 'body,'" I told him. "But what meaning does *fen* contribute to the word?" He drew the character 分.

"You know what this character means, right?"

"Yes," I said. "It means divide."

"Right. Now suppose you have a plate of food, then you divide it up like this." He used his hand to make five or six cuts in an imaginary plate.

He kept writing. "Now take 分 and add 亻, 'person.' It becomes 份."

"Oh, I see," I said. "When you take what you have divided, and give it to a person, it becomes their portion."

"Yes," he said. "That is the part just for that person."

So in Chinese, your identity was your portion, your portion of the whole.

During my Chinese lessons with Zhang she mentioned the family tree at her grandfather's house. Zhang was her surname, the surname of nearly everyone in her ancestral village, where her grandfather was born. On this family tree every single man listed—for there were only men on the family tree—had the same surname, Zhang.

The second character also had meaning, for it was the generational character. All the men of the same generation had the same Chinese character as the second character in their name, making it easy to see each generation pass to the next.

But what she found interesting was that the third character, the only character truly unique to the individual, often was also tied to the family. If a family had four sons, the third character of each of the four sons, when said together from eldest to youngest, would be a phrase of great meaning.

For example, the first character would be the family surname, in this case, Zhang, written as 张. The second character would be the generational name, for example, Mei 美. The third character for eldest son might be 鹏; for the second son, 程; for the third son, 万; and for fourth son, 里. Thus their names, when written in order, would look like this:

First son: 张美鹏 (Zhang Mei Peng)
Second son: 张美程 (Zhang Mei Cheng)
Third son: 张美万 (Zhang Mei Wan)
Fourth son: 张美里 (Zhang Mei Li)

The last character was the only character truly ascribed to each individual, but in a case like this, the last four characters said together formed the well-known saying:

鹏程万里

peng cheng wan li

roc . . . distance . . . 10,000 . . . li

This *chengyu* refers to the roc, a mythological bird of enormous size and strength, and its capability to fly such a long distance as ten thousand li (about three hundred miles). But it has come to mean, as all Chinese understand, "Will have an exceedingly bright future."

A child thus named would know where he belonged and where he came from. His sense of identity would be clearly defined in terms of family and clan. Just like the child himself, his own name would achieve its greatest and truest meaning as one essential part of a greater whole. And in this specific case, by naming their four boys 鹏程万里, these parents would have emphasized that to have a bright future, the four sons must work together, each one doing his part.

This practice is rarely used now. There is only a single child for each generation, so generational names or links with names of siblings are impossible. But I thought a child of those previous generations would certainly have known who he was and where he came from. It would have been impossible for him to forget. Each time his name was spoken he would have been reminded of his identity, of his portion of the whole.

Chapter 21

COLD

❁

THE FIRST WEEK OF DECEMBER I FINALLY MAILED A LETTER TO GRACE'S foster mother. I'd had her address for more than two years, but writing her was something I could easily put off, especially since it would require careful wording as well as translating.

One night Grace and her dad were having their nightly wrestling match on our bed while I was in the kitchen cleaning up after dinner. Since our apartment was so small, our bedroom doubled as a secondary living room. I could hear Grace squealing with delight.

"Do it again, Dad!"

He whirled her through the air like an airplane. Flying like an airplane was one of her favorite activities, second only to being chased. Or swinging from monkey bars. Or playing hide-and-seek. Grace stretched her arms out and laughed.

I laughed too. You couldn't help laughing when Grace was laughing. Chris plopped her down on the bed.

"Do it again, Dad!"

"Daddy's tired."

"Just one more time."

"All right." Up she went into the air, shrieking happily. That girl was all about fun.

Grace's foster mother often came to mind at moments like this, as I thought about what she was missing out on. I knew I needed to establish contact. So I wrote a letter and Zhang translated it for me. Then I went to a photo shop, printed two pictures of Grace, and sent the envelope registered mail to Jiangxi province.

❁

December brought with it brisk winds and cold days in the classroom. We hauled our layers of long johns and smocks out of storage, and purchased new down-filled winter coats for the children. We knew winter had arrived when we saw our first pomelo of the season.

I had never seen a pomelo until coming to China. Its massive size makes it tower over its younger cousins in the citrus family. It is like a giant, delicious yellow grapefruit. After slicing it into halves and then quarters, we peeled away segments and ate it like an oversize orange.

Grace and Katherine were always excited when they walked into the kitchen and saw a pomelo on top of the water cooler.

"Katherine, Mom bought a pomelo. Mom, can we eat it now?"

"Grace, you get the trash can, I'll get our stools. Mom, you can start slicing it up."

The three of us girls sat on stools in the kitchen, the garbage can in the middle, necessary for the peelings, seeds, and membrane we disposed of in the course of eating the tasty slices. Andrew didn't care for it, and Chris usually came into the kitchen after we'd polished it off.

"Didn't any of my girls save me a slice?" Chris would ask.

"Nope," they said, with no remorse whatsoever.

But the advantages of the pomelo were not only taste. It also left off an aroma of clean-smelling citrus that permeated the entire kitchen. This was no small matter, for the drains in the floor often had us waking up to smells that were not nearly so pleasant. I usually bought one and placed it strategically atop the water cooler for a few days before we broke down and ate it, then quickly replaced it with another.

The approaching winter also meant I had to bundle up the children for their walks to and from school, something I could never do to Chinese standards. One day as the kids and I returned home from the kindergarten, we were met by Mr. Jia. He quickly took me to task for the children not wearing enough clothes.

I had a prepared speech in Chinese for such occasions, one in which I was getting quite well practiced: "Mr. Jia, American children, compared to Chinese children, are not used to wearing so many clothes. American children prefer to be able to move their arms and legs." I always said this with a smile, and it usually brought gracious nods of comprehension, if not actual approval.

But Mr. Jia was not put off so easily as the others. With a wave of his hand he completely dismissed my carefully crafted soliloquy.

"*Leng!*" he said. "The children are cold!"

The character for *leng*, meaning "cold," is written 冷. It has two parts: the first, 冫, means "ice," and gives the character its meaning. The two drops signify ice crystals. These ice crystals are also seen, in a slightly varied form, at the bottom of the character for winter, 冬. The second part of the character, 令, gives a clue to pronunciation. But I needed no hints to pronounce this word. I heard it all winter long.

I looked at Katherine and asked her: "*Leng bu leng?*" Are you cold? She shook her head no.

I turned to Grace. "*Leng bu leng?*"

She also shook her head no.

I turned to Mr. Jia with a slightly smug "told you so" expression on my face.

But he was not to be deterred. "It doesn't matter if they say they are not cold. They will still catch cold if you continue to dress them with so few clothes!"

Mr. Jia, as our minder, knew that in the past few days one child or another had spent a day home with a cold. I didn't know what else to say. He decided he had made his point, and so I was left to herd the children upstairs to our apartment.

As I reflected on this conversation, I realized that Mr. Jia had blown right over the line of polite inquiry used among people who considered themselves strangers or acquaintances. He had landed squarely in the domain of giving pushy child-rearing advice, whether welcome or not, usually reserved for grandparents or other close relatives, or basically those who felt they also had a personal stake in these children. In short, by gruffly taking me to task, he had signified our closeness.

Over the weekend Mr. Jia went to Beijing to meet his nephew who was flying in from Canada. On Tuesday morning as I left early to catch the bus to the new campus, I saw that he had returned.

"How was Beijing?" I asked him.

"Hen hao," he said smiling and beaming. "Very good." He paused, then added, "I saw Mao Zedong."

I was intrigued, but unfortunately I had a bus to catch so I couldn't continue the conversation.

That afternoon in my Oral English classes we were covering the conditional form: "If (something happened), I would (verb)." To practice this I divided the students into discussion groups of four or five students and gave them hypothetical scenarios designed to allow them to practice this form freely. One of the scenarios was this: "If you could be anyone in the world, who would you be?" By this time I was on my fourth two-hour class of the day, and quite tired. I walked among the aisles, absentmindedly listening to the students, but primarily just making my presence known so they wouldn't be tempted to lapse into Chinese.

As I was walking suddenly the phrase, ". . . and I would fight with America!" pierced my consciousness.

Involuntarily I stopped. "What did you say?" The entire group of students got wide-eyed, then laughed nervously.

Betty, an articulate student in the same group, tried to cover for the student. "Uh, he said that if he could be anyone in the world, he would be the president of China, and then he would become friends with America."

"That's not what he said."

The student finally spoke for himself. "I said that if I were president of China, I would fight with America," he admitted.

"Why?"

"Because of Taiwan," he said. "Our country had the chance to get Taiwan back and America interfered. Now our country is not complete."

I understood now. "All right," I said, trying to reassure him.

After eight hours of classes I caught the 6:00 p.m. bus home to the old campus. Darkness came early on these winter nights, and I stared out the window looking at the oncoming cars and the neon lights. The bus pulled into town and was turning left at a busy intersection when I saw a peasant herding a group of about thirty sheep across the road. He sent the sheep forward, in the dark, directly into the path of our turning bus. Traditional China was headed for a confrontation with modern China, and I wasn't sure who would yield, the sheep or the bus. As it turned out, the sheep stopped and let our bus pass.

The next day as I waited for the taxi to bring me to the new campus for my Chinese lesson, I finally had the chance to chat with Mr. Jia about his trip. He proudly showed me his tickets to the Forbidden City and told me about standing in line and then filing past the preserved body of Mao, lying perpetually in state.

"Did you ever see Mao when he was alive?" I asked.

One time, he told me, when he was a twenty-two-year-old soldier marching in a parade in Beijing.

"I didn't know you were a soldier," I said, quite surprised. Truthfully, one of the greatest benefits of all those hours spent laboring in the study of the Chinese language was finally getting to know these people who were so precious to our daily life, to get to ask them those questions that my inadequate language skills had never allowed me to before.

"Oh, yes, I was a soldier," he answered. "I even fought in Vietnam." He paused, then, with a mischievous twinkle in his eye, took aim at the sky with his finger and added, "I used to shoot down American airplanes!"

"Really!" I said. "My father also fought in Vietnam! He was in the air force."

"When was he there?" asked Mr. Jia.

"Let's see," I said, thinking out loud, "I was born in 1970, my parents got married in 1969, so it had to be 1968."

"In 1968," Mr. Jia said, looking at me, "that was when I was in Vietnam. 1968."

Then, unexpectedly, with his revelation and my own, with this knowledge that he and my father had fought on different sides of the same war, that Mr. Jia had tried to shoot down the planes my father was flying in, we suddenly felt the emotional weight of history between us. This man, this surrogate grandfather, who had sat on our couch drinking Chinese whiskey, who had taught our kids Chinese, who had brought us to the kindergarten to pick up our children, had been my father's sworn enemy in a war neither of them had forgotten.

We felt an awkwardness between us, stranger for it being the first time we had ever felt such. Words seemed necessary to fill the uncomfortable lull.

Mr. Jia spoke first. I picked up a few words about communism and democracy, recent acquisitions to my vocabulary, but my broken Chinese prevented me from getting much more than he was trying to explain why his country needed to fight the United States in Vietnam.

I tried to tell him that this was a different time, that Americans feared communism back then.

"Of course we are friends now," I feebly added.

My taxi pulled up, so I picked up my book bag and got ready to go. "So, you must love Mao Zedong," I said to Mr. Jia.

"Of course, *mei you Mao Zedong, mei you xin Zhongguo*," he said. "No Mao Zedong, no new China."

I turned and waved and left for my Chinese lesson. As the taxi coursed through the streets of Tai'an, I stared out the window and thought about Mr. Jia and Vietnam, about my students and Taiwan. I thought about the land of my fathers, and the land in which I now chose to live—and the sometimes vastness of the separation between them.

The taxi pulled into the new campus, and I strode purposefully to my office. Zhang was already waiting for me.

"Zhang," I said as I unlocked my office door, "what happened between the United States and Taiwan? My students mentioned an incident, and I don't know anything about it."

"Oh, yes," Zhang said. "Everybody knows about this. You don't know?"

"Come on Zhang, this must have been a long time ago. When did it happen?"

"Quite soon after Liberation," she said. "I don't really remember, but I know I learned this in school; we all did, of course. I rarely think about this anymore, because I know there is nothing I can do to change it. But the students are still young and the memory of learning this is fresh in their minds."

"How exactly did the United States interfere?" I asked.

"I really don't remember the details," she said.

I felt I had to explain my country's foreign policy thirty years before I was born, so I attempted: "You know, that was a different time. Back then Americans were afraid of communism, and the two biggest countries of the world had just become Communist, and smaller countries like Korea and Vietnam were on the verge. We saw ourselves as not interfering with China, but rather as supporting those who were fighting communism. It was the Cold War. But that was so long ago."

I later did some research. I found that in 1950 President Truman, fearing the Mainland would attack Taiwan, sent the U.S. Navy's Seventh Fleet to patrol the waters between Taiwan and China. War had just broken out on the Korean peninsula, and Truman feared the encroachment of communism not only from the Soviet Union, but from red China as well. What was for China the foremost event preventing the unification of their country was for the United States but a minor act in the overall Cold War drama.

In Chinese, the Cold War is written literally, just as it is in English: 冷战. The word for war is put together the same way as the word for cold: one radical signifying meaning, the other signifying pronunciation. In this case, the right part gives the character its meaning, for 戈 is a pictograph of a spear; 占 has an unrelated meaning, but lends its pronunciation, *zhan*, to the entire character.

"But Zhang," I said, "the world is different now and the *lengzhan*, the Cold War, is over. America and China have been friends for thirty years. Why do students still learn about this minor incident?"

"Because our country is still not whole, we still don't have Taiwan back," she said plainly.

❀

Then one day, only a few weeks after I'd sent my letter, we received mail with a Chinese return address. I knew it had to be from Grace's foster mother. I opened the envelope and stared at a letter addressed to me, written in handwriting I could not decipher.

Sally from the foreign affairs office was in her old campus office, so I brought her the letter. She quickly scanned the letter, then turned to me.

"She says she's so happy you've written to her," Sally translated.

"She couldn't sleep for several nights after Zhi Chun (Grace) left. She was worried about her, wondering how she was doing."

"Anything else?" I asked.

"She mentioned that there are two brothers and a sister in the house, and they miss Grace too."

Then Sally looked at me strangely. "Who wrote this letter?" she asked. "Are you sure this is her foster mother? Look, she wrote that Zhi Chun has been a joy 'since her birth.' And see how she signed the letter?" Sally pointed to four characters at the bottom of the letter: 知春妈妈, meaning "Zhi Chun's mama."

I felt unsettled. Since a fellow Chinese thought it worded strangely, I couldn't dismiss it as cross-cultural miscommunication.

When I had my next Chinese lesson with Zhang, I showed her the letter.

"I agree," said Zhang, "The way it's worded, it's hard to tell whether she is the birth mother or the foster mother." She thought for a moment. "I wish we could call her," she said.

"Well, we can," I said. "Look here. She gave her phone number."

She had not given the city code, so we searched on the Internet and were able to find it. I handed Zhang my phone and she dialed. We sat at the table listening to the phone ring.

"Wei?" Zhang said. "Hello?"

Zhang explained who she was and why she was calling. I could hear excited chatter on the other end. Zhang turned to me. "It's not her, it's her neighbor. This is her neighbor's phone. Her neighbor is running over to get her now."

Zhang got back on the phone. I could hear her talking slowly, distinctly—even more so than she did with me—saying, "Can you speak Mandarin? Do you understand me?"

Zhang put her hand over the mouthpiece and whispered to me: "Really this is difficult. It's like they are speaking a foreign language."

In Jiangxi province the local dialect was Gan, quite different from standard Mandarin Chinese. Additionally, since Jiangxi is a mountainous province, even neighboring villages might have trouble understanding one another, so great is their difference in dialect.

One question we were able to put to rest. Zhang asked her if she had given birth to Grace, and the answer was a clear "no." I was relieved to know that she was Grace's foster mother and not her birth mother. That would have opened up a lot of complications that I wasn't sure we were ready for. Zhang thought that the foster mother said Grace only came to live with her when she was a few months old, but wasn't quite sure.

I got on the phone. I wanted to hear her voice. She was excited and talking so quickly, and in my own excitement, I couldn't understand a word she was saying, nor could I even remember how to speak Chinese myself. Finally I gave up and said the only thing I could recall: *xie xie, xie xie.* Thank you. Thank you.

I repeated these words over and over, frustrated, for I knew they were inadequate. I needed to say thank you for taking care of our daughter. Thank you for loving her first. Thank you for showing her in those vulnerable early months that she was deserving of love, care, and protection. Thank you for loving her even though you knew you'd have to give her up, and that in so doing, you would get hurt.

But all I could say was thank you.

I hoped we could visit soon, and now we knew to bring an interpreter, one who could speak Gan. And I made a mental note that, to make a good impression, I had better bundle the children up tightly so they wouldn't appear cold.

Chapter 22

圣诞节
CHRISTMAS

❋

SOON CHRISTMAS WOULD BE HERE AGAIN, AND WE CONTEMPLATED SPEND-ing our second Christmas in China. Most holidays where our culture had provided a smorgasbord of activities had been emptied by coming to a new country. Christmas merited hardly an asterisk on the Chinese calendar, a workday, like any other. But while Chris and I could perhaps survive on memories, we could not raise our children in a tradition-less environment. We realized, with some nervousness, that we had a clean slate, an open stage, to build our own holiday traditions.

Last year we had been so overwhelmed that we didn't put that much thought into Christmas. We made room in our suitcases for the children's stockings and a small nativity scene. I read nightly from a collection of Christmas stories we had brought. We also sang Christmas carols, usually "Jingle Bells," on the way to school. But China just didn't feel festive at Christmas.

But one day we returned to our apartment to find on a small tree on our doorstep, replete with ornaments and lights, a thoughtful gesture from our foreign affairs office. And in the week leading into Advent, we received packages sent from our friends and family, filled with candy canes and other reminders of Christmas with which to decorate our home.

Many retail shops and supermarkets had three large characters displayed in the windows: 圣诞节. I was familiar with the last character, *jie*, and knew it meant "festival." From that, plus the jolly pictures of Santa on either end, I was able to deduce that the phrase meant "Christmas." The characters seemed so strange and foreign-looking, and the word for Christmas, *Shengdanjie*, stirred up no particular holiday mood.

"Merry Christmas" was such a festive greeting; *Fröliche Weinachten* evoked memories of drinking *gluhwein* at Christkindlmarkts in Germany. *Joyeux Noël* made me wish I could attend midnight mass at a French cathedral, and *Feliz Navidad* made me want to get up and sing. But *Shengdanjie Kuaile* (Happy Christmas)? It was difficult to remember, awkward to pronounce, and it had no familiar ring or cadence to it. We accepted the idea that in China, Christmas would be a subdued celebration.

We were expected to cover Christmas in depth with our students, a task we took to heart. We received a great amount of joy from listening to our students sing Christmas carols for the first time, as well as hearing them read the Christmas story from the Gospel of Luke.

A group of us foreign teachers practiced singing "Silent Night" in English and Chinese. Chris and two others sang it at a festival of music Christmas Eve night at the Three-Self church. The Christmas service was crowded. A few latecomers huddled precariously just inside the canvas quilts draped over the doorways, glad not to be outside braving the cold, but once inside barely able to even stand up straight for all those sitting in the aisle.

The church was all decked out for Christmas. Long strands of tinsel in various shades—silver, gold, red, green, hot pink—draped from the central chandelier. The overhead screen was flanked by two large Chinese lanterns. Colorful blinking lights lit up the nave.

This year, our second Christmas in China, I resolved to be more purposeful about our Christmas celebration. I spent an evening pulling some classic Christmas literature off the Internet to put together as a booklet, so that I could read from it nightly to the children. I also purchased *A Christmas Carol* from Amazon, and hoped to begin reading it as soon as it arrived, provided it didn't arrive too late and the Dickensian language wasn't above the level of the children. Chris and I also decided to start a new tradition from an idea in home schooling literature called a Jesse Tree. Here, one symbolic ornament, each representing an Old Testament prophecy of the Christ child, would be placed on a tree during the Advent season.

Were we in the United States, we never would have put so much thought into Christmas. We would have happily and joyfully attended our parties with extended family, brought our contributions to potlucks, gone shopping for hours, taken the children to see houses lit up with Christmas lights—all happy memories. But here in China we had no culture and no family to pull us along in the prevailing current, so we had to invent our own traditions.

❀

Our second year I noticed considerably more Christmas decorations around Tai'an than the previous year. The first year I didn't see Christmas trees for sale anywhere. Although our foreign affairs office had brought us one, I had no idea where they found it. But this year was different. On the shopping street of the new campus there were artificial trees available for purchase. Even our Jiayuan supermarket had a Christmas display. The moment I went up to the supermarket's second floor I was immediately confronted with an abundance of tinsel and oversize snowflakes dangling from the ceiling. Not only could I buy an artificial tree, but there were tinsel trees and plastic Santa faces on the windows, and glitzy ornaments and sparkly snowflakes hanging from the ceiling. The clerks were even wearing Santa caps.

But something was not working about the whole Christmas display at Jiayuan or, for that matter, with Christmas in Tai'an or even in China generally. At first I thought it was the gaudiness of the Christmas decorations, but that wasn't it. It wasn't the absence of snow either, for I had spent festive snowless Christmases down south in Georgia. Finally I realized. There was no Christmas music. While shopping upstairs at the supermarket Chinese pop music was playing. Although a stuffed Santa with a sled sat in front of the Zhong Bai department store, while purchasing gifts for our children we heard the lilting sounds of an *erhu* piped through the loudspeaker. China had imported Santa and even Christmas shopping, but Christmas music, so important for setting the Christmas mood, had not yet made it into the country. Chris and I resolved to make sure our children heard carols in our home, and to teach our students the songs we had grown up with.

In the weeks leading up to Advent our children all caught colds. After a week or so of us nursing the children back to health, Chris and I got it. Mine was the worst I'd had in years, giving me a sore throat, cough, congestion, and sinus aches. But the cold was centered in my eyes, which were continuously weepy and bloodshot. We muddled through, trying to squeeze in holiday events around our work schedule and making an effort to feel festive despite our infirmity.

On Christmas Eve, Katherine brought enough candy canes for her entire class. When I picked her up, she was very excited.

"Mom, all my classmates loved the candy canes!"

"That's wonderful," I told her.

"But that's not all," she said. "My teacher told them that since tomorrow was Christmas, they should all bring me a Christmas present."

I was sure Katherine had heard incorrectly. How indeed were forty students supposed to go home and return the next morning with a Christmas present?

"Are you sure?" I asked her. "Don't be disappointed if it doesn't happen. You probably misunderstood."

Christmas Day, like every Tuesday that semester, I was scheduled to teach for eight hours.

We had been singing Christmas carols throughout the month of December in class, the students learning two new Christmas carols each week. This was a difficult task, as I had to first sing each song once all the way through, then sing it line by line with the students repeating after me. Chris was the musician in the family, not me. I had never sung in public and was not comfortable with this. But each week it got easier.

It was Christmas Day, but with my sore throat and constant cough, I was in no condition to lead singing. Chris loaded my iPod with every Christmas song we had so I could at least play them some Christmas music. They had never heard any produced or performed version of these songs we had been learning; it had just been us singing a cappella. I didn't have a chance to preview any of the songs, so what we got was anyone's guess. First came a taste of the 1940s as we heard "Jingle Bells" sung in the style of the Andrews Sisters; they rocked to Mariah Carey singing "Santa Claus Is Coming to Town"; they listened respectfully as the Mormon Tabernacle Choir sang "Joy to the World."

Our last song was "Silent Night." Just one vocalist accompanied by a guitar sang the song as it was originally written, without any artistic ad-libbing or intricate vocalizations. Spontaneously, the students joined in singing this beautiful carol, one they had just learned three weeks previously. The whole room was filled with the voices of a chorus of angels singing these familiar words. From the podium I gazed into their faces, truly captivated by the Christmas spirit, singing earnestly out of the pure beauty and joy of the song and its meaning. My Christmas music had in fact arrived in China, in a way more meaningful than I could have hoped.

I later asked Mr. Jia about the characters for Christmas, 圣诞节. He told me they meant "holy . . . birth . . . festival"—Holy Birthday. So while my students may have never heard the Christmas story, their language still recognized its basic significance, all in just three characters. And those three characters expressed the essential meaning far more succinctly than the Latin-based expressions for Christmas I was more familiar with.

After lunch I returned for my afternoon classes. We were in the process of going over the answers to some reading comprehension questions when my cell phone, sitting on the podium, vibrated. It had been vibrating all day as I had been inundated by students sending me text messages with Christmas greetings. I gave it a cursory glance and saw on the display not an incoming text message, but rather something I had associated with home since childhood, my home phone number.

I picked up the phone. "Hello?"

"Merry Christmas!" said Mom and Dad.

I put the phone on speakerphone and on the count of three, all forty students in unison said, "Merry Christmas!" to my parents.

My parents were thrilled. The students were also delighted. This was better than anything a textbook could offer—it was The Real Thing. Mom admonished me to go see a doctor about my cold. The students chuckled; they had been telling me the same thing all day.

Finally, we said our good-byes. "We love you," said Mom and Dad.

"I love you too!" I replied. I hung up the phone. My students were gaping at me. Two girls in the back row brushed away tears and hugged each other. Parents and children rarely said those three words in China. They knew their parents loved them, but they knew from their actions, not because they had ever been told. The students had studied and heard about the importance of family at Christmas, but with that telephone call they saw it for themselves.

When I returned home after teaching, I was met by Katherine and Chris, each wearing opposite expressions on their faces.

"Mom, it really happened! It really happened! It was true, I told you!"

Before I could gather what she was talking about, Chris, his face full of consternation, asked me why it was that he had to carry home two huge garbage bags full of goodness knows what.

I surmised what had happened. Each and every one of Katherine's classmates had brought her, and her only, a Christmas gift. Some were new, some were old, some quite special, others a little worn, but each child managed to play a part in giving Katherine a Christmas I was sure she would never forget. Actually, none of us would ever forget this 圣诞节.

Chapter 23

独一无二
UNIQUE

❀

ZHANG WAS GETTING HER DRIVER'S LICENSE. ALL YEAR SHE HAD BEEN taking lessons and now she had passed three of the four required tests. Some of my students were doing the same, reporting it proudly during such Oral English conversational topics as "What did you do over your summer vacation?"

Getting a car or a driver's license was completely unnecessary for most Chinese since buses, trains, or taxis could take you anywhere you wanted to go quite cheaply. It was also inconvenient: parking lots were non-existent, parking spots rare, and horrendous drivers plentiful. Nonetheless, the driver's license, followed by the car, was still highly coveted.

Cars had dominated the other countries I had lived in. In Germany, the home of BMW, Porsche, and Mercedes-Benz, fast cars ruled the roads. In the early years I remember speedsters in the passing lane flashing lights on their roofs to signal to other cars: they were coming and get out of the way. But after reunification the autobahns became overcrowded and the *Stau*, the traffic jam, put the brakes on Germany's roadrunners.

Japan was also famous for its carmakers. While living in Japan we drove a Toyota Town Ace Van, shaped like a shoe box turned on its side—long and thin—necessary in a country of narrow lanes called streets that somehow two-way traffic was supposed to negotiate. Our van had two rows of seats in the back that could swivel around completely or even be folded up out of sight. And we bought it cheaply, because the Japanese preferred new cars; the only used-car market was thrifty American servicemen. Our van was equipped with extra mirrors on the hood and rear that allowed us to get within an inch of the car in front or behind, a required skill. Every once in a while we saw Cadillacs or SUVs on the roads; they looked completely out of place and awkward in Japan's warren of narrow streets.

China had not yet reached full automobile saturation. Mr. Jia drove a three-wheeled motor scooter with an open bench in the back. Three-wheeled trucks with cabs and beds were also a common sight, along with homemade contraptions, their motors and belts completely exposed. Once as I returned from dropping the kids off at school three donkey carts went by in the opposite direction, a stark contrast in a country that added twenty thousand new cars to the roads each day. For in China the dream was to have a car. And like the other countries I had lived in, China's automobile preference reflected its personality. No bright colors, no rear spoilers, no shiny hubcaps, China's choice was a black four-door sedan, impeccably cared for, blending in with all the other black four-door sedans already on the roads.

When I first started teaching I asked the students to introduce themselves in English to me and to their classmates. I gave them a short list of topics: age, hometown, hobbies, and something unique about themselves. The students all did fine, with the exception of the last question. They tried to find some way around it, and had a difficult time pointing out their uniqueness to others. A few of the male students in the class said, "I am just a common man. There is nothing unique about me."

I dropped that question from then on, deciding that while Americans were quite proud of what made them distinct as individuals, Chinese modesty did not allow them to comfortably express such thoughts.

I brought it up in office hours, saying that I thought we Americans would never so quickly discount our uniqueness; perhaps we even believed it defined us. In discussing this, Kevin told me he thought a country needed to reach a certain level of development before the people could worry about such things. When a farmer was spending all his hours tilling the soil and bringing food to the table, there was neither time nor motivation to think about independent ideas.

Much later, as I looked up a word in my Chinese-English dictionary in the U section, I stumbled across the Chinese word for "unique." It was quite a clever formulation using four concrete characters to express this abstract concept: *duyiwu'er*, written 独一无二, literally meaning "only one, not two." I decided to ask my tutor about this word, as I was sure it must have a story.

Zhang told me that most of the time in Chinese this word was used to describe objects. For example, Mount Tai was *duyiwu'er*, the Great Wall of China was *duyiwu'er*. She said that it was rarely used to describe a person. Mao Zedong was certainly *duyiwu'er*, but it would be inappropriate to use this term to describe one's colleagues or friends.

She continued. Most Chinese people could be described by a different combination of characters, though one no less interesting linguistically: *congzhong*. A quick look at the two characters making up this word, 从众, show that they are both made up of the component *ren*, 人, meaning "person." The first character, *cong*, shows two people, one behind the other, with the meaning "to follow." The second character, *zhong*, shows *ren* three times for the meaning of "many people" or "crowd." Put these two characters together and you have "follow the crowd" or in everyday speech, "be just like everybody else."

I asked Zhang if this was considered a positive trait, but on this point she demurred. "It's not positive, it's not negative, it is simply descriptive of Chinese people," she said. She then taught me a Chinese proverb:

枪打出头鸟

qiang da chu tou niao

We went through each of the five characters in turn: "gun . . . shoots . . . out . . . head . . . bird." I was confused about the meaning.

"Now imagine a flock of birds on the ground," said Zhang. "But one bird's head is just slightly taller than the rest . . ."

I nodded in understanding. "Ah . . . that's the bird that will get shot."

"Yes!" she said, pleased that I understood. "This traditional proverb expresses what Chinese people feel is the danger of standing out from the crowd."

"But today among young people the idea is a little different," she continued. "Of course we all know this proverb and are familiar with this idea, but at the same time, we know we must stand out if we are to be successful."

❀

Chris and I were playing Scrabble that night after the kids were in bed. I told him about my class with Zhang that day and what I had learned about the Chinese and their phobia about being unique.

"Unique. That would make a great word to play this Q I'm stuck with. But I would need two Us, and I have none," Chris said.

"We Americans derive so much of our identity from being unique. But the Chinese don't. It's completely different with them. Their identity comes from their belonging to a group—family, hometown, university, and so on," I said.

F-A-Q-I-R, Chris spelled.

"And what is that?" I asked.

"A faqir is a Hindu ascetic," he said.

"You did not know that."

"Look it up," he challenged. "My brain is filled with all sorts of useless trivia." I ignored him and starting looking at my letters.

"It is interesting," Chris said. "Our students certainly all look Chinese. But they still try to look and dress alike. There doesn't seem to be an effort to look different from anybody else."

I spelled E-A-S-I-E-R with my letters and pushed Enter.

"Is that the best you got?"

"The computer gave me all vowels and one-point consonants!"

"Sure, likely excuse."

"I wonder how China's large population affects the psyche of the individual?" I wondered out loud. "I mean, there are so many of them, their education is identical, they are easily replaceable. And official Darwinism teaches them that they are not a unique creation."

"Just one more zygote out of a massive Chinese gene pool," Chris said.

"But how does it feel to honestly believe that you are just like everyone else? That you are not unique?"

"It's not that they don't think they are unique," Chris said. "They just don't proclaim their uniqueness. It's not the same."

"That's true," I admitted.

"But enough conjecture. It's your turn."

❀

I wrote a story about this word "unique" and sent it out to many of our family and friends. A fellow ERRC teacher e-mailed me that she had a similar experience when she taught mid-level Chinese government officials. After she returned to the United States, one of her students sent her the following e-mail about uniqueness.

Mrs. C,

Thanks for your good advice to us about not being afraid to show our uniqueness. I am very interested about the topic concerning whether one should express his uniqueness in public or not. First of all, I want to tell you something about our traditional culture. When we were young, we were told that "A good child is one who is obedient," or "Modesty is the best virtue of people." I think the culture developed in this way because China experienced a long history of feudalism. The emperor controlled everything including people's thoughts. Those who didn't obey the emperor's order were killed. If you wanted to be successful, you had to infer what the rulers liked to hear. In order to protect themselves and their families, most people preferred to hide their uniqueness. That is why your Chinese students like to say: "just like everybody else."

However, now China is facing up to a changing world. We need great innovation. We need unique characters and special thoughts because the road we should walk is so unique and different from other countries. Therefore I agree that it is time for Chinese to change their habits. If you have many Chinese friends, you will find they all have splendid thoughts and like to discuss things in private. But if you want them to say the same thing in public, they will always say, "I have nothing to say, I agree with the others." So I think what also needs to change is government itself, especially the government's policy about speech. The government should let people believe they have the real freedom to speak in the public and won't be punished afterwards. What's more, the government should take some measures to encourage people to do so since Chinese people have been afraid to be punished for their speech for over five thousand years.

Only by this will our nation be full of creativity and hope. That's my opinion about "uniqueness." Maybe we can discuss other topic through e-mail. Hope to hear from you soon.

Wish you happy every day.

❁

I remembered going to Katherine's class one day last fall during art class. On the table in front of her was an almost completed drawing with a house in the center, and two trees on either side. In the air were a few birds and clouds.

"What a great drawing!" I told her.

"No, it's not that good," she replied.

"Yes, of course it is. What do you mean it's not good?"

She pointed to the blackboard. "See. I just copied it. It's not like I drew my *own* picture."

I looked at the blackboard. Sure enough, there I saw a house framed by two trees, with birds and clouds in the sky. Looking around, I saw virtually identical pictures in front of each child.

A few days later I showed up at her classroom again. I could see through the windows that the children were outside, so I walked through the classroom and observed them through the window.

Here, recess was not the same as in the United States. Children were not allowed to run around and climb and play however they chose. The teacher went out with the children and led them in an organized activity. The school day started with morning exercises. The entire school lined up in formation by class, two-year-olds on up. Marching to the beat of music amplified through the loudspeakers, the children followed their teacher's motions to the routine. By the time they were older, that is, four or five years old, they knew the routines by heart. Even afternoon playtimes were organized, with the teacher as the leader. This frustrated Katherine to no end. She just wanted to play. She saw the playground equipment and wanted to climb and run and jump. But that was not allowed.

As I gazed out the window I saw all the children lined up in two rows as the teacher instructed. All the children except Katherine. Katherine was in the back performing an individual ballet dance, sweeping her arms up to the right, then up to the left, pointing her toes and twirling about with a flourish. Not even five years old yet, already she had been shaped by her Western upbringing, sensing somehow that she was unique, that she was allowed to be an individual. Not only that, but that this was her right and one she was not willing to give up, no matter how many Chinese children lined up without a murmur of protest.

Chapter 24

灶王
THE KITCHEN GOD

❖

IRECEIVED A TEXT MESSAGE FROM GRACE'S "OLDER BROTHER" THE DAY Zhang and I called her neighbor's phone. I didn't see the message for a few hours. I responded, but then heard nothing for a week.

Some days later I received another message in which he explained that his cell phone had been broken for a while. I was curious about this family's role in Grace's life and I had some specific questions I wanted to ask. But it was not Chinese custom to get right down to business. Relationships have to be built first. So we first texted back and forth about pleasantries.

"How are you enjoying that cold weather in Shandong?" he asked me.

"It's not bad," I said. "How is the weather down south?"

"Much better than where you are," he said.

"How old are you?" I asked.

"Twenty-two," he replied.

"Can you speak English?" I asked, hopefully.

"No," he replied. He had little education. "How is Zhi Chun (Grace) doing?"

"She's doing well. She's healthy and happy. She goes to Chinese kindergarten and is learning to speak Chinese."

"My mother and father miss her very much. They want you to come for Spring Festival."

"Thank you very much for the invitation," I said. "Unfortunately we can't come this year. Perhaps next year."

Finally, I asked some more specific questions: when Grace began to live with them and for how long. But I got no answer.

It felt so strange that I could communicate with this family now by text message. I wondered if we did visit how we would do in this situation: two families with so little in common. Would we commit cultural blunders? Would they think we were elitist and rich? Would we find common ground? In fact, we did have common ground: a child whom we both loved. But would that be enough?

My Chinese tutor could not communicate with the foster mother in spoken Chinese, but the older brother and I, a peasant and a foreigner, could communicate through *written* Chinese. My written Chinese was not that stellar, but neither was his. Neither of us could communicate in a sophisticated fashion, but in our simple use of the characters we understood each other reasonably well.

❁

That week in Extensive Reading the unit title was "Festivals and Holidays." The passages dealt briefly with the origins of Christmas, Easter, Valentine's Day, and Halloween. Finally, one passage contrasted the celebrations of Chinese New Year in China and in the United States. According to the textbook:

> After the house is cleaned, it is time to bid farewell to the Kitchen God (灶王, pronounced *Zaowang*). In Chinese folklore, the Kitchen God is regarded as the guardian of the family hearth. He is considered the inventor of fire as well as the censor of household morals. As the folktale goes, the Kitchen God leaves the house on the 23rd of the last [lunar] month to report to heaven on the behavior of the family. At this time, the family would do everything possible to obtain a favorable report from the Kitchen God. On the evening of the 23rd, the family would give the Kitchen God a ritualistic farewell dinner with sweet foods and honey. Some say this is a bribe; others say it seals his mouth from saying bad things.

When I first read this passage I thought it described something rather kitschy or folksy, an antiquated custom, certainly not something still practiced in today's China where modernization and economic development were the only known gods. So I asked the students if this passage about the Kitchen God was true; surprisingly, they all nodded their heads and didn't seem to think it anything other than a straightforward description. After class I met my former student Amy for lunch. I asked her about the Kitchen God.

"When I was growing up, my mother always hung up a picture of the Kitchen God on the day he arrived," Amy said. "Then she prepared a table full of sweet treats. My younger sisters, younger brother, and I begged to be allowed to eat these, but Mother refused. She would stand firm that they were first for the Kitchen God."

She smiled at the memory.

"Our mother told us that if we ate these, our mouths would become swollen. We were too frightened to eat them after she said that. But the next day, after the Kitchen God left, we were finally allowed to eat them.

The Kitchen God is written in Chinese 灶王. The first character, containing fire, 火, and earth, 土, together in one character, means "an old-fashioned earthen hearth with an open fire." The word used here for "god" is usually translated as "king." It shows three levels 三 representing heaven, humanity, and the earth. The vertical line is the person who connects all three levels: the king. In this case 王 is an apt depiction because it is the Kitchen God's job—according to tradition—to leave the mortal realm to report to heaven on the affairs of the family. The Kitchen God is the link between heaven and earth.

灶

HEARTH

王

KING

THE KITCHEN GOD

"On one certain day right before Chinese New Year, my mother forbade all talking whatsoever," Amy said. "She was worried that we children might say something to anger the Kitchen God, so she determined it best that no one say anything at all."

"Amy, it sounds like your mother really believes in the Kitchen God," I said.

"Oh, yes, she truly believes that he is real."

"How old is your mother? She sounds very traditional."

"Forty-seven years old," she told me.

Amy told me more stories about her childhood. She told me about the matchmakers who were constantly introducing young men to her mother as marriage prospects, and how she turned them all down until she agreed to marry Amy's father, a man five years younger. She told me about the family struggles: her paternal grandmother had emphysema and died three days after Amy's paternal grandfather was released from jail. Her father's grandmother, Amy's great-grandmother, was the family matriarch, raising her father and his brother although she was widowed. It was this woman who pressured Amy's parents to keep having babies until they had a son, and they obliged.

Amy was the eldest, followed in successive years by two younger sisters, and finally the long-sought-after boy. But though they had appeased the great-grandmother, they were now in grave violation of the one-child policy.

"During this period we were always running away."

"What do you mean, running away?" I asked.

"The police would come around looking for families with more than one child. So we would have to run away to our uncle's home or another relative's home. Sometimes the police would be walking in our neighborhood and our parents would cover the babies' mouths to stop them from crying, but, of course, doing so only made them cry even more."

Amy talked of being poor and not having enough to eat, of living in shabby homes and always being afraid. I was entranced by her stories.

"Amy, you should write a book," I said. "You have lived a traditional childhood, an interesting childhood, but this way of life is fast disappearing in China. In fact, your own child won't be raised in this way, and probably won't be able to understand it. Even if it doesn't ever get published, you should have this history for your own child to understand."

"Well, I know you say it sounds interesting, but really, it was a difficult time for my family," she said.

The next day in office hours I brought up the Kitchen God. I had nine students that day, a range of countryside students and city kids, and with that, a range of views about the Kitchen God. The country students could describe the elaborate preparations their grandparents or parents made for his arrival and departure, although they said they didn't believe in the Kitchen God themselves. I asked if their parents or grandparents still believed in him. They weren't sure. Perhaps it was half belief and half tradition, they said.

The city students knew of the Kitchen God but were unfamiliar with the associated customs; they listened to the country students in rapt attention just like me, somewhat shocked that such practices still occurred. These traditions had faded away in city life, one student told me.

I thought about this. The village was the bearer of Chinese traditions. Some of these traditions were viewed as backward and superstitious, and therefore not in line with the developed nation China wanted to become. The further they strayed from the village, whether that be measured in terms of time (how many generations since the family were peasants) or distance (what level of municipality in the hierarchy—small town, town, city, big city), the more distant the traditions of old China became. Where they stood on the Chinese rural-to-urban scale and how long their family had been away from the village were fairly accurate barometers of their general worldview.

I reflected back to Amy, the first in her family to leave the village, now an English major at our university. I remembered my first day of class with her last year, when I passed out 3 x 5-inch cards and asked the students to give me their name, student number, and a few sentences on why they chose English as their major. I had forgotten most of these responses, except for Amy's: "I love English. It has opened up a whole new world for me."

Amy, raised in the village, never having left Shandong province, brought up to respect the Kitchen God, was now studying English, a language that exposed her to new and foreign ideas, gave her access to technology, allowed her to read nineteenth-century British literature and to watch Hollywood movies. English caused her to look outward and forward, a great departure from her traditional village childhood.

She simultaneously existed in two distinct worlds: the traditional Chinese world and the modern Western world. What's more, she seemingly did this without any internal conflict, completely at peace with who she was and where she came from.

❁

After not hearing anything for several days, I texted the foster brother asking if I could ask him a few questions. Monday, I received a reply—yes, I could. So I asked when Grace began to live with them and for how long. I received a reply quite soon. But though I understood each character and could tell it was referring to a date and time, I could not comprehend the meaning.

He used the character for "month," 月, but instead of prefacing it with a number, 1 月 for January, 2 月 for February, and so on, he wrote 正月. What was that? I stared at my cell phone. I was so close to getting some good hard information about our daughter's early life, which was such a mystery to us, yet I was stymied.

I forwarded the message to Sally at our foreign affairs office. She called me and explained that he had used the lunar calendar, not the solar calendar, which explained my confusion. China uses both the Gregorian calendar and the lunar calendar. Most festivals, such as Spring Festival and Mid-Autumn Festival, are determined by the lunar calendar. Engaged couples use the lunar calendar to set an auspicious wedding date. Peasants rely on the lunar calendar to plant and harvest according to the phases of the moon. In fact, the lunar calendar in Chinese is called *nongli*, which literally means "agricultural calendar." 正月, Sally told me, was the first month of the lunar calendar. To add to the confusion, Grace's foster brother was off by a year, writing that she came to live with them in 2004, which made no sense since she was born in February of 2003 and adopted by us in February of 2004.

Once we switched the year and converted to the lunar calendar we came up with a date: February 16, 2003. Now this made sense, for it was the same date Grace's paperwork listed as her abandonment date. But the confusion wasn't over, because he said she was "born" on that day, and also added "at 6 o'clock in the morning." How could they know this if they were but her foster family? I thought we had settled this question with

Zhang's phone call, but the wording used in his message reopened the question.

"This just underscores for me the huge potential we have for miscommunication with this family," Chris said. Getting into contact with them was much more my idea than his.

"To begin with, we have a completely different language and culture," he continued. "But not only that, our educational level, income, and general exposure to the world are completely different."

"Well, we have experience living in China," I said. "That should mitigate some of these factors."

"But our experience is quite limited. We are only familiar with academic life on a university campus in northern China. That is a world away from a mountain village in Jiangxi."

I knew he had a point. But I still felt we owed it to Grace to try.

I received another text message from the older brother during a break on Tuesday between final exams. He told me they did not know who gave birth to Grace, that they were the foster family. To have this question settled again was a great relief.

I asked him if he could speak *putonghua*, Mandarin Chinese, and suggested that I call him. He said he could. So I did. I was excited to talk to him. But my Mandarin was not good enough for me to express my questions clearly. A few of my students were still in the classroom. One of them volunteered to translate.

"They want you to come for Spring Festival," the student said to me.

"We would really like to," I said. "This year we can't, but perhaps next year." She translated and told him over the phone.

"Ask him about their life together with Zhi Chun (Grace)," I asked the student.

She listened on the phone for a few minutes.

"They want you to know they treated Zhi Chun as their own daughter, taking her with them wherever they went. They miss her very much."

My student went back to the phone, listened for a while longer, then turned to me. "He said that Zhi Chun would always *fu zhe qiang* to try to go outside to play with the other children."

"*Fu zhe qiang?*" I asked. "What does that mean?"

My student was at a loss as to how to explain it to me. She looked around the room. Then, moving to one side of the classroom, she began walking along the wall, with her hands moving along the wall as she walked.

"Ah, I understand," I said. *"Fu zhe qiang."* She was cruising, as we said in American baby parlance. I later looked up the words in the dictionary. *Fu* means "to support with the hand," *zhe* adds an "-ing" to the word, and *qiang* means "wall."

But my "ah" wasn't just because I understood the word; rather, I finally felt a connection with these people I had such trouble communicating with. I knew then that their Zhi Chun was truly our Grace. When we adopted Grace this was exactly where she was in her gross motor skill development: using the bed, the wall, the chair, anything, to cruise to where she wanted to go, not yet confident enough to walk on her own. And where she wanted to go was usually where other people were, for our daughter was without a doubt a social creature.

At that moment I wanted to call this family back, to tell them I knew and I understood.

I wanted to tell them that three weeks later she started to walk on her own. That now she was the most coordinated and agile child we had ever seen, able to run and jump and dance with abandon.

I wanted to tell them that she would eat just about anything in sight, and even if she didn't care for it, she still would have two or three helpings just to make sure. I knew they would nod and laugh and tell me a similar story.

I knew they would love the tale of when we stayed in the hotel in Nanchang, the capital of Jiangxi, waiting for the adoption to be finalized. Grace wasn't used to high chairs and felt trapped and confined. So Chris would put Grace in the high chair and quickly give her some food to distract her long enough for me to hasten to the breakfast buffet and bring Grace a larger plate of food. If she liked what she saw on the plate better than what she had in her mouth, she would reach into her mouth, pull whatever it was out, and throw it to the ground so she could immediately start eating the new food before it passed her by.

Yes, they would laugh.

Finally, I wanted to tell them that she was sad and melancholy for those first few months after we adopted her. She was so unhappy. We thought that was simply her temperament, though we knew now that her true nature was to radiate happiness. I wanted to tell them that she had cried for them and though we knew little about what had happened to her that first year before she became ours, we knew she had been loved and had loved in return.

I wanted to call them back and tell them these things. But I knew I had no hope of communicating this by phone across a language barrier that seemed at that moment impassable.

So I just sat there in an empty classroom with my thoughts, processing all that had happened, all that I had just learned, thinking back to earlier times, picturing Grace living with them in this village, *fu zhe qiang*, as she searched out her companions.

Then a thought came to me.

When we were in the adoption process I remember excitedly chatting with my mother about all that we were going to teach our future daughter about Chinese culture.

She frowned. "Won't this only confuse her and make her feel different from everybody else? Isn't it better to raise her only as an American?"

In fact others have expressed similar opinions, even the Chinese writer Nien Cheng, author of *Life and Death in Shanghai*.

I considered my mother's ideas, but quickly dismissed them. I had given a great deal of thought to our child's identity—as an individual, as an adopted child, as a Chinese-American. I thought the lure of needing to know about where she came from should be acknowledged and nourished. Also, this child, as yet unknown to us, was meant to be adopted into a family that admired Chinese culture and desired to learn more about it. We would not be genuine if we intentionally chose not to teach our daughter about her own culture. So this question about Grace's identity had been with me for years, even before her adoption.

I then realized that this foster family was the answer. If my daughter, who was destined to grow up to be a freedom-loving, fashion-conscious, well-educated, technology-savvy, English-speaking, Western-thinking American woman, was able, at the same time, to understand the values and the worldview of these peasants from Jiangxi, to know the rituals of the Kitchen God and to have the deft fingers required to make dumplings; not only that, if she could feel comfortable with, connected to, and at home with these people who had truly loved her, then not only would she understand the land from whence she came and her first year of life, but she would understand the traditional China, for the countryside was the caretaker of this culture. She would know who she was and where she came from. She would be firmly rooted, both legs of her bicultural self—Western and Eastern—planted firmly on the ground.

It seemed a formidable undertaking to ask of a child, to grasp two cultures and pull her identity from both; but then, my student Amy was pulling off a similar task with aplomb.

Last year, we were on the sidelines for Spring Festival, foreigners, because it was truly for the Chinese. We stayed holed up in our small apartment, waiting for the buses to begin running again, for the supermarket to reopen. But if we could be invited, expected, eagerly anticipated guests at a Chinese home for Spring Festival, how different that would be.

Chapter 25

丝

SILK

❀

AT OFFICE HOURS ON WEDNESDAY I MENTIONED THAT I WOULD BE GOING to Shanghai as the first stop on our winter vacation.

"Shanghai," snorted Qingdao Cathy. "I hate Shanghai."

"Oh, you've been there?" I asked.

"No, I've never been there," she admitted. "But when I took the train home for Chinese New Year a lady from Shanghai put her stuff on the overhead shelf above my seat. I put my stuff on top of hers—after all, it was my seat and she shouldn't have put her stuff there in the first place. Then her Barbie toy got broken and she started yelling at me that her city was more developed than my city. I told her how dare she come to my city and yell at me!"

❀

Before we left for vacation, I brought our graded exams to the home of Mr. Jia, who had agreed to deliver them to the English Department on the new campus. I had never been to his home before. He invited me into the master bedroom and cleared some things so I could sit on the bed and watch TV with him and his wife. Even before Mr. Jia took me on a short tour, I was struck by how small their apartment was. Recently I had been requesting that our foreign affairs office give us a bigger place. I asked if perhaps they could join two apartments or give us another small apartment for storage space.

But the visit to Mr. Jia chastened me. Who was I to complain about my apartment when Mr. Jia, the manager of our building, lived in one even smaller and far older than mine? And his had bare cement floors.

❀

We left for Shanghai on the D-train, China's fastest train.

Our family had a pattern for boarding trains. First, Chris would help me board with the children and get our bags situated. Then, with a camera in hand and a smile on his face, he would walk up and down the platform taking pictures of the cars, engine, and conductors. He was like a little boy, transported back to happy childhood days spent with his model trains. As they blew the final whistle, he'd leap aboard and rejoin us.

I also liked train travel. I liked staying close to the earth, crossing over rivers and through cities, so much better than leapfrogging in by plane. On the train to Shanghai we passed through the countryside of Shandong and Jiangsu provinces, sometimes right through the middle of a village, it seemed. Out our windows we peered directly into courtyards hemming in chickens, pigs, and livestock. The courtyards were attached to dwellings with three generations under one roof: the Chinese definition of happiness. Life had not changed here for decades, perhaps centuries.

We met our guide, Eric, the next morning. Eric was a Shanghai transplant. He was from a village in neighboring Jiangsu province but had come to Shanghai as a college student studying tourism. He now could speak the local Shanghai dialect, he proudly told us.

Our guidebook, *The Rough Guide to China*, said that Shanghai's history and geography had given this city an outward perspective; foreign customs and ways had been accepted and fashionable here long before they were anywhere else. Our guide confirmed this.

"People in Shanghai will be very friendly to you. They like foreigners," he told us. "Actually, Shanghai people don't really like other Chinese people. They feel since Shanghai is China's most developed city, they have more in common with foreigners."

"What about you?" I asked. "Do Shanghai people like you?"

Eric laughed. "Well, they didn't like me at first, since I was a country boy from Jiangsu. But I have been here five years now and can speak the local dialect, so now they like me."

After strolling along the Bund, the riverfront of the old International Settlement and now Shanghai's banking sector, we went to "Chinatown." Eric told us that Shanghai was so modern and Westernized, it needed its own Chinatown. What he referred to as Chinatown was, according to *The*

Rough Guide, actually Shanghai's old city, contained by the old city walls dating from the eleventh century and never incorporated into any foreign concession. It became somewhat of a Chinese ghetto during the late nineteenth and early twentieth centuries when it was hemmed in by the British, Japanese, French, and American concessions. We strolled through the same pedestrian area and Yu Yuan garden that I had seen seven years previously.

On that first visit to Shanghai, the last stop on our eight-day tour, I had felt as if I were no longer in China. Amid the modern hotels and tangled freeways, I saw nothing around me that seemed remotely Chinese. I hoped during this visit to find something to draw me to this city, since it had played such an important role in Chinese history.

As we drove over the freeways and contended with the traffic, I asked Eric if there were any older neighborhoods or historic buildings that we could visit.

"But I just took you to Chinatown," he replied with a quizzical look.

"But isn't there anything else, perhaps not so touristy, but reflecting Shanghai's history?"

He seemed to search his mind, but then shook his head.

"No," he said. "In Shanghai everything is new."

I continued to press him. "But what about the old foreign concessions?" Shanghai had a long history as a treaty port with foreign enclaves carved out by Western powers and Japan.

"Sure," he said, "I'll take you to the French Concession."

But he didn't bring us to the French Concession. Instead, he brought us to Xin Tian Di (New Heaven and Earth), designed by an American architect and built in 2002, a trendy area near the old concession. Xin Tian Di boasted sidewalk cafés, upscale retail, and Western restaurants built in a European courtyard style. It was nice, but it was new; I was looking for Old Shanghai.

In trying to pack lightly I had left my other guidebooks at home, but when I returned and read about Shanghai, I was greatly disappointed to learn that we could have visited the former homes of Zhou En-lai, Sun Yat-sen, and Soong Qingling, but those would have to be saved for our next visit. And I learned that while much of the former French Concession was being razed to make way for skyscrapers and modern buildings, a small corner remained.

Despite the history we were looking for but didn't find, today's Shanghai might as well be New York or Chicago. I was glad I lived in Tai'an, for to live in Shanghai would be to live the lifestyle of a Western ex-pat. I preferred my Chinese life. While the amenities of the big developed city were nice, something was lost.

One evening Katherine and I went to the hotel beauty salon for haircuts. I always came home depressed after a haircut in Tai'an and thought I might have better luck in fashionable Shanghai. But Katherine and I walked out just as disappointed with our new coifs, despite having paid 192 yuan compared to Tai'an, where I paid 30 yuan for me and the children were usually 10 yuan for all three.

Afterward, we took the kids to McDonald's for dinner. At least at McDonald's the prices were the same as in Tai'an, but this McDonald's had security guards posted at the doors. It also had a homeless man who grabbed up Andrew's uneaten fries, extra ketchup packets, and sweet and sour sauce the moment we left the table.

In a country fixated on development, Shanghai is the pearl. From its skyscrapers to the TV tower in the newly developed Pudong area opposite the Bund, everything is modern and developed. It is the showpiece. Everything here was clean; even the air didn't have the dust I had grown accustomed to.

But I resented Shanghai. I didn't feel comfortable with its name brands, its clean, antiseptic feel. I didn't feel comfortable around its fashionable women, knowing my kids were wearing clothes bought from a street market, now torn and stained by the Shandong winter. I just didn't feel comfortable here. Coming straight from America, I would have. But coming from Shandong province I felt like a country bumpkin—wide-eyed, naive, not fitting in.

❀

Our next stop was Hangzhou, a two-hour train ride southwest from Shanghai, and the hometown of my Chinese friend Shentu, my classmate from Waseda University in Tokyo. After completing her Ph.D. in chemistry in Japan, she had returned home to her job as a professor at Zhejiang University. She made reservations for us at the Lily Hotel, close to the famous West Lake. After arriving at the hotel the children and I rested while Chris went exploring. By the time he returned around three thirty with pizza from Pizza Hut, we were famished. We considered ourselves lucky to have found a small pizza restaurant in Tai'an, but Pizza Hut it was not. This pizza was so delicious, and so familiar, that we stuffed ourselves.

Shentu came by around 5:00 p.m. after giving an exam at the university. Apart from a few gray hairs and her professional, fashionable attire, she looked exactly the same as during our student days in Japan. She took the girls and me on a walk to West Lake. My first impression was that it hardly seemed like China—not in an overly urban and developed way like Shanghai, but there was a different ambience, an atmosphere pleasing to the eye, something I didn't usually associate with China. China was certainly interesting; it was always striking; but it was not usually beautiful. But this place, Hangzhou on the shores of West Lake, was beautiful.

The lake and the surrounding areas were filled with tall trees and abundant vegetation. Green foliage was everywhere. That alone made me feel transported to a different place, for my China was brown, not green. As we walked along manicured sidewalks and wrought-iron fences we saw teahouses lit up with lights, not gaudy colored lights left over from Christmas, but long strings of white lights that, in the cool mist around the lake, provided a romantic atmosphere. The children enjoyed exploring the interweaving paths along the lake.

For dinner Shentu had booked a private room at the hotel restaurant. The waitress stood at her side for at least twenty minutes while Shentu happily discussed the menu with her. Unfortunately, we had just had our gullets stuffed with pepperoni pizza. We did our best, but to Shentu's consternation we only picked at the food, barely making a dent in the feast she had ordered. Our conversation consisted of exchanges like this:

"Shentu, the deep-fried pumpkin is very good."

"Good. Eat another one. Do you like the beef soup?"

"Yes, it's delicious."

"Good. Eat more."

She urged us to eat, continually suggesting this or that dish and if we showed the slightest interest, putting a large serving onto our plate. The situation was not helped by our picky eaters, Katherine and Andrew, who ate nothing at all. Even ever-hungry Grace just nibbled at her food.

The last plate to arrive was the customary fruit platter. The orange slices were juicy and delicious, and finally the children ate to Shentu's expectations. She was thrilled.

"Oh, shall we get another fruit platter?" she asked.

"No, no, that is not necessary," I said.

"Yes, yes, can we?" exclaimed our girls.

Shentu was off and soon the waitress returned with another platter filled with orange slices. I was deeply embarrassed, but Shentu looked on in satisfaction as they ate.

The next morning she picked us up at the hotel, bearing a bag of oranges in her hand for us to have in the room. Then she took us in her car to drive the periphery of West Lake.

"Wow, Shentu, you have a car!" I said.

"Everyone does here," she replied.

As we took in West Lake by day it seemed like we were in a Swiss lake town. West Lake was surrounded on three sides by mountains, one side by city. The whole area was landscaped, maintained, and immaculate. Even the apartment buildings were beautiful, no drab functional apartment blocks here. We took a boat ride to two islands in the center of the lake, the second of which enclosed four inner lakes. The children loved tramping through bamboo gardens, over zigzag bridges, and along covered sidewalks.

After returning, Shentu took us to lunch at a local restaurant featuring the city's specialty: Hangzhou *dianxin* (hors d'oeuvres). Leaving us at the table, she left to order and returned proudly with a stack of steamed bamboo trays containing a variety of dumplings as well as some soup. Chris enjoyed the meal, and I did my best, although a lot of it was seafood, to which I have an aversion. But the kids hardly touched it, which Shentu's eagle eye did not miss.

"Why don't I run across the street to McDonald's? I'll get them a hamburger. I'll be back in ten minutes."

She reached for her bag. Only after much coaxing did she stay. But after our necessary round of bathroom breaks before heading off, she saw her chance again.

"I'll be right back. Ten minutes."

I could see she was resolute. "No! You mustn't!" I said.

She seemed to waver, but then glanced down at our table of mostly uneaten *dianxin*, and determinedly picked up her purse. Thankfully at that moment Chris emerged from the bathroom. He came to my aid and only with both of our strenuous objections did she agree to forgo her run to Mc-Donald's.

That evening Shentu had a university function. Not wanting to leave us unattended, she arranged for one of her students to escort us to dinner. We really just wanted some free time to explore without the pressures of hospitality, but how to tactfully convince Shentu? I told Chris he must stay and help me so we could present a united front. The two of us together convinced her that we would be all right in Hangzhou for an evening by ourselves.

The next day was Saturday and we awoke to pouring-down rain. Shentu suggested that instead of seeing Hangzhou's famous temple, which would require some hiking, that we go to one of two museums: tea or silk. We opted for the China National Silk Museum and spent a more enjoyable morning at a museum with our three children than we thought possible. Andrew was fascinated by the life cycle of the silk worm and the display of the pupa and cocoon; Grace enjoyed seeing the progress of Chinese fashion through the dynasties; and Katherine, after a short lesson on the Chinese character for silk, 丝, enjoyed finding more examples of this character and 纟, its radical, in various other characters in the museum display, such as the colors red, 红, and green, 绿 (describing the red and green *qipao*—Chinese silk dresses—in the museum displays), and the character for paper 纸 (which was originally made from silk).

Chris and I were fascinated by the history of silk presented by the museum, the largest silk museum in the world. The Chinese learned how to produce silk at least by the third millennium BC, then carefully guarded that secret for two thousand years. In China's silk-producing provinces, all the women in a family devoted six months each year to tending silkworms, spinning threads, dyeing cloth, and embroidering. The beginning of the silk season each year was inaugurated by the empress herself. Silk embodied luxury; initially, only the emperor was allowed to wear garments of silk. But eventually it came to be used by all classes of society. The Chinese produced fishing line, musical instruments, and rag paper out of silk; at one time, lengths of silk were even used as currency.

After we finished touring the museum, Shentu announced that we were going to KFC for lunch. She was determined that on her watch, our children were going to eat, and KFC was the answer. We also thought it a wise choice, and I felt relieved of the pressure of having to get our children to eat to please Shentu.

"Make sure you don't let Shentu pay. She's paid for everything so far," Chris whispered to me as he took the kids to find seats near the play area. I ordered our usual meals and a few extras we had come to enjoy. She ordered a small meal for herself.

But when I tried to pay Shentu looked at me absolutely horror-stricken. I quickly backed off, realizing that to pay, even though she had paid for everything up to this point, was to insult her.

That afternoon Chris took the children back to the room for naps and Shentu took me on a driving tour of the old and new campuses of her university. Zhejiang University, one of sixteen national key universities of China, has five campuses and about forty thousand students. When she brought me back to the hotel, we agreed she would pick us up at five for dinner at her home.

We were met in the lobby by Shentu and her husband, He Ping (pronounced Huh Peeng). They led us outside and He Ping motioned us toward his car, a silver BMW—one year old, fully loaded.

Chris gazed admiringly at the car, then our eyes met. "I guess it was all right to let Shentu pay at KFC," he said.

Shentu and He Ping brought us to their home on the tenth floor of a modern high-rise nearby. They had a spacious three-bedroom apartment with hardwood floors and beautiful views. No bare cement in sight, perhaps not even in the parking garage. There was a flat-screen TV and a completely modern built-in kitchen. Everything was bright and well lit, and in their bathroom, there was not only a Western toilet and shower, but a Siemens washer/dryer combo.

Thus far I had been to the home of a *bing* seller in Tai'an, to the home of a peasant in Dongping, and to Mr. Jia's home on our campus. But this was the first time I was in the home of the other side of China: the wealthy side. Their standard of living was certainly higher than ours here in China, perhaps even higher than ours in the United States. The last time we were guests of Chinese hospitality we were in a village with a hay-filled, fly-infested outdoor stall for a bathroom. The distance between my previous experiences and Shentu's penthouse was so vast, I could hardly get my head around it.

And less than a week earlier I had visited our dear Mr. Jia and had been humbled as he took me around his cramped apartment with its dim lighting, bare cement floors, and worn furniture. How could I ask for more, even ask for two apartments, when my colleagues lived uncomplainingly as they did? But seeing how Shentu lived made my compass arrow swing right back around. Shentu was a professor just like me. Why couldn't I live to her standard?

Shentu lived with her husband, He Ping; her sixteen-year-old son, He Yue (pronounced Huh Yway); and her mother. Her husband, very kind and easy to converse with, was the manager of a thirty-employee chemical plant. He was originally from a village in Anhui province, west of Shanghai. I asked Shentu how it was being a city girl married to a boy who grew up in the countryside. She said it was complicated, but didn't elaborate. He Ping worked late hours. Shentu usually came home from the university at around 7:00 p.m. and ate dinner with her mother. Her mother had lived with them, doing most of the cooking and cleaning, since Shentu's father died of cancer about ten years ago. Her mother did not speak Mandarin Chinese, only Hangzhou dialect, which was distinct since Hangzhou was geographically quite removed from Beijing, upon whose dialect Mandarin Chinese is based.

Since He Ping grew up in Anhui province, his native dialect and the Hangzhou dialect were mutually unintelligible. This had several ramifications for Shentu's family. First, she and her husband had always conversed in Mandarin, their common language. Since they talked to each other in Mandarin, this was the only Chinese dialect their son knew. Even though he now lived with his maternal grandmother, he had never learned to speak the Hangzhou dialect, so he could not communicate with her. When Shentu studied in Japan her husband, son, and mother lived together. Her mother cooked and cleaned then as she did now, but her son-in-law and grandson could only communicate with her through a few words and gestures.

Shentu sent her son to reside in the dorms at his high school. He returned home on weekends only. While they lived close enough to the school for him to commute, living at the high school allowed him to completely focus on the college entrance exam, only two and a half years away. But there was another reason he resided at the school. Shentu felt her son had grown too accustomed to the attention he commanded at home as the only child. At school he had to learn to be one of many instead of the one that many doted upon.

It was a dilemma many Chinese parents like Shentu and He Ping face: how to properly socialize an only child. Every other year for Spring Festival Shentu and her family went back to her husband's village in Anhui province to see his family. She said her son disliked these trips but they forced him to go. He had grown up with the wealth and privilege of the city and could not relate to rural life. This was compounded by the language problem. He could not understand the Anhui dialect of his paternal grandparents.

When we arrived, Shentu made the children welcome in the living room with a coffee table stacked with all their favorite treats: chocolate cakes, peanuts, and candies. Then she, along with her husband and mother, busied themselves in the kitchen while we watched TV and conversed with her son, He Yue. He Yue spoke excellent and confident English.

Once the food was ready, we were treated to a delicious feast. Crab legs, pounded rice, cabbage, vegetables, all delicious. But as usual the children weren't overly enthused.

"Have another chocolate cake," said Shentu. "Eat more."

The children, with mischievous glances at their mother, happily complied. Andrew was tired and growing frustrated with opening peanuts, but Shentu would not consider my tending to him.

"You must go to the table. Eat more. It's no problem."

The children calmed down and we were able to just sit around their dining room table and enjoy the conversation. He Ping several times lamented China's one-child policy. "How we wish we could have had another. A boy and a girl would be perfect!"

I was sure after an evening spent with our three he would change his mind. But he didn't seem to.

"Your son speaks excellent English," Chris told Shentu.

She said they had sent him to England for a two-week home stay last summer. I remember chiding Qingdao Cathy a few weeks ago for this being her standard of wealth. Our students were all English majors and the majority of them had never left Shandong province. I knew not a single one who had been to another country or even flown on an airplane. Many rode a train for the first time to get to the university. Foreign exchange rates were not in favor of Chinese going abroad. My salary, sufficient for daily life here, if converted was just a few hundred U.S. dollars a month. But Qingdao Cathy, although so rich relative to her classmates, had adopted this skewed barometer of wealth. I had told her this was ridiculous.

Yet here I was, in the presence of it, not reading about it in the newspaper or hearing about it secondhand. Rather, this was my own friend who had sent her son abroad.

Hangzhou changed our perspective about China. It is a historic city, but also a modern city. Other Chinese cities have not done well with this dichotomy, but Hangzhou has managed to preserve its history while achieving a level of development equal to that of any Western city. It has managed development beautifully, not at the expense of its Chinese-ness like Shanghai. Its West Lake epitomized 山水 (*shanshui*), "mountains, water"—the traditional Chinese ideal of art—together with arched bridges and tiled-roofed pavilions adding minimal artistic accoutrement to the natural beauty, like a perfectly balanced Chinese ink painting. Hangzhou showed what China could be, that it could develop without losing itself.

And in Hangzhou Shentu showed us the other side of the new China, the affluent side. Not all Chinese wear the cotton trousers of Shandong peasants; some wear garments of the finest silk.

Chapter 26

香港
HONG KONG

❦

AFTER TAKING THE OVERNIGHT TRAIN SOUTH FROM HANGZHOU WE arrived in Shenzhen, adjacent to Hong Kong. I always thought taking an overnight train with soft sleepers would work perfectly for our family. Often when I made such plans involving our children they completely backfired. But in this instance, it turned out exactly like I thought it would. We had our own private cabin equipped with two sets of bunks, a total of four beds. Chris and Katherine slept on the two top bunks. Grace and Andrew slept together on one of the bottom bunks with their heads at opposite ends. I occupied the other bottom bunk. During the day the children amused themselves for hours just climbing up and down the bunks; at night, they were easily lulled to sleep by the train's gentle movements and slept the whole night through.

I didn't sleep quite as easily as the children, and woke up periodically to take a peek out the window at the landscape going by. I knew the dark train was taking us south through Jiangxi province. Our sleeping Grace had no idea that she was in her home province for the first time since leaving almost four years before, albeit just passing through. I lay awake, thinking that we must take our children on a proper visit to Jiangxi province soon, at an early age, or they'd likely develop into a Qingdao Cathy, incapable of not looking down on her country classmates; or like Shentu's son, He Yue, unable to relate to his Anhui grandparents.

In Shenzhen we passed through customs, departing mainland China for the Hong Kong Special Administrative Region. We took the MTR—Hong Kong's subway system—to the Kowloon peninsula of Hong Kong, then dragged our bags to the Star Ferry to cross to Hong Kong Island. From there, we caught another ferry, and forty-five minutes later we were on Cheung Chau Island, the site of our winter conference with our organization, ERRC.

Cheung Chau Island (pronounced Choing Chow), a fishing village since the Ming Dynasty (1368–1644), chose to leave its quaint narrow alleys and footpaths untouched instead of widening its streets to allow for the introduction of the automobile. To this day it is only accessible by passenger ferry, and while it has its share of bicycles, scooters, and even motorized carts, there are no cars or trucks. It is a perfect blend of an interesting culture unspoiled by tourism, yet still having the amenities we craved after a semester on the mainland.

The island is shaped like an hourglass, with the village crowded onto the narrow isthmus in the center and clinging to the overlooking hills. The ferry docked on one side of the island and we walked five minutes across the isthmus to the island's only hotel, which overlooked the water on the other side.

After settling in we walked back along the main drag that overlooked the harbor, filled with colorful fishing vessels. We poked our heads into a tiny grocery story with four short aisles—we found Skippy peanut butter, canned tuna fish, mayonnaise, four different types of breakfast cereal, parmesan cheese, granola bars, an assortment of candy bars, beer from around the world, and English-language newspapers. If we could just take this small grocery and transplant it in Tai'an, how different our life would be.

In the early evening I strolled along the waterfront, looking at tiny shops with colorful clothing and purses for sale. There was a delightful tie-dyed skirt but the one on the rack was too small. I wanted to inquire if they had larger sizes, but no English was spoken by the shopkeeper. I only heard streams of confounding Cantonese. On a whim I asked if she could speak Mandarin. *Hui!* (She could!) We conversed easily, although I unfortunately found out that she had no other similar skirts of a larger size. But how easy the Mandarin seemed, how familiar, how flowing after just a few days of listening to that incomprehensible Cantonese!

Chris, the kids, and I walked to an Indian restaurant for dinner, leisurely, as there were no cars or traffic to continually watch for, that constant hazard in mainland China. We fed our family on a set menu for two with Indian naan bread, chicken, yogurt sauce, curried potatoes and cauliflower. After dinner we walked along the harbor road containing an assortment of fishmongers. The children were delighted to see a squid that would ink himself and turn the surrounding water brownish-purple at the slightest scare. We took a circuitous route back to the hotel, walking through narrow alleys where the third-floor awnings on opposite sides were just inches from touching; I'm sure on a windy day the laundry of one invaded the airspace of the other.

Cheung Chau Island had the feel of spending time in someone's neighborhood. For the most part, the local residents were simply going about their daily lives. We spent our time walking past community centers, playgrounds, schools, small homes, and corner grocery stores. We saw the elderly doing their morning exercises and young families spending time together. Commuters returning home on the ferry after working all day in Central Hong Kong shared the street with uniformed schoolchildren, garbed in gray V-neck sweaters over crisp white shirts. The neighborhood was dotted with Thai clothing shops, Indian restaurants, and other signs that we were entering that region of the world that was a delightful hodgepodge of Southeast Asian cultures.

Our retreat ended and the next morning we were flying to Thailand. Instead of going back to Central Hong Kong or remaining at Cheung Chau, we decided to spend the one intervening night on Lantau Island, one short ferry ride away. Lantau would have been just another outlying island if not for the new airport and, more recently, Disneyland. But there were no hints of those in Mui Wo, a small community thirty minutes away by ferry from Cheung Chau Island. I would stop short of calling Mui Wo charming, but then nothing seemed charming when viewed from under an umbrella. The rains started when we arrived and the weather remained wet for our entire less-than-twenty-four-hour stay.

A cluster of homes and shops, more modern than on Cheung Chau, faced the ferry terminal, their only choice, as several hills rose up vertically right outside the town. The harbor was quiet, with one lone sailboat. Together with the rain, water, and misty mountain ranges I almost felt transported back to the San Juan Islands of my home state. I ordered some take-out Turkish food just because I could. While waiting for our hummus and kabobs I walked through the local grocery store. It was bigger than the one on Cheung Chau Island, and I was treated to such a colorful display of fruit it hurt my eyes.

As I was browsing I saw a box of flaxseed granola cereal with pumpkin seeds. I was amazed. I vaguely recalled a former life where I used to bake my own granola and our children routinely asked for flax flakes for breakfast. It seemed a lifetime ago.

I stared at the box, not knowing what to do. We were flying to Thailand in the morning and our bags were already stuffed. What was I going to do—carry on a box of cereal? But how could I walk away now that I had seen it?

I remained incapacitated, knowing I couldn't take the box with me, yet not able to leave. At last, shoulders slumped, I left the supermarket and went out into the rain to retrieve our takeout.

The next morning the taxi arrived early at the appointed stop, as did we. The moment we were inside the driver pressed his gas pedal down and we went flying around the traffic circle and up the winding road that led out of town through the mountains. The seat belts in the back did not work; I tried, even though we were no longer accustomed to wearing them. Katherine quickly started complaining of motion sickness; I rolled down the window, but soon was feeling it as well. I took off my jacket in an exaggerated fashion, accompanied by deep sighs, hoping the driver would catch on, but to no avail. As we crossed over the mountain range the road narrowed into one lane of traffic, which we had to share with oncoming buses and a herd of cattle that ranged freely. Never did the driver let up speed, except to slam on the brakes to avoid a collision, which happened twice, sending us flying into the back of the front seats. He seemed not to notice. How happy we were to look from the heights above and see the airport below.

After two weeks in Thailand, we returned to Hong Kong for the last leg of our monthlong journey. This time we stayed at the Salisbury Road YMCA at the tip of the Kowloon peninsula. Four years earlier we had stayed here when we adopted Grace. It had been her first birthday, Valentine's Day, and we were almost ready to fly home nearly three months after receiving our referral.

When most people involved in adoption talk about the wait, they mean the wait until referral. Referral is when you are matched with a child, when you receive her name, her picture, her vital information. But for me, the most excruciating wait was not before but after the referral.

We received our referral November 17. We knew from my Internet research that we should go to China in four to six weeks. There were more documents to fill out. We had to receive travel approval from China. Finally, we needed our official appointment at the U.S. Consulate in Guangzhou that would process Grace's immigrant visa.

But the timing was terrible. First, we ran into Christmas. As usual, for two weeks little American government business would be conducted. But immediately following Christmas was Chinese New Year, and for two weeks the Chinese government would all but shut down.

But I held out a glimmer of hope. There was one week in between these two holidays. If we could squeeze into China that one week, the first week of January, we could get her sooner.

We had her picture now. We had been matched. Now every day that went by was a day she was without her mother. She needed me. These early months were critical for our bonding, for our life together. We needed to get to China immediately. There was no other solution.

I fired off an e-mail to the adoption agency, making sure they were aware that we had to go for this one-week window. They said they would try, but I shouldn't get my hopes up.

And then, I did what I usually ended up doing when the problem was completely out of my own control. I prayed.

For days I waited for news from our adoption agency. Finally it came: we couldn't travel early. We would have to wait until the end of Chinese New Year. We could plan to travel in early February. I was devastated.

As evening approached I took Katherine and the infant Andrew upstairs. Katherine lay in her bed, and I nursed Andrew in the rocking chair, absentmindedly staring at the pictures of Chinese children on the wall that I had stared at hundreds of times before during our bedtime rituals. Early February! A full month longer than the normal wait. The nine-month-old we had met through her picture would be days shy of her first birthday before we could lay our hands on her. I glared angrily at the ceiling, wondering why God had failed me this time. Couldn't He, the Master of the Universe, see that in this particular instance, I was correct? Didn't He realize that this little girl with the bald head and penetrating eyes needed her mother?

I stared at the picture of a little girl in black pigtails hanging on the wall. It was the first picture I had noticed when I had looked through the hundreds of farmer's paintings on my first trip to China, back when I was pregnant with Katherine. It was this picture that had given me the idea to decorate my child's nursery with these pictures of Chinese children, painted boldly in primary colors.

The pigtailed girl was holding a lantern, a typical Chinese lantern with a Chinese character emblazoned on the front. I stared at the lantern. The character was familiar. I looked at it again. There was no mistaking it. It was Fu, the Chinese character for "blessing," "happiness." It was Fu, the first character in our daughter's name, Fu Zhi Chun. It was the same Fu.

福

BLESSING

I had looked at these pictures countless times. I was intimately familiar with the Chinese characters in my daughter's name, tracing them in my mind over and over. Yet I had never noticed that they were the same. Not until that exact moment.

"Why do you still insist on questioning Me?" asked the Ancient One, to the place deep in my soul. "Aminta, please be still. I'm in control of all of this, every last detail. Make no mistake: this was *My* plan from the beginning. And the next time you begin to question Me, remember that you had a painting of your daughter hanging on your wall. It was hanging there before you had any notion of adopting this little girl who, by the way, I've loved far longer than you."

And I became still. And for the moment, at least, stopped questioning.

❁

At the YMCA, everything was the same as four years before: the same great view, the 山水, mountains and water, the same light show from the skyscrapers on either side of Victoria Harbor. As before, I stared out the hotel window at the continuous sea traffic on the narrow strait between

Kowloon and Hong Kong Island. Hong Kong, in the Chinese language, means "fragrant harbor." To form the character for harbor, 港, the Chinese simply added the water radical 氵 to 巷, the word for alley or lane. As I watched this water alley I thought it was an apt description, although today the constant traffic of container ships, cruise ships, ferries, and hydrofoils made it seem less a water alley and more a water superhighway. Incense, at one time produced north of Kowloon, gave Hong Kong its 香 character, meaning "fragrant."

Four years ago I remember thinking I could easily live here, for it had all the Chinese things I loved and admired, but also the Western amenities to make me feel comfortable. Now, for the past year and a half we had been deeper into China than I ever imagined back then. Four years ago we were toting a four-month-old and a one-year-old. (Katherine had stayed home with my mother.) Andrew had been the perfect age to travel at that time—still nursing, happy, not yet mobile. And I had to admit that had we traveled one month earlier, as I had wanted, his immune system would not have been as developed.

Now, we had three preschoolers, and they were hungry. We went to dinner at T.G.I. Friday's because we had to get in all our Western meals while we could. It cost over 800 Hong Kong dollars. Hong Kong dollars and Chinese yuan had achieved near parity in value. Since my monthly salary was 3,600 yuan, I had just spent more than one-fifth of my salary on one quite marginal dinner. Yes, it was time to go back home.

The next day was Valentine's Day, Grace's birthday. We were celebrating her fifth birthday in the same hotel in Hong Kong where we celebrated her first birthday, ten days after adopting her. We had made plans to spend the afternoon with Garlum, my friend from language studies in Japan. Garlum took us to Stanley, a small community on the southern tip of Hong Kong Island, away from the busyness of Central. After spending an enjoyable afternoon with her, the taxi dropped us off at IFC (International Finance Center), a huge modern mall in Central. We were to meet friends from our hometown in Washington State who were teaching locally at the international school. We weren't supposed to meet them for another two hours, but it didn't make sense to take the ferry back to Kowloon only to take it back again, so we decided to just walk around the mall until dinnertime. We were immediately impressed with how new and modern this mall seemed.

"Is this an airport?" Andrew asked.

Many malls in the United States have grown tired-looking, often nearly deserted after a heyday perhaps twenty or thirty years previous. But in Central Hong Kong that which was not new and modern did not survive. A newspaper article I read while there said that the average life span for a building in Hong Kong was thirty years; some buildings had even been torn down seven years after being built. Property values were so high that the buildings themselves could be discarded relatively cheaply to make room for new buildings that would bring in greater revenue.

It was our last day in Hong Kong. We hoped to stock up on a few grocery items that we couldn't get on the mainland. The mall had a supermarket, so off we went.

The Story of Qiu Ju, a 1993 Chinese movie directed by Zhang Yimou, stars Gong Li as a pregnant village woman seeking justice after her husband is kicked in the groin by a village elder. She travels with her sister-in-law from their village to the town to lodge a formal complaint. The two women are brushed off by the officials. Undaunted, Qiu Ju continues to the next bigger town. Never receiving the justice she desires, she continues to take her case to the next higher level until finally, after riding in oxcarts, trucks, and buses, she arrives with her sister-in-law in the big city.

At this point the artistry of the movie shows distinctly the difference between these two women of the village and the high-heeled business-suited city folk bustling around them. It is not so much their country clothes, simple hairstyles, or tanned skin that distinguish them, but rather the disorientation evident in their faces as they cling to each other, looking around, appearing somewhat dazed.

This was the exact feeling I had walking with my husband and three children in this high-end supermarket in this high-end mall in high-end Hong Kong. The aisles were crowded with fashionably dressed Hong Kongers. After a month of traveling, we were wearing the last clean clothes we had left as we pushed our cart along, overwhelmed by the immense array of cheeses, cereals, and pasta. Deli counters were filled with every cheese imaginable, even buffalo mozzarella, which I hadn't had since I enjoyed Caprese sandwiches in Europe. The health food aisle held not only the flaxseeds I was shopping for, but also wheat germ and granola. While the other shoppers moved deftly to pick up exactly what they needed before commuting home, we looked here and there with confusion, not knowing what merited adding weight to our already heavy suitcases.

As we prepared to leave, I thought about this city bridging two cultures, this Hong Kong mixture of East and West. Hong Kong people have been exposed to the West far longer than mainlanders, but are they just as Chinese? What exactly makes someone Chinese anyway? And something I had been wondering since I moved to China: Could Chinese culture withstand China's opening to the West?

I wondered why Chinese culture was so strong; why China could boast nearly five thousand years of continuous civilization; why Chinese was the only language to have maintained its ideographic characters, while others, such as Egyptian hieroglyphics, had faded away to mere archaeological interest; why Chinese who went abroad, whether to Singapore or Malaysia, Canada or the United States, still retained their culture even after generations. The only answer I came up with was the strength of the family, the core of the culture.

Western culture is alluring. It might be the greatest challenge to Chinese culture yet. But while Western culture pervades the world outside—ads, Internet, shopping, TV, movies—the home is still Chinese. Chinese culture, like all other cultures, is passed down as mother's milk, bedtime stories, scolding, and bundling up to prevent cold. Over meals it is taught with the proper use of chopsticks; after dinner it is passed down as the parents check over notebooks filled with rows of Chinese characters; in the in-between times, Chinese culture is passed while giving children lectures that their future—meaning not just theirs but their entire family's—is dependent upon their studies. It is passed down in the kitchen over the folding of dumplings and the slicing of potatoes, and in setting out food for the Kitchen God. Grandparents pass it as they hold a child while he pees on the sidewalk through his split pants, and parents pass it when their child sleeps with them until she is seven years old. Finally, it is passed as both generations raise a child with their expectations and hopes.

From the outside, with its skyscrapers, rapid transit systems, and Disneyland, Hong Kong appears very Western indeed. But inside, inside the home, the incense still burns, and the fragrance is very Chinese.

Chapter 27

蛋

EGG

❀

WE RETURNED TO TAI'AN IN FEBRUARY. THE TREES WERE STILL BARE OF leaves and everything had maintained the brown hue as before we left. But there was one subtle change. The New Year's couplets, faded after a year of sun and wind, had been replaced by bright red ones. The Chinese traditionally pasted these couplets, usually containing messages of hope or luck for the coming year, on the sides and top of each doorway during Spring Festival.

The morning the kids went back to school I woke up early. I'd been waiting for this day, since we had spent the previous ten days cooped up in our small apartment. As I dressed Grace, she complained about all the layers I wanted her to wear.

"Grace, it's cold outside. I don't want you to be cold!" I said.

She remained unconvinced. I decided to take her out on the balcony/laundry room to demonstrate to her firsthand how cold it was outside. Picking her up, I opened the door. We were greeted by a completely unexpected scene: three to four inches of freshly fallen snow covering our courtyard, sidewalks, trees, and bushes.

Suddenly, the entire mood of the morning changed. The routine was exchanged for the magical. The children went from grudgingly putting on their required layers to yanking on pants and zipping up boots with frenzied excitement. Snow! We'd never seen snow in China; last winter, although cold, had remained dry. This winter we left in January before the big snowstorms of 2008 hit the area. All complaints about going to school were forgotten. The children delighted in making footprints along previously untrodden areas and sliding down the hill.

❁

The last week of February was unusual, for while the children recommenced their studies in their kindergarten, Chris and I didn't start teaching until the following week. We had a week to ourselves with no children. We used the time to prepare for classes and do some reading and writing around the two key events of each day: bringing the children to school in the morning and picking them up in the late afternoon.

By noon on Friday, we had completed nine round-trips to the kindergarten along Ying Sheng Road. That stretch of road from the campus front gate to the Jiayuan supermarket on the corner truly felt like our street. At least four times a day we walked along that block, to and from the kindergarten. Kitty-corner from the supermarket was an intersection crammed with fruit sellers, so we would often go there to pick up some bananas or tangerines or the occasional pomelo to bring home. On the other side of the street was the *bing* seller I frequented almost daily. Further down toward the campus gate was the beauty shop I took the children to. The first time I went there they welcomed me as if they already knew me. They had seen us on our daily walks to and from kindergarten. In fact, everybody on Ying Sheng Road knew us: the American family with the daughter who sure looked like she was Chinese. Once I had given a few of them our explanation—that we had adopted Grace a few years before from Jiangxi province—that information spread along the street. Sometimes, if I took just the girls to the store with me, a complete stranger would come up and ask me where *didi* (little brother) was.

Along that section of Ying Sheng Road nobody really looked twice at us anymore. Why should they? They saw us four times a day. They knew our story and accepted our presence on the street.

I well remember last year during our first semester, when I fixated, while trying to herd our children along Ying Sheng Road, thinking that there had to be a better way to get the children to school. Fifteen to twenty minutes one way was well within walking distance by Chinese standards, but with three children, at least one of whom wanted to run ahead, one of whom was prone to falling behind, and one who wanted to whine and be carried, it seemed a huge daily burden.

Consumed with the search for solutions, I would probe the perimeter of the campus for shortcuts, sure there must be a better way to make this twice-daily journey. But I came up with no alternative but the well-traveled route. We considered getting a three-wheeled bicycle, similar to a grown-up tricycle with a cart in the back for the children to sit, so at least they would all be contained. But these bikes proved unwieldy and the uphill portion would have had to be walked, so we dropped the idea.

"Why not arrange for a taxi to meet us at our courtyard every morning and bring us to school," I thought. We discussed this with Lucy, our taxi driver friend, but she was hesitant to commit. Going-to-school hours were also prime earning time for taxi drivers. Finally, we decided that what we really needed was a little red wagon. We searched online and found the perfect model, only to discover that the company did not ship to China.

So, despite our grasping at solutions, we were left walking our children to and fro each day, right along with the other parents and grandparents. But this week, as I recalled our failed efforts to solve the problem, I realized it was different now. Chris and I made this walk admiring the mountains and sky, which had been particularly clear and blue lately. We chatted with those walking with us. We practiced poetry memorization with the children. Or sometimes we just lost ourselves in thoughts about the day or our children or our students. We had accepted the situation and were now content.

This had required some learning and some unlearning of the problem-solving and innovative inclination that was part of our American culture. Chris and I, both admittedly type A personalities, fell right into this stereotype: always looking to improve on the good, continually seeking greater efficiency. We always quickly, and proudly, came up with new ideas. We had been taught by our culture: "Whenever you identify a problem, always propose a solution."

Contentment itself was something we had to learn from the Chinese people around us. Historically, particularly in the last century, the Chinese had proven themselves capable of bearing quite a lot: occupation by Japan followed by civil war, starvation after the grossly misnamed Great Leap Forward, and capricious and catastrophic government decisions. They usually hadn't had the ability to change their circumstances. And they had emerged with the ability to be content in tremendously hard situations.

I recall before we left on winter break, Zhang and I discussing our teaching schedules for the spring semester. In the fall Zhang taught twenty hours per week, well beyond a full teaching load. But in the spring she was only assigned eight hours.

"Which do you prefer?" I asked her.

"Well, it doesn't really matter," was her reply. "If I teach a lot of hours I earn more money, and that is good. But if I teach fewer hours I have more spare time, which is also good."

Frustration seemed to come slowly, and willingness to accept inconvenience, easily. Things that drove us crazy—last-minute changes to our teaching schedules, sudden power outages, getting paid late (and not being informed that we would)—left our neighbors and colleagues unfazed.

Sometimes we did long for more willingness to solve problems, such as when one of our gas burners wouldn't light. If I needed to cook with both burners, I had to awkwardly light a toothpick from the working burner and bring the flame to the second burner. We brought Mr. Jia up to have a look at it, and demonstrated the problem.

"Yes," he declared, "It is certainly broken. Just continue to light it with a toothpick."

Our walks to the kindergarten were much more enjoyable now that we were learning to be content. And when I returned home and saw my tiny apartment, I now saw how bright and cheery it was, in spite of its small size, and thought, perhaps we might just continue to live here, without searching for a bigger place, a better place, a place that would rectify the shortcomings this apartment has. Perhaps we should instead be content here.

The week went by quickly, and it was time for Chris and me to think about teaching again. I kept telling myself that my teaching schedule wasn't fixed until I started teaching. Although I didn't allow myself to make lesson plans, each schedule I received I still bought into, and could not resist making mental preparations and plans, coming up with ideas, picturing the faces of my students on the first day of class. Chris and I decided to check e-mail one last time before bed on Friday night, with classes starting Monday, and there was an e-mail from the English Department in our inbox, an ominous sign. It was a complete schedule change, requiring a shift in thinking on everything from who was bringing the children which day to when Chinese lessons would occur.

The Sunday before classes started everything came alive again as students reinhabited the campus. With the clear sky, slight breeze, and sunlight it was a perfect day to open the windows, hang some laundry, and *shai beizi*, "sun-bake the blankets." Fences, rocks, and shrubs, even Ping-Pong tables and badminton nets were strewn with pastel-colored comforters.

As the days went by, we slowly began to see signs of spring. In the morning, the children could once again do morning exercises at their kindergarten; in the afternoon, it was warm and light enough for them to play ball after school in our courtyard. The long johns had been put away, and the children could wear their winter coats unzipped, sans hats and gloves. Pineapples on a stick were once again available at the fruit and vegetable stands.

But there was one milestone of spring that we completely forgot about: the haircut. Every year on the second day of the second lunar month, which this year fell on March 9, Chinese boys typically got their hair cut for good luck and an auspicious start to the new year. When I picked up the children from school I could see the scalps of all the newly shorn heads. In contrast, our Andrew's strawberry blond hair, already starting to get a little bushy, looked unkempt and stuck out at various angles thanks to his long nap that day.

❁

When I taught my students about Easter and showed them decorated Easter eggs, marshmallow chicks hatching out of eggs, and Cadbury Creme Eggs, they asked me why eggs were so important at Easter.

I had never thought about it before.

"I suppose an egg is a symbol of birth, and in this way, it is a symbol of spring, the season of rebirth," I told them.

When I learned the Chinese character for egg, 蛋, I immediately noticed that its bottom half, 虫, meant "insect." What did insects have to do with eggs? Wouldn't the bird radical have been much more meaningful? I looked up the upper radical, 疋, but it had been used so frequently as a component of characters that its original meaning was unknown.

I asked the other teachers as we waited for the bus, but most of them gave me strange looks.

"It just means 'egg,'" my colleagues said. "We've never thought about the different parts before."

"But there must be some reason for the insect," I said.

"I think it's because some insects lay eggs too, and 蛋 refers to all eggs, not just chicken eggs," suggested one teacher.

That day when I returned to the old campus after teaching, Mr. Jia was in the duty room. I asked him about 蛋.

"Well of course," said Mr. Jia, who raised chickens as a boy in his village not far from Tai'an. "Chickens eat insects. They can't lay eggs if they don't eat."

Everyone had a different story.

❁

Saturday night before Easter Sunday Chris waited until the kids were asleep, then retrieved all the candy that he had purchased from his various hiding places around our small apartment. He got to work, fastidiously stuffing the plastic eggs he had brought from the United States months before for this exact purpose.

On Sunday before we left for church Chris dropped off a paper bag filled with the plastic eggs with Mr. Jia in the duty room so the children wouldn't find them while we were gone. After church, Chris retrieved the eggs and hid them around the courtyard. I went upstairs to relieve the babysitter and bring the children.

The kids had a great time with their own personal Easter egg hunt, for there is hardly anything as fun as a good treasure hunt when you are a child. When they had finished and taken their eggs upstairs to open, Katherine immediately started complaining.

"My eggs don't have anything in them," she said.

Grace opened a few and found a bag of M&M's. That only added to

Katherine's consternation and in frustration she searched all her eggs for what she thought was a noticeable dearth of treasure.

Chris pulled me out of earshot of the children.

"I remember specifically filling each of the three large eggs with a bag of M&M's each. Then I put them at the bottom of the sack."

He paused. "But when I picked up the sack from the duty room, the three large eggs were at the top of the sack and were empty."

Someone had rummaged through the eggs. Not only that, they had taken some of the candy meant for our children.

I was completely at a loss.

Chris said, "Well, we'll just have to learn from this experience."

But what was I supposed to learn? I had this information, but I didn't know where in my brain I was supposed to file it. Should I put it under the heading: "Mr. Jia is not trustworthy?" Emotionally that was very hard to do. Could our beloved Mr. Jia have done this? We certainly couldn't ask him now, for just the asking would result in a loss of face that would damage our relationship in the future, and the relationship was too important to risk that.

Or should I let Mr. Jia off the hook and let the culture take the fall instead? We knew Chinese culture had different views on privacy than our own. Did the culture allow for something that to us seemed such a breach?

I had my tutoring session with Zhang the next day and I was anxious to get her opinion. But in this case, she offered no clear-cut explanation. While Chinese culture was certainly less private and more open, still, someone else's stuff was someone else's stuff.

"Perhaps Mr. Jia's granddaughter went through a few eggs," she offered. I admitted that was a possibility, as she had been there at the time.

Finally, I chose to believe that while I wouldn't know or understand what had happened, our kids had in fact received plenty of Easter candy and had not suffered. And that Mr. Jia was the same person before as he was after.

❁

A few weekends later, I got up Saturday morning and got ready to take a shower. I felt for the bathroom light switch, hoping the light would come on. For the last few months we had felt lucky if the bathroom light turned on in the morning. More often it only flickered; usually, though, there was no response at all. We then had to unscrew the light fixture (in the dark), rotate the bulb until the light came on, and then screw the light fixture back into place.

That morning when I turned on the switch there was not even a flicker of light. I went to the kitchen to get the screwdriver. As I reached up on tip-toes to rotate the lightbulb it suddenly sent out sparks. The bulb exploded into small glass fragments raining down on me and cascading all over the bathroom floor.

The small explosion tripped the circuit breaker, leaving the entire apartment without power. Our children, who had been happily engrossed watching a video, started howling at the sudden loss of power. I slipped on some clothes and went out into the stairwell, flipped the circuit breaker, restarted the video for the children, swept up all the glass, and took a shower (in the dark).

I started to prepare our customary Saturday morning breakfast of French toast. But when I opened the fridge, there was only one egg to be found. I went to put on my shoes so I could buy some eggs, and in my grumpiness sniped at my husband. He sniped back. I walked out the door to the campus grocery store muttering about my terrible morning and dreading the day to come.

Surrounding the small campus grocery were many outdoor vendors set up to provide students with their Saturday breakfast of noodles or egg and vegetable soup. I walked past them into the store and told the proprietor that I wanted eleven eggs—*"Wo yao shiyi ge dangao."*

He looked at me rather curiously and repeated, *"Shiyi ge dangao?"*

I became irritated at his seeming inability to understand my Chinese. I confirmed firmly, if somewhat curtly, *"Dui. Shiyi ge dangao."*

In our town we did not buy eggs in one-dozen cartons like back home. Rather a pile of eggs, along with a few downy feathers, were located in a large plastic bin. Normally the salesclerk placed the desired number of eggs in a plastic bag and weighed them. We paid by the weight, then gingerly carried them home.

I waited for the proprietor to fetch me the eggs, but then noticed that he appeared to be putting several items resembling pound cake into a plastic bag. To my horror, I suddenly realized what had happened. Instead of saying *shiyi ge jiDAN* (eleven eggs), I had said *shiyi ge DANgao* (eleven cakes). In Chinese, egg is pronounced *dan*. The character for egg (蛋) is present in both words, but egg is called *ji-dan*, chicken egg, while cake is called *dan-gao*, egg pastry.

I quickly tried to correct my mistake before he put any more cakes into the bag. *"Bu hao yisi!* I'm so embarrassed!" I said. "I said DANgao, but I meant jiDAN."

Everyone burst out laughing.

As he put the cakes back, I tried to add, *"Wo SHUO cuo le"* (I spoke incorrectly); but what came out instead was *"Wo DA cuo le"* (I dialed the wrong number).

The entire store, along with the students outside, erupted into laughter. I smiled weakly. The proprietor dutifully filled my bag with eleven eggs. As I was walking out, he amusedly said, "Are you sure you don't want to try a cake?"

I walked back into my apartment, deposited the eggs on the kitchen counter, and announced to my husband, "We are just going to have to start this day over, because I just ordered eleven cakes instead of eleven eggs."

I turned on my heel, retreated into the bedroom, and burst into tears. My husband and children found my mortification quite humorous. Chris put his arm around me, and the children piled onto me sympathetically, and we did in fact start the whole day over.

That summer I was sitting on the courtyard steps with Mr. Jia and some of his friends, one of whom spoke a little bit of English.

"I met an American," Mr. Jia's friend told me. "His name was Dan. *DAN!*"

He repeated what he said in Chinese for the benefit of Mr. Jia and the others, and they snickered.

"Egg! His name was egg! Can you imagine?"

Chapter 28

语
LANGUAGE

Human speech is like a cracked tin kettle, on which we hammer
out tunes to make bears dance when we long to move the stars.
—GUSTAVE FLAUBERT, *Madame Bovary*

❊

WHEN WE FIRST ARRIVED IN CHINA WE FOCUSED ON WORDS. LIKE
toddlers, we pointed to and named the objects of our daily life. But now
in our second year, we were stringing those words together into sentences and
paragraphs, into language. Living as we did in a bilingual world, we became
acutely aware of language. We studied one language while teaching another.
Our children attended school in Chinese, but spoke English at home. Chinese
characters—neon, flashing, painted, or, most commonly, affixed to a red banner—challenged us every day to understand their meaning.

On my way to the new campus I noticed a red banner on the China
Telecom building. It had several Chinese characters on it. The first two
I had recently learned: 继续, meaning "continue." Continue what? I
wondered.

A few days later I asked Zhang about the Chinese term for "liberation,"
since my students often used that term to refer to the events of 1949. 解放,
she informed me. The next day when the school bus passed the China Telecom
building, I noticed that I was now able to read not just two, but the first four
characters. After "continue" came the two characters meaning "liberation."

The following week we discussed Mao Zedong Thought (毛泽东思
想). That helped me with the remaining two characters on the banner, for
they were 思想, the "thought" in Mao Zedong Thought. So I could now
read the entire phrase:

继续解放思想
Continue Liberation Thinking

The moment I put it all together, I saw those exact six characters on the back of the bus we were following.

As we approached the old campus, there they were again on a billboard on Ying Sheng Road.

The next day I saw the phrase at a bus stop. I had been blissfully unaware of this propaganda barrage all along, but now that I recognized it, it was everywhere I turned. I could not escape these words, this silent broadcast of language.

The Chinese character for "language," 语, puzzled me for some time. I saw the radical for "words," 讠 —the simplified version of 言. I also saw "the mouth," 口. Words and mouths have a lot to do with language so I understood those components. But what I didn't understand was why the Chinese character for the number five, 五, stood atop the mouth. Five what? Five mouths? Five people? Why was there a five?

It was my habit to mull over these linguistic mysteries and then pounce upon the first Chinese person I saw who might be able to explain them to me. When I came downstairs from my apartment I saw Mr. Jia. Perfect, I thought.

I wrote the character for Mr. Jia and asked him why the number five appeared in the character for language.

语
LANGUAGE

"No, it's not a number five," he said. "In this case the five and the mouth are one unit." He wrote it for me: 吾.

"We don't use this character so frequently anymore, but in classical Chinese it meant 'myself.' So, if you put the whole character together it means 'the words,' 讠; 'of myself,' 吾; and that is 'language': 语."

The words of myself. I was satisfied with his explanation, although now I wondered why five and mouth together meant "myself." Perhaps the five mouths meant the five senses, and here the mouth was not a literal mouth, but rather a means of sensual intake. I sense therefore I am: "myself."

❊

When I dropped Grace off at her kindergarten class I noticed an announcement in handwritten Chinese characters on the door. I always paid attention to these signs because I didn't want the children to miss out on anything. In the past these announcements had informed parents of the date and time for the New Year's program, that textbooks had arrived and payment was required, or that the next day school would be closed because a student had developed hand, foot and mouth disease. So I stared at the announcement and tried to make out the meaning as best I could. All I was able to ascertain was that on Monday, something was starting.

I pointed to the sign and asked the teacher. She went and retrieved a book for me. I looked through the book and immediately recognized it. It was a book designed to introduce the Chinese characters to children based on easy-to-remember poems. Katherine had tried to use a similar textbook in the fall. It took one basic character and then changed its meaning by adding radicals. A catchy rhyming phrase helped the children remember the changes in meaning. The problem was the characters became complex quite quickly, and often were rather obscure. Katherine quickly became frustrated; since it was an elective, we allowed her to drop this study.

So I was quite wary when I saw the textbook Grace's teacher presented.

"This is good for Chinese children," I told her. "But perhaps too difficult for foreigners."

At this she shook her head. "But Grace can do it. She understands everything we teachers say, every word. She speaks Chinese just like all the other children. I really think she will have no trouble with this textbook."

When we first came to China I thought Andrew would do best with the acquisition of Chinese, followed by Katherine, and finally Grace. After all, Andrew had started talking when he was eight months old, and before his second birthday could count to ten in three languages. Katherine like-

wise was a very verbal child. Grace, on the other hand, was in speech ther-
apy for almost a year before she learned to express simple phrases. She had
always been active, energetic, and social, but didn't seem to have a real
academic bent. She was never very interested in her ABCs or writing her
name, and books didn't hold that much fascination for her. I didn't think
that language was her strong point.

Yet now, after a year and a half in Chinese school, it was Grace who
was bounds ahead of the other two in Chinese. While Andrew could easily
memorize a list of words and Katherine would assiduously and artfully
copy the characters, Grace could actually speak the language. I'm sure the
Chinese she heard as a baby left an imprint upon her brain, left channels
through which language could flow. Even though she wasn't yet talking
back then, the paths had been formed nonetheless. Once she was back in a
Chinese-speaking world, the synapses that held those bits of early language
exposure refired and reconnected.

But there was something else. We believed Grace was so successful
picking up Chinese because at her very heart, she was a social creature.
The playground was her natural habitat. I had never seen a child so friendly
as our Grace, or one with such a magnetic personality. And it was all the
easier to recognize in our family since Katherine and Andrew were by nature shy and reticent, even standoffish. Grace could go into any new group
or class, regardless of whether Western culture or Eastern, and quickly
make herself the favorite. On the way to school we often heard her classmates calling out her name. She would turn, smile, and wave happily at
them.

"Grace, you have so many friends," I often said.

"Yes, I know. Really a lot, right?"

I recall once on a flight a little girl was sitting kitty-corner from us.
Once Grace saw her, she was almost physically in pain that her particular
seat did not allow for interaction. While Katherine and Andrew could retreat
into private mental worlds and play happily by themselves, for Grace this
was an impossibility; she required company.

Every semester on the first day of class I told my university students,
in an effort to encourage them to participate freely in the class, "Learning
a foreign language is not academic, it is social." They might memorize a

word, hear it, write it, even recite it, but it would not be *their* word until they used it to express their own thoughts, until it became part of language. *The words of myself.*

❀

Andrew, unlike Grace, had seemingly gone months without uttering a single Chinese word other than "thank you" or "good-bye." While Katherine and Grace easily slipped into Chinese as their play language, Andrew never did. *The words of myself.* For Andrew, his words were in English.

I hoped that he just insisted on using English at home or with us, but spoke Chinese at school.

"Does Andrew speak Chinese in class?" I asked one of his teachers.

"You shihou," she told me. "Sometimes."

It was not an answer to inspire confidence. When we first moved here I was sure Andrew would be the first to pick up Chinese. He loved language. He was the youngest, and should have been the most impressionable. He started off well, but had been in a slump for quite some time. I consoled myself by remembering that he had learned to read during these months, and perhaps that required so much concentration in English that it simply smothered any attempts by Chinese to take residence in his young mind.

Mr. Jia had brought up an electrician in another attempt to fix our bathroom light. While the electrician was busy in the bathroom, Mr. Jia sat on the couch with the children. They were delighted to have him—Andrew in particular. Andrew made room for him on the couch, then cuddled up close to Mr. Jia and put his head on his shoulder. Mr. Jia asked him about the Winnie-the-Pooh book he was reading.

Andrew had been obsessed with Winnie-the-Pooh lately. It started when we read A. A. Milne's *The House at Pooh Corner* at bedtime, and continued when we rode the Winnie-the-Pooh ride at Hong Kong Disneyland. To my surprise, Andrew began to tell Mr. Jia about his book *in Chinese.*

Zhe shi yi ge daxiong. This is a bear. (Pooh)
Na shi yi ge xiao zhu. That is a small pig. (Piglet)

He was then a little stumped, but Mr. Jia told him the words for "kangaroo," *daishu* (literally meaning "pocket mouse"); "donkey," *lu* (for Eeyore); and *laohu*, meaning "tiger," for Andrew's beloved Tigger. I sat there in wonder, listening to my little boy speak Chinese.

The next day when I picked Andrew up from the kindergarten I brought along Hong, who babysat the kids occasionally. I wanted to use this chance to get a brief report from all the teachers, since Hong could translate for me.

But before she even saw that I had brought a personal translator, Andrew's teacher excitedly told me that *jintian ta shuo hen duo putonghua*—today he spoke a lot of Chinese! From her tone, this was obviously a departure from previous patterns. Finally, some of Andrew's words were in Chinese.

Our first year here, although the gates did not open until five, I routinely picked up the children from kindergarten between three and three thirty. In my childhood, school dismissed promptly at three fifteen, making me sure our children would all turn into pumpkins if I didn't fetch them at the same time. While I felt calm and productive throughout the day, by three it was as if the drugs had worn off. Nervous and jittery, unable to concentrate, I could think of nothing but the pressing need to get the children and release them from institutional confinement as soon as possible. Speed walking along Ying Sheng Road, I would arrive at the school gate, then either climb over the locked gate or call the kindergarten office and ask them to let me in.

Katherine, Grace, and Andrew would play together at the playground while their classmates toiled in the classroom, then we would walk slowly back home. My actions had some benefits. I think it helped ease them into this complete immersion, and besides, they were still quite small. If I was home early that day there was no reason for them to remain cooped up.

Gradually, however, we changed. The children realized that they were missing out on snack time if I arrived too early, so they asked me to postpone pickup time. Then I would show up to find them engrossed in an art project that they didn't want to leave unfinished. We then realized that it made no point to pick up the children merely a half-hour before everyone else, especially since it gave our children and us an aura of special treatment, something we tried to avoid. So finally we arrived at the gate along with the hordes of other parents and grandparents.

But now we realized what our efforts to protect our children from too much school had made them miss out on. Now when we picked them up our children ran out to the playground, each soon surrounded by a group of classmates. After school they finally had the chance to play freely with their friends. We would sit and watch from the side, amazed at the Chinese flowing so effortlessly from their lips. At last, the language was coming for them. *The words of myself.* They were children. And their words were expressed in play.

❀

In early June, Teacher Wang, a retired radiology professor who lived in the building opposite us, told me her family from America had come for a visit. Her son and daughter-in-law were both scientists at a Department of Energy lab in Tennessee, and they had two sons, eight-year-old Max and his baby brother.

Our children were so excited to have a playmate who spoke English, and after school they eagerly ran to the courtyard gate of Teacher Wang's house to ask if Max could play. Katherine's excitement surprised me. I thought she was perfectly content with all her Chinese-speaking friends. I followed them around as they played and laughed together speaking in English. Our children sounded awkward at first, for Chinese was their play language.

I noticed a difference between them. Katherine's English was more mature and grown-up sounding than Max's, naturally, because she usually spoke English with her parents or other adults. Max, on the other hand, had learned most of his English from his classmates, and he peppered his prose with "What the . . ." or "Dude!"

Katherine sometimes looked at him in confusion: "What are you talking about?" she would ask. Though Katherine's language was more mature, at the same time, it was more innocent, not having been exposed to the playground variety of English.

Max's mother explained that when he was born, her parents had come from China to help take care of him for the first eighteen months. After that he went to day care. Not knowing any English, he always played apart from all the other children. The teachers at the day care advised his mother to speak to him in English so that he could fit in and socialize with his peers.

This they did, hoping to get him comfortable in one language and culture before adding another. However, in Max's case, once firmly ensconced in the English-language world, he had little interest in Chinese. He would not answer when his parents began speaking to him in Chinese again. They took him to Sunday afternoon Chinese lessons, but he learned little. Currently at home they spoke to Max in Chinese, but he always answered them in English.

I thought about Teacher Wang, as she proudly watched her grandson play in the park. Out of love she had sought out English-speaking playmates for him; yet, he was unable to communicate with her, his own grandmother.

I listened to Max talking as he ran around the park with our children, his speech dripping with the various inflections of kidspeak, yet lacking the polite speech children should use when speaking with their elders. He had learned to speak English horizontally, completely from peers. It was missing that vertical element that came from regular speech with adults. I began to feel proud of our children and their sophisticated English: their big words, their large vocabularies, their complex sentences.

"I'm glad my children aren't exposed to such playground pulverization of the English language," I thought. "Won't their grandparents be so proud of them when they come to visit? Won't they compliment me on my children's way with words?"

But then I stopped. I began to wonder how our children sounded when they spoke Chinese. They certainly spoke the Chinese of the playground variety. Our children knew how to insult each other and call each other names in Chinese, and did so with much more ease than they did in English. In fact, when Katherine was angry in English she usually switched to colloquial Chinese to deliver her insult: *Ni shi yi ge da huai dan, ni shi yi ge xiao huai dan!* You are a big bad egg, you are a little bad egg! I realized that in listening to Max, I was hearing what my own children sounded like in Chinese.

I knew then that we had to broaden our children's linguistic world. People in our lives like Mr. Jia were even more important than I had realized, for they could give our children what Chris and I could not: interaction with authority figures in Chinese. They could speak to them in adult language, correct them when they spoke impolitely, and admonish them when they spoke out of turn.

Afterward I asked Katherine if she had had fun with Max and she nodded her head. "But it's so strange that he looks Chinese but can't speak Chinese!"

Max was a completely American kid in a Chinese body. He seemed more American than Katherine, and Katherine more Chinese than Max.

The words of myself. Perhaps more than our ethnicity or our appearance, it is our words that ultimately define us.

Max returned to the United States and our girls returned to speaking Chinese when they played outside with their friends. Actually, Grace and Katherine returned to speaking Chinese almost anytime they were together—at dinner, in bed at night, doing homework at the kitchen table. Chinese was the special language of sisters.

This made me happy. After two years in China, language would be no impediment, no wall, between Grace and her cultural heritage. The mysteries of her culture would be open to her. She could communicate with kids her age who looked just like her, comfortably travel anywhere in China and speak to anyone, and hopefully, one day, thank her foster family for caring for her that first year. I had wanted her to know Chinese to help bind her to her culture. That it had created a sisterly bond between my two daughters was just an added bonus. Language: *the words of ourselves.*

Chapter 29

西方

THE WEST

In reacting to contemporary events, we tend to forget just how deeply implicated we are in how China came to experience and view the modern world.

—ORVILLE SCHELL, *Newsweek*

❋

THUS FAR IT HAD BEEN A DIFFICULT 2008 FOR CHINA. THE YEAR BEGAN with China believing that this was their year, the Olympic year. This was the year China would show itself to the world, and the world would take notice: China was no longer weak, no longer poor and undeveloped, no longer backward as it once was. The world would see the shiny new airport terminal, the Bird's Nest stadium, the Water Cube aquatic center, and the new subway lines.

But while we were enjoying ourselves in Hong Kong and Thailand in January, historic snowstorms paralyzed many regions in southern China. Just as they dug themselves out from the snow, riots erupted in the streets of Lhasa, the capital of Tibet. This was followed immediately by the Olympic torch's ill-fated debut through international capitals, where pro-Tibetan demonstrators grabbed the headlines. Instead of greeting well-wishers as it traveled from London to Paris to San Francisco, the torch was met with opposition and condemnation. My students became angry, upset that the West was "using Tibet" as an excuse to malign China, wondering what the West really thought of China, humiliated when a CNN anchor labeled the Chinese "goons and thugs."

As representatives of all things Western, we had to answer for this. Our students asked questions like "Isn't this an excuse to keep China down? Doesn't the West want to keep China from growing stronger?"

During my Wednesday morning Chinese lesson, I spent the entire first hour talking (in English) about Tibet, with my normally apolitical (albeit Communist Party member) teacher.

"Why are there demonstrations?" Zhang asked me. "I don't understand it. I'm really so worried about this. I'm worried for the Olympic Games. Why would Western countries protest against our torch? What do you really think of us?"

I sighed. "It's complicated. But you must understand, since we were children, we were taught that communism was bad and democracy was good."

"You were? We were taught the opposite!" She laughed.

"So we have a hard time trusting countries that are not democracies," I explained.

"But why does the West concern itself with Tibet? We all know that life there is much better than when the Dalai was the ruler. I don't understand why you like the Dalai, when we know he is such a terrible man."

"Well, we have this image in our mind of a peaceful Dalai Lama who was chased out of his home by the Chinese army and who has now devoted his life to serving his people. How could we not like somebody like that? Besides, the Dalai Lama has said that he is against the current violence. In fact, he said he will resign if it continues, for such violence is against Buddhism."

"He said that?" She thought for a moment. "But, you know the Dalai is not just one person. There's a whole group around him."

"You mean the 'Dalai clique,'" I said. I remembered reading this pejorative phrase in *China Daily*.

She continued. "Yes, the Dalai, along with his 'clique,' is really masterminding affairs within Tibet. And they are manipulating your media about it too. So how can you think that he is actually a good person?"

"We just have a different idea, Zhang. We have a different image in our mind. We see him as . . ." I tried to think of an appropriate metaphor. "We see him as similar to Martin Luther King Jr." I said. "They are in the same category. The Dalai Lama, like Martin Luther King, is fighting for rights, fighting for freedom. In our eyes, we see the Tibetans as you see the blacks in America."

She looked at me strangely, then began to nod her head.

"Okay, I think I understand," she said.

She thought for a moment. "So you think he's like Martin Luther King. I understand your thinking now. But I still can't agree."

Later that week I read that Nancy Pelosi, Speaker of the House, was encouraging Bush to boycott the opening ceremonies of the Olympic Games because of the crackdown in Tibet. I knew the effect this would have on those around me, on all the Chinese people. I awoke in the middle of the night. Huddled over a glowing laptop, I began to write. Then after a few hours of spasmodic slumber, I woke again on a nocturnal jaunt in search of pen and paper to write more words that had burst through my subconscious. My brain, its contents under pressure, had words that demanded to be let out, exiting through my compulsive pen. Only when the words were written down would peace—and sleep—return. The next day, I turned this untidy bundle into an opinion piece and optimistically thought I might submit it to the *Washington Post* or the *New York Times* so that people, hopefully policy makers, would know that such a snub would do lasting harm to our bilateral relationship, not to mention deeply hurt ordinary Chinese people.

The next afternoon, I went to the *New York Times* website looking for how to submit an opinion piece. But I found the editors had already written one of their own. They had expressed an opinion completely contrary to mine. They were urging Bush to boycott the opening ceremonies as an expression of support for the Tibetan people.

I felt completely deflated. I had something urgent to say, but no one would listen to me, a mere English teacher in a small city in China. I left to pick up the children from their kindergarten, smarting about my voicelessness as I walked along Ying Sheng Road. Later that evening I submitted my opinion piece to the *Seattle Post-Intelligencer*. It was never published.

I continued to ponder this issue. I thought of the reaction I might get if I expressed my opinion in the United States, to these editors, even to my own family. I remember my father's raised eyebrows reproaching me when I mentioned during his visit that I thought communism was just a system, a neutral framework, not inherently good or evil. I had felt dismissed. What would people say about me now?

"You are too close to the situation," they might say.

"You have lost your objectivity."

"Maybe you have Stockholm syndrome, and you are identifying with your 'captors.'"

I could hear their nay-saying voices in my head. How was it possible that I was so at odds with the prevailing opinion in my own country? Had I really gotten too close to China, learned too much, lost my objectivity? Perhaps. But I didn't think so. No, I knew I hadn't. I knew there was a political correctness surrounding the Tibet issue, particularly media coverage of it that was preventing them from being objective.

Then I received an e-mail from Kimberly, one of my freshmen.

Dear Mrs. Arrington,

Recently, I am confused by some political issues. When the Olympic torch was carried in Paris some Tibetan separatists intended to damage it. And things like last year the German chancellor met the top separatist, the Dalai. I want to know, what are foreigners' opinions on Tibetan independence? Especially foreigners from Western countries like you.

Also, some Western media organizations such as CNN and BBC, have churned out untrue and distorted reports about the riots last month in Lhasa. Some photographs on their website had been deliberately cropped to denigrate China which misled the public about the recent protests in Tibet. What do you think about this?

Mrs. Arrington, I wrote this letter without any hostility. All I want to know is simply foreigners' real opinion of China. I wish you could give me the answer carefully and honestly.

Thank you very much.

Kimberly

Our organization advised us to stay away from political topics, and gave us a list of items, most of which started with the letter "T," that we should not bring up in class. But I had always tried to be genuine with my students, and in any case, they were the ones seeking me out. They were feeling mistreated at the hands of the West, and I was a Westerner they knew. I hoped after almost two years here, they trusted me. I thought I owed them answers to their questions.

On Tuesday in my freshman Oral English class, I started the class by letting them ask questions about Tibet.

"This is not about trying to determine who is right and who is wrong," I told them at the outset, "but rather, this is so we can understand each other better. I am not an expert on Tibet. I have never been there, and I have never spoken with a Tibetan. But I can tell you something regarding Western notions about Tibet."

Qingdao Cathy started off with the first question.

"What do you think about this person," she spat, "the Dalai?"

I told them that in our Western mind, we had an image of the Dalai Lama: a peaceful bespectacled monk garbed in saffron, kicked out of his country, only hoping for a peaceful end to this confrontation. I mean, he's barefoot! As I did with Zhang, I compared him to Martin Luther King Jr., saying that we viewed the two similarly, both fighting for freedom and rights for their people, both using nonviolent means to do so.

When I said this there was murmuring and shaking of their heads.

"No, he's not like Martin Luther King. He's a separatist!"

"But there you are perhaps not quite correct." I had to choose my words carefully, for I didn't like to even imply that their media was feeding them an incorrect picture.

"The Dalai Lama has said many times that he does not want independence. He says that Tibet is so small it cannot be its own country; that it must be part of China."

The students looked confused.

"He has also said that he supports the Olympic Games and thinks they are good for China."

They wrinkled their brows. "He really said those things? We have never heard about this."

They asked about the recent press reports of the riots in Tibet and the wide coverage in the Chinese press about biases in Western media coverage, which singled out CNN and the BBC for cropping pictures or showing pictures of police beating Tibetans in Nepal, but labeling the policemen as Chinese.

"You in the West say you have a free press," they challenged. "So are these the ways of a free press?"

"It was wrong for the press to do this," I told them. "But, to be honest, the Chinese government contributed to this problem because they didn't allow Western journalists into Tibet."

I continued. "In our Western mind, when someone does not allow the media to see something, we just assume you are doing bad things. If you weren't doing bad things, why not let the press in to take lots of photos and write lots of stories? Since journalists couldn't see, they fabricated. It was still wrong, but the Chinese policy indirectly contributed to it. And, since the media couldn't get to Tibet, they went to Dharamsala, the Dalai Lama's headquarters in India, and took their version of events for the truth."

I tried to explain the political correctness in the West concerning the Dalai Lama, but I found the term "political correctness" itself difficult to explain.

"Well, movie stars support the Dalai Lama," I told them.

"Like who?" they asked.

"Richard Gere."

"Who's that?"

"Well, how about Brad Pitt. He made a movie about the Dalai Lama."

"What?" Sighs of dismay. "Not Brad Pitt!"

I said that I rarely read anything negative about the Dalai Lama, and had never heard about the feudal society of serfs he had supposedly presided over as a teen ruler, until I came to China.

"In the West, you know we don't know very much about China," I told them. "I think many people in the West think that there are two kinds of people living in China—Chinese and Tibetans." They shook their heads and started murmuring.

"But we have fifty-six different ethnic groups in China."

"I know you do. But most people in the West don't know that. They think you are all the same, that you are all just Chinese. Except for the Tibetans." I drew my breath and continued. "In fact, I didn't know this either. I didn't know until I visited Guangxi province last year that there were so many different peoples in China, most with their own distinct language and culture. And most of them live here peacefully, in fact, more happily than most minorities living in Western countries. Actually, we in the West could even learn from you."

Andy, the class monitor, was shaking his head. "I still can't believe Brad Pitt," he said.

"Well, you should go to Tibet. Then you can see for yourself," a student told me.

"I would like to do this, but I can't."

"Why not?"

"Because Americans are not allowed to go to Tibet right now."

Silence.

Afterward I walked over to Kimberly and asked if I had answered her questions.

"Yes," she told me, "but I still don't really understand, what does the West think about China?"

The West. The big bully in the game of globalization. The West attracts the Chinese while simultaneously provoking feelings of disgust or resentment. Usually this term is combined to form separate but related words: Western technology. Western culture. Western religion. Western philosophy. Western governments. In Chinese it is written 西, and the word is just as loaded. 西餐—Western food, 西服—Western clothes.

Whether in English or Chinese, whether West or 西, this word makes a distinction and assigns people into camps. It can just as easily be defined by what it is not: not Eastern, not Oriental, not Communist, not like us. And for the past two hours I had been the representative of the West, needing to explain its mind-set, justify its actions, defend its approach.

"The West is not seizing on the Tibet issue to hurt China," I told Kimberly. "It genuinely thinks it should help people, especially those desiring freedom. Unfortunately, we sometimes try to help with a simplistic idea about the situation, not bothering to learn, frankly. You know we Americans are not good at learning foreign languages."

"But when the Dalai ruled Tibet they were serfs, you know, slaves. The rulers cut off the arms of the people and did all sorts of violent things. They have a much better life now."

I wanted to ask her why, if they had such a better life now, they were protesting. But I knew she would tell me the Dalai clique was masterminding the protests. And really, that was not her question. She felt the West was looking down on her, and she wanted to know why.

"America is a little afraid of China—it's so big, and has such a big army. There is an idea that as China grows richer and stronger, a confrontation between our two countries is inevitable."

"Don't they know that we have never invaded other countries? For us Chinese, our land, our territory is sacred. This is the most important thing. But we don't want the land of other countries. We're not like Japan. We've never been imperialistic. Don't they know this?"

She shook her head and gathered up her books to leave. I watched her and the other students file out of the classroom. I thought they would appreciate a greater understanding. But they seemed crushed. The world was not as simple as they had been led to believe. I had splattered mud on their mental picture of the vast blue skies over Tibet's Potala Palace. And the West, which they admired, held a view so contrary to the one they had been taught and which they had believed wholeheartedly.

Later that week I had lunch with Seven and Miriam.

"Seven?" I had asked, when he first told me his name.

"Yep, Seven," he replied confidently. "Just like the number."

The class monitor, Seven was a natural leader who told me his dream was to "become a great man in China." He once told me, as if confessing, that he was a Communist Party member.

"Of course you are," I told him.

"You knew this?" he asked incredulously.

"No, I didn't know. But I guessed it. You are the type to be a party member. You are the class monitor, you are ambitious, you love your country, so of course you would join the party."

"Actually, my grandfather joined the party. He fought against Chiang Kai-shek. My father also is a party member. And now me. So you see this is important for my family."

Seven and Miriam made an unlikely pair of friends. Miriam, who had shown us the old church buildings, was a Christian from the countryside nearby Tai'an. She would never join the party, but loved her country as much as Seven. Both were interested in international relations, though Miriam lacked the ambition of Seven. We had been meeting throughout the semester specifically to discuss these issues. The questions started immediately.

"Is there a bias in American reporting toward China?"

"I think there is," I had to admit. "There is pressure to insert negative items in reporting about China." I had realized this as I read the various news stories about the riots in Tibet. While censorship and propaganda certainly limited the free press of China, political correctness limited ours.

"Is this official pressure, from the government?" Seven asked. He then checked his cell phone for the latest headlines about the president of Taiwan's visit to Nanjing, which was occurring that week.

"No, not official pressure," I told him. "Grassroots pressure. Perhaps people have grown to expect negative reports; a completely positive report on China would seem strange to us."

"But why?" Miriam asked.

"It's complicated," I told her. "It has to do with Cold War history, when the world was so clearly and neatly divided into two camps: communism and democracy, evil and good, not free and free. We were raised to fear communism, taught that it was evil."

I continued, thinking the issue through myself as we talked. "And even though governments change, it takes a long time, decades, for this to trickle down to the thoughts and views of ordinary people."

On May 12, all such discussions ceased. We received news of the devastating earthquake in Wenchuan, Sichuan province. I remember consoling students as we talked about the estimated ten thousand killed, only to read the news the next morning and see the number climb unimaginably higher. But most of the time I felt that there was nothing I could say. There was nothing I could do but watch in shock as I saw schools that had turned into rubble, parents mourning their only child, families living in tents, motherless and fatherless children. I wrote nothing about the earthquake. For nearly two weeks, I wrote nothing about anything.

Chris and I received e-mails from family and friends wanting to be sure we were okay. We received other e-mails from those who knew we were far from the epicenter but still wanted to get in touch with us, to let us know they were thinking of China.

My friend Donna e-mailed me: "I am relieved for you guys, but grieving for those families who live in the area of the earthquake. As a mother of four little ones, I can hardly stand to look at the photo slideshows on the Internet and see mothers cradling their dead children. Along with the tragedy in Myanmar, it just all hits me in the primal mother gut and leaves me in tears."

And a few days later an e-mail from our friend Janice: "In light of all that has taken place in China over the last several weeks and months, I wanted to send an e-mail assuring you of our prayers. I know this is a tragic time for the people of China. Moving around the world has taught me one thing for sure. All people are basically the same. They love their families and want the best for them. They laugh and cry and hurt all the same."

Ordinary American people were deeply affected by the suffering of ordinary Chinese. Images of hurting and struggling Chinese people went straight into American homes where they were watched by ordinary American families. There was direct communication, people to people, not government to government and trickling down.

The earthquake also affected the grassroots feeling between China and Japan. The Chinese were deeply moved that Japanese teams were among the first to arrive to help in the difficult work of finding survivors. On TV they saw footage of collection boxes in Tokyo, and they heard reports that the Japanese had donated several million yuan toward earthquake relief. My students told me that for many of them, this changed their view of the Japanese.

The Japanese, for their part, deeply felt the Chinese pain, for the specter of earthquakes was something they were familiar with. The Chinese and Japanese governments had worked on a cautious and functional friendship for years, but it had not resonated with the people, it had not trickled down. The response of the ordinary Japanese to the earthquake changed this.

I thought about what Janice wrote.

All people are basically the same. They love their families and want the best
for them. They laugh and cry and hurt all the same.

Looking back, I could see that some of the anti-China protests were a backlash against China using the Olympics to "show off." I didn't see it at the time; perhaps I *was* caught up in it myself. I knew the historic wrongs China felt from the Opium Wars to the unequal treaties, from the Treaty of Versailles to the Rape of Nanking; I hoped for their sake that a successful Olympics would heal these wounds. But the Chinese do have some issues with pride. And no one likes a show-off.

But the earthquake changed all that. Instead of showing off material prosperity, development, or technology; the earthquake, far from Beijing's Bird Nest and Shanghai's Bund, showed the world the humanity of China. It showed the Chinese people, working, loving, crying, surviving, overcoming. And this was what the world really needed to see to change its opinion of China.

It was this side of China—its humanity—that had always been my China. I so wish it hadn't taken a disaster, but at last, I felt their China and my China were drawing closer.

Chapter 30

女

WOMAN

❦

DURING ONE OF MY EARLIER TUTORING SESSIONS WITH ZHANG SHE had explained the organization of the English Department so I could understand who was who. I couldn't help but notice that although the majority of teachers were women, the leadership was primarily men.

"When it comes time for promotion," she said, "they usually will hire a man instead of a woman." She said this with no bitterness or resignation whatsoever. She expected it.

"If I were hiring," she said, "I would prefer a man to a woman myself."

"Why?" I demanded. "You are a great teacher. What about Hu? Is he a better teacher than you?"

"No, of course not," she said.

"What about Zhou? Is he better than you?"

"No."

"Then why would you not hire the best teacher?"

"Well, someday I want to have a child and I won't be focused completely on teaching; I'll be focused on my family as well. A man can be focused completely on his job."

"That's not true," I retorted. "A man will be focused on basketball or watching TV or playing chess or some kind of hobby. Just because he isn't taking care of the child or cooking dinner doesn't mean he's working on class preparation; he's just doing something different."

"I never thought of it that way before," she said.

I felt pleased to have raised her awareness level.

❁

When I first moved to China, I thought I would be entering a society where men and women were equal. Communism, whatever its faults might be, was theoretically an egalitarian doctrine. Mao Zedong had emancipated the Chinese women, famously declaring that women held up half the sky. When Mao and the Communists came to power, women were publicly made equal; they were declared comrades. Women were expected to work for the revolution alongside the men, in direct divergence with the Confucian ideal of women ruling only the domestic sphere.

In the United States, I had often been the only woman or one of few women in an office. In the first few weeks that I rode the teacher bus here in China, I happily noticed the large number of women on board; in fact, it seemed a roughly fifty-fifty split. In China, most women rarely took more than a few months off when their child was born. Grandparents moved in to care for the baby, and the mother returned to work. Thus, there was no experience gap in China that handicapped American women who took time off to raise children before returning to the workforce. I enjoyed in China what I perceived to be an egalitarian atmosphere.

But as I went about my normal routines I began to realize that my perceptions were just a thin crust; scratch the surface and one soon reached the bedrock of history and tradition completely contrary to my initial ideas.

As an example, each class of students was assigned a monitor, a class leader, who organized the class and liaised with the university administration. The monitor was invariably a male student. This fact stood out because in most of my classes I taught English majors, who were 90 percent female.

"Why is the class monitor always a male student?" I asked my students.

"We've never really thought about this before," they said. "It has been this way since primary school."

"It's because boys are born with natural leadership qualities," one female student told me.

One class of freshmen told me their faculty adviser had insisted that a male student be chosen as the class monitor. I couldn't believe such overt discrimination. Then I found out that this faculty adviser was a woman.

The lack of women in leadership was not just among the students.

There was also a noticeable dearth of women in leadership positions in the administration and among the faculty. I talked to Teacher Chen from the English Department about this.

She nodded her head. "Yes, the traditional ways are still strong. You know we have a saying." She wrote it down for me:

头发长，见识段

Hair Long, Worldview Short.

"It is this idea," she said, "that keeps women out of leadership. In the old days women stayed in the home, so they didn't know much about the world. Of course things are different now, but the idea is still there."

Several months after my initial conversation with Zhang the two of us had lunch with another colleague from the English Department, Zhao. Zhang and I recalled our initial conversation about women in leadership. But I was shocked when she told me that I had not changed her thinking at all. She had simply demurred to be polite.

"No, I still think the same. Men are better suited for leadership because they don't have so many family responsibilities."

"Besides," added Zhao, who had received her master's degree in Shanghai, "men are better at making decisions; women tend to waffle a bit more. They make one decision but then they change their mind. It's not good for leadership."

I was flabbergasted. I was hearing words that raised my ire and put me in full battle mode. But whom was I supposed to fight? Against whom should I begin flinging my verbal arrows, launching my justifiable assault? These words were from the women themselves, from these articulate, well-educated, modern women who were my friends.

The Chinese women were discriminating against themselves.

It has been this way for thousands of years, going back to Confucius (551–479 BC) and even earlier. His writings had been the staple diet for generations of Chinese students, all the way up to the twentieth century. Modern subjects like math, science, and English now crowded Confucius out of the curriculum. But while the writings of Confucius were no longer subject matter, his teachings about women, obedience, order, and government had morphed into Chinese culture, making the two all but indistinguishable.

Perhaps it was our proximity to Qufu, the hometown of Confucius, that meant that while Beijing was open-minded, and Guangzhou progressive, Shandong people still acted as if the old sage might be looking down on them, and never dared to stray too far from his conservative ideals, especially in regard to the status of women. Confucius taught a strict hierarchy of obedience in relationships, with women in the deferential and submissive position. He stated:

> Women and people of low birth are hard to deal with. If you are friendly with them, they get out of hand, and if you keep your distance, they resent it.

Ban Zhao (AD 45–116), an eminent female historian of the Han Dynasty (206 BC–AD 220), codified traditional Confucian thinking into her *Lessons for Women*, a widely circulated instruction guide for her daughters. She outlined the "four virtues" as such:

> There are four edifying behavioral characteristics for women: the first is womanly virtue (*fude*), the second is womanly speech (*fuyan*), the third is womanly manner (*fuyong*), and the fourth is womanly merit (*fugong*). What is womanly virtue? She does not distinguish herself in talent and intelligence. What is womanly speech? She does not sharpen her language and speech. What is womanly manner? She does not seek to be outwardly beautiful or ornamented. What is womanly merit? She does not outperform others in her skills and cleverness.

Together with the three traditional "obediences" for women (when a woman is in her maiden home she obeys her father; when married she obeys her husband; and when her husband dies she obeys her son), these were summarized in a four-character Chinese proverb, 三从四德 (three obediences, four virtues), which had long been part of traditional Chinese thought. Even the character for women, 女, most experts agree, is a pictograph of a woman in a kneeling, submissive posture.

Mao sought to change all of this. He was the anti-Confucius, giving women the right to divorce and own property; setting quotas for women in civil-service positions, and putting as much money into women's sports as men's. But what he could not change, was millennia of thinking.

Whenever I talked to a Chinese woman about the status of women in China, she usually supplied me with a *chengyu*:

嫁出去的女儿，泼出去的水

To marry off a daughter is like pouring out water.

三个女人一台戏

Put three women together and you have a drama.

男尊女卑

Man is superior to woman.

There seemed to be no limit to these sayings. And every woman knew them. I ran into Chris's Chinese tutor and asked her about women and Mao and tradition.

"Yes, Mao gave us the right to divorce, to own property, to get educated." She sighed and seemed pensive. "He told us we held up half the sky. But we don't really believe this. None of us do. Here is a better phrase to describe the status of women in China." She wrote down four characters and translated them for me:

重男轻女

Respect men. Look down on women.

"The problem," she added, "is that we women even think this of ourselves. And we have thought this for so long now, that it is hard to change."

In traditional China, throughout a woman's life, various occasions put her firmly in a place of submission and powerlessness. It started with birth.

In the *Book of Songs* (1000–700 BC) is found this poem:

> *When a son is born,*
> *Let him sleep on the bed,*
>   *Clothe him with fine clothes,*
> *And give him jade to play . . .*
>   *When a daughter is born,*
> *Let her sleep on the ground,*
>   *Wrap her in common wrappings,*
> *And give broken tiles to play . . .*

Having a son was one of few things that could change a woman's status. Throughout her life, a few key events could change her fate: a good marriage, the death of a woman with higher status in the household, but most of all, the birth of a son. A son gave her derivative status as his mother. It meant someday she would be a mother-in-law herself, perhaps the only power she might ever wield.

But there was something else. In a world where a woman possessed little—neither status, nor possessions, nor learning, nor freedom, nor power—a son was the one thing in her life that would truly be her own. Her natal family was not hers to keep. She would always be a stranger in her husband's home. A daughter would eventually marry out and leave her. But a son was hers, and would always be hers. So it was natural for even little girls to go to the temples and pray that someday they might be the mother of many sons. It was this—the cult of the son—that began this pattern of discrimination of women against their own gender.

Demonstrating this cult, at birth, sometimes a daughter would be given a name such as 招娣, meaning "calling for a little brother," thereby voicing her parents' disappointment in her birth and their hope for a little brother next time.

As a young daughter grew up, she might hear her father say that she was 赔钱货—"inventory that creates only loss." Her family would have to struggle to prepare a dowry for her, only to have her become the possession of her husband and mother-in-law. Even into the last century, she prepared for her own marriage at the age of seven or eight by going through the excruciatingly painful foot-binding. Only with bound feet, created at the price of freedom—for she would never be able to walk fast or far—could she hope to achieve a good match and a good future.

Once a grown woman, she would be confined to the inner realm of the home. This was reflected in the language. A classical term for wife was 贱内, meaning "humble inside," while the husband was termed 外子, "outside person," reflecting his expected preoccupation with external affairs. Once married, it was her primary duty to produce sons. If she did not, this provided a legal reason for her husband to take a concubine.

Once her husband died, she should obey her son. Not only that, she was bound by a "cult of chastity," forbidden to remarry out of respect for her dead husband, regardless of her material circumstances. Of course China has changed much since those days. But these traditions remained in force even into the last century.

China's modern women have no such constraints. Most happily determine their own destiny, no longer subjected to the whims of fate. Women are now entrepreneurs, teachers, and corporate managers. While their grandmothers couldn't travel as a result of bound feet, and their great-grandmothers were confined to women's chambers by tradition, their mothers marched with Mao, who declared an end to the old days.

But though their feet can now wander, and though today's Chinese women go to work daily in factories and universities, in businesses and government, I wondered if their minds had broken free from their grandmothers' constraints. For although their bodies had left the women's chambers, their spirits seemed reluctant to travel far.

China is justly proud of its long history and rich culture. But culture doesn't only mean art, language, poetry, architecture, and ceremony, all of which China has in abundance. It also means duties, obligations, manners, rituals, and traditions, and China's long history has layer upon layer, which have become more intricate and complex as the centuries have passed. These layers are not easily disentangled because China happened upon the twenty-first century. In the case of China's women, culture gives them not only their identity, but also their limits.

I often thought about limits when I thought of the Chinese. There are the limits of the household registration system, called *hukou*, which stipulates the city in which each person is allowed to live and work. Then there are the limits imposed by their relationship-oriented society. My students' dreams are necessarily tempered by the knowledge that they can go only as far as their relationships, or their parents' relationships, can take them. Their own abilities are but a secondary factor. There are the limits put upon education, where knowledge is limited to the textbook, and must conform to the limits of the "one correct answer."

The Chinese characters themselves have limits. Some characters representing ideas that have obvious boundaries, such as the characters for garden, 园, country, 国, or prison, 囹圄, contain literal boxes. But whether a 口 is there or not, an imaginary box puts limits or boundaries on each character. These boxes are on the notebooks children use to practice writing. No stray tails or curves should go outside the box.

And I often mused whether, like the Chinese characters with those invisible boxes, women are boxed in by their self-deprecating ideas. Seeing these limits accepted by my students, especially by my female students, limits that were already intolerable to my young children, made me understand better who I was.

I might disagree with the war in Iraq, be embarrassed by my country's occasional arrogance, and abhor the violence and decadence shown in the movies that we export around the world, but I couldn't disown this country that had pushed my bounds so far, that had told me my abilities, my imagination, my work ethic were my only limitations. Perhaps it was this, more than anything else, that made me an American.

And it was this that distinguished me, as an American mother, from the Chinese mother Grace might have had. As the mother of two daughters, I hoped that they too would know no limits but their own dreams.

Chapter 31

运动
SPORTS

Mencius [had a] famous argument that the man who works with his mind rules and man who labors with physical strength is ruled. This idea, I am afraid, greatly and negatively affected Chinese men's attitude toward physical exercises for perhaps over one thousand years.

—XU GUOQI, author of *Olympic Dreams: China and Sports, 1895–2008*

❀

SOMETHING HAPPENED FOR THE FIRST TIME IN OUR ALMOST TWO YEARS in China: it rained for more than twenty-four hours nonstop. It rained all day and we still heard the rain pounding as we put the children to bed. When I took the early morning bus to the new campus it was still lightly drizzling. Not until mid-morning, when my Chinese lesson finished, did the rain finally stop. I hopped into a taxi for the ride back to the old campus. On the way I fixated on Mount Tai. Thanks to the rain washing away all the pollution, it looked greener than I had ever seen it. The taxi dropped me off on the street so I could add money to my cell phone. That was when the real surprise awaited me: I beheld all the bright colors and clear definitions on this so familiar street. I felt as though I had been living in an out-of-focus world for nearly two years and suddenly everything had become clear and crisp.

That weekend I spent a lot of time outdoors watching the children as they played. When I looked at the mountain, there were great swaths of kelly green amid the dark evergreens—new leaves signaling the arrival of spring—clearly defined, as though the Painter had used broad brushstrokes to paint patches of deciduous among the pine trees; although, in his flourish, some drops had flown off the brush leaving scatterings of deciduous trees here and there.

❀

Friday was the annual sports meet for our university, always held in the spring. Last year we were not invited to attend and I had felt left out, although Chris and I had used the day to climb Mount Tai. This year I decided to be there no matter what.

I started by riding an overcrowded bus. Standing all around me at 6:50 a.m. were fellow teachers, wearing identical sweat suits, with black leather loafers to complete the ensemble. China's fitness culture is far different from America's. Daily life—climbing stairs, walking home laden with groceries, hanging laundry, biking to and fro—usually provides activity enough for most. For the elderly, there is also Tai Chi, and for the younger generation, basketball and Ping-Pong.

The Chinese word for "sports" intrigued me, because both characters, 运动 (each of which mean "to move"), contain the radical for "clouds": 云. My research found that in their traditional forms, 運動, they each had different components, not related to clouds at all. So the decision to use clouds must have occurred at the time of simplification this century.

I asked Mr. Jia about this.

"Well," he said, pointing at the sky, "clouds move, don't they?"

I suppose they do.

❀

When the bus pulled into the new campus a little after seven I saw classes of students standing in formation, wearing the matching warm-up suits they were issued as freshmen for mandatory military training. I walked into our university's stadium and found a seat. My only other time here was when I gave a welcoming speech to the freshmen last fall. Then, as now, I was the only Westerner.

The stadium was strewn with red banners containing giant white Chinese characters. I ran into Christina and Edie, two of my regulars from office hours. They asked their monitor for permission to sit with me instead of with their class in the bleachers. They gave me a *baozi*, a steamed bun filled with a spicy meat patty. I was grateful since I hadn't eaten breakfast.

Behind me, a pair of elderly grandparents sat with their grandson. The grandmother had just a few yellowish teeth poking out of her gums. The grandfather said to me, "You have three children, don't you?" His grandson attended the same kindergarten as our children.

At 8:00 a.m. the ceremony started. First, girls dressed in red plaid miniskirts, white shirts, and red ties marched in with the Chinese flag. Then, each class marched in formation around the track and in front of the reviewing stand, composed of the various university deans and vice presidents. As they approached the reviewing stand, they changed to a smart goose step. They continued past the stand to the back of the track, then marched onto the field itself.

Edie turned to me. "When we see this," she said, gesturing to the formations on the field and the marching students still pouring into the stadium, "the only thing we think of is that China has *so many people*."

After all the students marched by, it was time for the faculty. They marched in formation like the students, holding large red flags with gold characters announcing their department. They forwent the goose step, instead waving to the reviewing stand or doffing their caps.

After the national anthem, there were several mass demonstrations: aerobics, Tai Chi, Tai Chi with swords, and so on. By this time Edie and Christina had been chased away by a gentleman who said that this area of the stadium was only for teachers. In fact, there were still seats left, and these were taken by other students I didn't know. One of them decided it was his job to facilitate my experience, and continually told the people standing in front of me to sit down or to put their sun umbrellas away so they didn't block my view. I found the entire situation uncomfortable. At one point I turned around to take a picture of the people behind me, the grandparents and their grandchild. The student decided he needed to position and pose everybody, meaning that whenever I tried to take a shot, his long arm appeared in the picture.

With the ceremony over, the meet itself began. I only ever saw the hundred-meter dash, for there were several heats. As the heats got ready, the drums would beat and students would cheer *jia you* in unison. I was quite relieved when my student facilitator told me he had to leave and could no longer help me. But to my chagrin, he was quickly replaced by another student. This student sat quietly for some time, then suddenly looked at me and said, "Do you mind if I ask you several questions?"

I realized, too late, that I was trapped by someone wanting to practice his spoken English.

"Well . . . no, it's okay," I said weakly.

"Where are you from? What is the name of your hometown? Are you married? Is your husband a teacher? Do you have any children? Why does the American flag have fifty stars?" all came in rapid succession.

At that point, I decided that I had experienced the gist of the sports meet, and it was time for me to depart. After answering a few questions, I politely excused myself, walked to the main gate, and caught the No. 9 bus back into town. Many students had the same idea, so I ended the event as I started, by standing on a crowded bus. China has *so many people*, I thought to myself.

❀

Our children had their annual sports meet the following week. The teachers had organized several relays in which parents/grandparents and children were teammates. On Tuesday, I taught all day, so Chris and Katherine enjoyed the event together. Chris made quite a spectacle of himself trying to get a small hula hoop repeatedly over his six-foot-two-inch frame bedecked with camera equipment.

On Wednesday it was my turn, with Grace's meet in the morning and Andrew's in the afternoon. Grace took off the moment the teacher yelled *"Kaishi!"* (Start!) and would have won several events had she not been teamed up with me. Unlike her father, she particularly excelled at lithely crawling through hula hoops. Andrew certainly didn't win any heats, but he had so much fun, he didn't notice. We were just happy that he set his books down long enough to participate. Some of the events were familiar to us (the three-legged race), and others not so familiar (throw the balls into mother's apron).

At the university sports meet I had to needle my way in just to observe. But in the kindergarten sports meet, I ran relays, carried children on my back, and caught balls in my apron; in short, I was a vital participant, not just allowed, but expected. I realized that our life in the kindergarten was the most authentically Chinese part of our life in China. In our jobs we spoke English, were titled "foreign teachers," and had offices separate from the rest of the faculty. We lived apart from the others in the foreign teachers' building where we ate some Chinese, but a lot of Western food.

But in the kindergarten, we were the same as everyone else, apart from having three children. Our children started the day lined up outside performing choreographed morning exercises. They carefully wrote the strokes and flourishes of Chinese characters, ate tofu and *mantou* for lunch, and, after naptime, practiced math and Oriental dancing. After school we stood with the crowds of other parents and grandparents to pick up our children, spoke Chinese to their teachers, watched our children play with their classmates on the playground. Then we all walked home together, the children arm in arm with their friends, we parents perhaps picking up some groceries and *bing* on the way.

❁

We had enjoyed the cool crisp April weather and felt so lucky that spring lasted an entire month this year, unlike last year when it was over in a week. We enjoyed seeing the peach blossoms and the wisteria, and walking under green leafy arches along the alleys of the old campus. Many a strong spring wind blew the pollution away, revealing the mountain and its various shades of vermilion.

But May arrived and the heat descended abruptly. We were now sticky and sweaty everywhere. In a rush, we pulled the giant duffel bag of summer clothes off its closet perch, exchanging quilted pants and turtleneck sweaters for shorts and T-shirts.

Middle-aged men pulled out their chess tables and stools, moving about flat round wooden pieces with Chinese characters imprinted on the top, red for one side, black for the opposing.

The children discovered two cherry trees nearby, one in our very own courtyard, the other in the park. Initially the cherries were sour, but the heat wave ripened them quickly. The children eagerly climbed trees and pulled down branches in search of soft, ripe cherries. The cherries were yellow and tangier than the red ones we were used to, but still delicious.

Like the previous spring, we planted beans in the courtyard, assisted by Mr. Jia. The children rushed downstairs every morning to inspect their beans, taking excited note of the progress.

And now, bikes. Last summer at home in the United States our children were the only ones their age who couldn't ride. We felt we were depriving them of a normal childhood. By the time we returned to China the cold weather was on its way so we decided to wait until spring. Chris and I looked at several of the department stores we frequented, but found the display of children's bikes both limited and expensive. We knew there had to be a bike store. But we didn't know where to find it or whom to ask.

Friday was the Labor Day holiday. Hong came over to watch the kids while Chris and I went to look once more for bikes. First we got haircuts, always a great treat. It begins with the shampoo, the first phase, done entirely sitting up in the chair. They would squirt some water on our heads, add shampoo, form a lather, and gradually massage it over the rest of the head. Only then would we go to the sink to rinse off. Back in our chairs, it would be time for the general massage—neck, back, arms, hands, fingers. Then the actual haircut begins. After that, back to the sink for a second hair wash. Then to the chair for final styling. The entire lengthy process costs 20 yuan, about $3.

At some point in my massage I thought that perhaps the hairdressers would know the best place to buy children's bikes. In my hometown, hairdressers knew who was getting ready to sell their house, who was getting ready to get divorced, and who was getting ready to get pregnant. The beauty salon was the central telephone switchboard for community information. Perhaps it was the same in China.

So I asked. My hair washer/massage therapist (a different person than the hair stylist) asked some of the others in the shop. After much conversing in Chinese, they told us: "Qingnian Lu."

Qingnian Lu! The same road as the church.

"Is it near McDonald's?" I asked in Chinese.

"Yes, it's south of McDonald's."

"How far?"

"Not far. South of McDonald's is the Tai'an Department Store, and about twenty meters south of that is where you can find the bikes."

The next day was Saturday. Chris and I decided to take the children to lunch at McDonald's, then walk south and see what we could find. We didn't have our expectations too high; after all, we had received all the directions in Chinese. But it was a beautiful day and either way it would be a nice walk.

Heading south across the intersection we saw the Tai'an Department Store. We continued walking and twenty meters later, just as they said, we walked into the biggest bicycle store we had ever seen. It was filled with bicycles, all jammed next to one another in a gigantic basement. The kids quickly found ones they liked, and we were delighted with prices about half the department store prices. They did a few test rides, and we did a bit of bargaining. Then, climbing into two taxis with three bikes and three children, we were off.

The first time Mr. Jia saw the bikes he asked me, "How much?"

I was a little nervous, because shortly before we had bought a new bookshelf/doll house for the children. When I had told him how much we paid, both he and his wife groaned loudly and declared *tai gui le* (too expensive). So I timidly said, "About two hundred forty yuan."

He nodded his head approvingly. *"Hai keyi,"* he said. "Not bad."

Feeling glad that I had not only found the best local place to buy bikes, but had also paid a local price, I began to carry the bikes down the courtyard steps so the kids could ride. As I did, a woman looked at Andrew's bike.

"It's beautiful!" she said in Chinese. "How much?"

"Two hundred forty yuan."

She nodded in approval. "Where did you buy it?"

I gave her the directions from McDonald's. She walked off.

I stood there for a moment. I, a foreigner, had just been asked by a local Chinese where to buy something. I sat down on the courtyard steps in great satisfaction.

❀

The gate of our courtyard opened onto the street. Mr. Jia often spent his time on these steps, greeting his friends or chatting with neighbors. I frequently sat on the steps as well. It was virtually always shady, thanks to the trees lining the sidewalk. I would watch the children ride bikes or play hide-and-seek—covering their eyes, counting *yi, er, san, si*—protected by the bamboo grove and overwatched by the old brick courtyards.

Sometimes when I brought the kids upstairs for dinner, Chris would stay out on the steps with Mr. Jia, just hanging out with him and his friends, chatting about this or that. One time Teacher Chen from our English Department stopped to chat for a while.

As she prepared to leave, she said to Chris, "You know, Mr. Jia and I were talking, and we said we no longer think of you as *laowai*, but rather as just part of . . ." She couldn't put her finger on the exact word in English she wanted to use.

"The community," Chris answered for her, "as part of the community."

She nodded her head vigorously.

"Yes," he told her. "We feel the exact same way."

Over the course of two years of sitting on those courtyard steps, while we swatted away the mosquitoes and listened to the crickets in the trees above, the people in our neighborhood had begun to take shape. The lady wearing the white baseball cap stringing a clothesline between two trees had an elderly mother in a wheelchair, whom she often took outside to get fresh air and practice walking a few steps. Next door to her lived Teacher Wang, whose son, daughter-in-law, and two grandsons lived in America. Across from the steps were the dumpsters, which The Trash Lady and elderly retired teachers would comb for treasures or recycling.

When I am old, I wondered, as I observed the many elderly around me, will I return to this place? Will I sit in the pavilion and close my eyes, and suddenly see our children when they were small, running around and playing in Chinese, with this mountain still in the background, gazing down at me then as it does now?

I looked around. The park was crowded with students reading aloud from their textbooks, preparing for finals. Grandparents walked by carrying their grandchildren. Some retired teachers went past us carrying home thermos flasks, freshly filled with hot water from the boiler plant. From an apartment above a middle school boy practiced his violin, and the sounds wafted out the window of his fifth-floor apartment.

I realized that in our months of hanging out on the courtyard steps, the neighborhood children had grown up. Mr. Jia's youngest granddaughter, born after we had arrived, was now walking around with a full head of hair. Prepubescent girls we often saw on the playground had sprouted, lost their baby fat, and begun to look like young ladies. Teacher Qi's son, once just a toddler, was now a big boy, talking a mile a minute.

Our own children had changed too. They used to play at a distance from the other children, engaging in their own English-language games. Now they were part of the neighborhood gaggle. Katherine would soon leave the kindergarten, where we had grown so comfortable, to start first grade at Ying Sheng Road primary school in the fall. Grace had enough hair for pigtails. And Andrew was finally potty-trained.

Tai'an was changing. Construction was occurring constantly. Luxury single-family homes and duplexes had just been built next to the five-star Ramada on Ying Sheng Road. Tai'an now scored a "6" on the McDonald's/KFC globalization index: three KFCs had been built in the two years since our arrival. We even heard rumors that a Walmart was being built and a Starbucks planned.

I watched my children happily ride their bicycles. I looked at Grace, laughing and playing with Katherine and their friends. She was five years old and, as of yet, had never asked me any complicated questions about her adoption. She never wondered why she looked different from everyone else in the family, never asked me if I was her real mom.

She was content to be in a circle of love, secure in her knowledge that she was the middle child, number two of three, linked to Katherine by bonds of pretty dresses and Barbies, and with Andrew by reading books and roughhousing, enjoying her role as the link between oldest and youngest. In our two years here, she had proudly learned Chinese, begun referring to herself as a Chinese-American, and completely adapted to her days in Chinese kindergarten. But fundamentally, when it came down to who she really was, she was still my Grace who loved life, loved people, and put herself fully into every single activity. I didn't really think she had changed at all.

That weekend a Chinese friend came to visit, and we took her to one of our local tourist attractions, the Dai temple complex, a fun place for children with labyrinths of interlocking courtyards and lots of stone animals to climb. The children enjoyed throwing bits of *mantou* into the fishpond, and when the fish had had their fill, eating the *mantou* themselves. "Can we go buy some more *mantou*?" they asked me.

"Well, I was going to take you to McDonald's," I said, sure that they would be so excited they would forget all about some bland steamed bread. But I got no reaction.

I repeated: "It's *mantou* or McDonald's. Which one?" All three children stared up at me, rather perplexed at the choice.

In the end we picked up a bag of *mantou* from an older gentleman on the street and continued on to the corner and bought Happy Meals at McDonald's. The children, without seeming to see any contradiction, contentedly ate bites of *mantou* from one hand while noshing on Chicken McNuggets from the other.

Chapter 32

自由
FREEDOM

❀

MY TUTOR ZHANG AND I STARTED A NEW LESSON IN MY CHINESE TEXT- book, and as usual, the first thing we did was go over new vocabu- lary. As I read down the list, I came to 千万别, which literally means "1,000 10,000 times not," but was normally translated as "under no circum- stances," or, colloquially, "not a chance."

千
1,000

万
10,000

别
NOT

UNDER NO CIRCUMSTANCES

After nearly two years here I still found this one of the most interest- ing facets of Chinese: how it used concrete pictographs to express abstract concepts. I gazed at the phrase for a while, then offhandedly commented to Zhang: "I like this one."

She started laughing.

"Why are you laughing?" I asked her.

"Because you treat them like they are people, liking this one and not liking that one."

I thought about what she said. "No, I don't think of the characters as people. It's more like I feel like I'm walking through an art museum. Each character is a work of art and some of them I really appreciate. I want to gaze at them longer and understand their hidden meaning."

❦

On Tuesday morning my students performed role-plays based on Chinese proverbs. At noon I had scheduled lunch with Linda and Milly, two of my students from last year. We ate at my new favorite restaurant, a Lanzhou-style beef and noodles joint run by some Muslim Hui people, one of China's minorities. Linda, Milly, and I talked about the proverbs. I asked them why most of these proverbs came from the Spring and Autumn (770–476 BC) or Warring States (475–221 BC) periods of Chinese history.

They thought for a moment, then Milly said, "It's because at that time there were a lot of scholars in China. And there was also lot of war and turmoil, so much wisdom was required of the people."

Linda added, "Not only that, but at that time, the thoughts of the people were free. They could say anything they wanted, and there would be no punishment."

"Really!" I said. "That's interesting. Has it always been this way in Chinese history?"

"No," she replied. "During the Qing Dynasty [1644–1911], you know the last dynasty in China, we say in Chinese, *wenzi yu*, it means 'character prison.'" She wrote down the characters in my notebook: 文字狱, then continued. "At this time the thoughts were not free, and the dynasty declined and China was weak."

"Also," added Milly, "during the Han Dynasty [206 BC–AD 220], the saying was *fenshu kengru*," and she wrote the characters 焚书坑儒. "The meaning is, 'burn the books, bury the scholars.'"

"What about now?" I asked. "How is the freedom of thought now?"

"Free," said Milly.

"Yes, completely free," added Linda.

Oh, come on! I thought. "Really, but what about the Cultural Revolution? Were the thoughts completely free then?"

"Well," explained Linda. "I think each dynasty starts out suppressing the people, but then gradually it becomes more free."

The following day during office hours we also discussed freedom, starting with mention of the CNN anchor who, referring to the recent violence in Tibet, had called the Chinese "goons and thugs." My students knew all about this. They were incensed.

"Why was he allowed to say these things?" they asked. "Won't your government do anything about it? Isn't it against the law?"

"First, most Americans don't agree with him," I said. "But it's about freedom. Should we put this man in jail just for stating his opinion, even if it is wrong, even if it is stupid?"

"Do you have the freedom to tell hurtful lies about other countries?"

"Well, yes we do, to a degree."

I mentioned my view that while freedom was of primary importance to Americans, Chinese held other values to be more important, such as harmony and unity in their society.

"Well, I don't know," said Christina. "I think freedom is very important."

"Yes, Christina, I know you do. But you are not like most," I countered.

She nodded in acknowledgment, then thought for a moment. "But I think Chinese people believe they *do* have freedom."

I thought about my conversations the day before with Linda and Milly.

Christina was still deep in thought. "How do you in the West think we don't have freedom?"

I really shouldn't answer this question, I thought. But once I opened my mouth the words just tumbled out. "Well, you can't say anything you want to in the newspapers. You can't change your government. You can't move to a different city. You can't have as many children as you want to. You can't worship God if you want to." I paused. "Those are the things that generally come to mind in the West."

But the Chinese don't think of freedom like we do in the West. Freedom is about the individual, and in China, the individual does not have primacy. In Chinese, the word for freedom actually contains the character for the individual self, *zi*, written 自. Together with the second character, 由,

it is pronounced *ziyou*, and has the literal meaning "let yourself" (do what you want to do). When I say the word "freedom" in English, I think of a true-blue ideal, something soldiers have died for. But when I say *ziyou*, it has sort of a self-centered ring to it.

I e-mailed my Chinese friend Ruby and asked her what Chinese people thought about freedom. She said the history books are filled with heroes who fought for freedom for their country or freedom for their people, but the idea of *individual* freedom seemed both strange and inaccessible to most ordinary Chinese.

This has nothing to do with their political system; rather, it has everything to do with their relationship-based society. Their parents have always told them what to do. Their grandparents have always told them what to do. Individual desires are subservient to family or group wishes. Duties and obligations abound. Make no mistake, their safety net is strong. But they are enmeshed in it, unable to extricate themselves, living their lives with the weight of others' expectations, constantly caring what others think.

Freedom, in such a society, has little place. Their lives are filled with real things like family and security. There is necessarily little regard for an abstract, out-of-reach concept like freedom.

The next week in office hours only two students showed up: Qingdao Cathy and Lucas. The topic that day turned out to be Marxism. As high school students, they had been required to take several classes titled "Politics." Actually, they were classical Marxist theory.

I was surprised that there was still such an emphasis on Marxist theory since China itself has followed the capitalist route for at least twenty years. I thought they had disposed of Marx when they disbanded the communes.

"Why are Chinese students still required to study Marxist theory?" I asked them.

"Because China follows Marxist theory," answered Qingdao Cathy.

I laughed. "How can anybody believe this when they walk out of their classroom to the shopping street and see so much capitalism?"

"But this capitalism is a stage in Marx's progression," she answered. "I don't remember how it works exactly."

"But there are no more communes!" I said. "China has moved away from communism and dismantled the communes. It has embraced the free market and capitalism. This isn't just me saying this. Go out on the street and look for yourself!"

"Yes, I know," admitted Qingdao Cathy. "None of us believe this anymore."

"So you cannot say that China is Communist."

"Oh no," said Qingdao Cathy. "We have not reached communism yet. Perhaps in a hundred years when everyone is selfless and can live together happily, then we will reach communism."

"Cathy, you're confusing me. You just told me you don't believe this, that nobody does."

"Yes, I know. None of us believe it," she said. "But we have to recite it on the exam. So there's no point in questioning it."

I stared at Qingdao Cathy. One moment she agreed with me, the next moment she disagreed. What was going on? It was like there were two voices inside her, contradicting themselves.

I then realized that she, like her peers, had to maintain two spheres of knowledge. One was that which was learned in school and subject to examination; the other was that which she really believed. Qingdao Cathy, at the moment, was confusing these two spheres, one moment speaking from one, the next moment from the other, saying completely contradictory statements, utterly confusing me.

She went on to elucidate the several levels of "heavens" before one finally achieved nirvana, communism, saying that perhaps about 2020 they would move up from socialism to the next level.

"But Cathy, you are not moving toward communism. You are moving away from communism. You were closer to communism in the 1950s than you are now!"

"Mrs. Arrington, I've been taught this for years. Two hours a week in office hours with you can't change all that teaching."

"Cathy, I don't want it to be me that changes your thinking. Go and think for yourself. Make your own opinion. Don't just accept what I say."

At that point Chris walked in, having finished his class early. I jumped at my target. "Okay, Chris, is China Communist or capitalist?" I asked him.

"Well, in its political system, it is Communist. In its economic system, it is Communist with many characteristics of capitalism."

"Very good answer!" I told him. My students applauded.

"Much better than yours," Qingdao Cathy said.

I had tried to remain dispassionate about China's education system. I understood the thousands of years of exam culture. I told myself it was just a system. The Exam was certainly flawed, but I understood its practical merits as a means of evaluating the students and assigning university placements in a country so large.

But what I could not understand was testing information that was outdated, or worse, testing fictitious information that was presented as truth. At this point, the exam system had degenerated into nothing more than the programming of minds; some would even consider it brainwashing. But everyone was willing to maintain these fictions and discuss these things as if they believed them, when everyone knew they were false.

❧

The following Tuesday in Oral English we continued listening and talking about famous American speeches. The first speech we had listened to was Martin Luther King's "I Have a Dream," followed by John F. Kennedy's 1961 inaugural address. This week I had chosen "Remarks at the Brandenburg Gate" by Ronald Reagan.

On Monday when I went through the speech myself, I realized that it referenced a number of Cold War–related historical events: the Berlin Airlift, the Marshall Plan, and the Strategic Defense Initiative.

So on Tuesday before we started listening to the speech, I first introduced these events. I explained that George C. Marshall was secretary of state after World War II. I displayed a map of Europe that showed the amount of Marshall Plan money each country received. I made the point that the United States gave money both to their friends in World War II, such as France, Great Britain, and the Netherlands, and to their enemies, such as Germany and Italy. I told them that the United States believed that to keep your former enemies in poverty was only to invite another war.

I also told them a little anecdote from the time I lived in Germany. One of my colleagues when I worked on our American military base was a German woman employed by the public affairs office. She once related to me a memory from her childhood. One evening when she was a girl, in the difficult years following the Second World War, her father was listening to the radio and heard, for the first time, about the Marshall Plan. He was so happy and grateful. These good feelings for the United States, ignited at that moment, never left him. He passed them on to his daughter, who learned English and eventually was employed by the American military.

But I needed to be fair. So, bringing up the map again, I told my students that while the Marshall Plan was kind and certainly generous, it was also strategic.

"Notice, the Soviet Union did not receive any money. Eastern Europe did not receive any money. The Marshall Plan was about promoting peace and rebuilding Europe. But at the same time, it was about preventing the spread of communism. We knew if the countries of Western Europe remained poor and devastated, it would be easy for the Soviets to move in and control them."

In this explanation, I continued a theme that I had emphasized as we listened to all the speeches: that this was the Cold War, and growing up in the context of the Cold War, as I had, where the world was dangerously divided into two camps, greatly affected American thinking today. I wanted my students to know that Americans still had a lingering mistrust of the idea of communism from this period. But, I always told them, Cold War mistrust had been primarily directed at the Soviet Union; it was only peripherally attached to China.

After like introductions of the Berlin Airlift and the Strategic Defense Initiative, we went on to the speech. We didn't have that much time for discussion afterward, so I broke them into small groups and simply asked them to discuss their general feeling about the speech. To my surprise, there was immediate commotion.

First was Qingdao Cathy.

"This is different history than we have learned before," she said.

"Well, that's good. I'm glad you're learning something new."

"But the problem is, this will not help me on my politics exam."

"Cathy, I am the wrong teacher if you want help on your politics exam. I know nothing about your politics exam. This is Oral English class."

"But this is presenting a different view."

"Good. I'm glad. That's the whole point. We should learn different views. Then you can understand the American perspective and the American mind. A different view is useful."

"But you don't understand."

"Understand what?" I asked.

"You don't understand the problem!" she said.

And then, although agitated, although trying to express thoughts she had not yet worked out herself in a language that was not her first, Qingdao Cathy achieved a clarity that cut through all the cultural barriers between us and made me finally understand, perhaps even made herself finally understand.

"The problem is, I am beginning to change." She collapsed back into her chair and sighed. "And that makes everything more complicated."

The entire class stopped their group discussions and turned their heads to listen to us. I raised my voice a little.

"I can't help you on the exam. But soon your exams will be over, and you must be able to use your mind and form your own opinions."

I took a deep breath and continued. "Isn't that the purpose of education? To use your mind? To broaden your horizons? To change? Every book you read should change you."

Class was now over. "Come to office hours tomorrow," I said quietly to Qingdao Cathy as she filed out of the classroom with everyone else.

As they walked out and the next class of freshmen walked in, I thought to myself: *What just happened?* Somehow I had trodden on areas I was not supposed to tread on, but how? For the next class I played the speech again, wondering what exactly had touched off the sensitive Qingdao Cathy. During discussion time, Kimberly raised her hand.

"We learned about this period in high school. We know about the Marshall Plan. But we were taught that the Marshall Plan didn't really help Europe. We were taught that it was intended only to control Western Europe."

Now I understood.

Again, we only had a few minutes left in class and I began to get a little nervous because I now realized that unknowingly I had presented a view counter to their official propaganda.

"Well," I told the class. "I gave you these speeches not to tell you that this thinking is correct, only so that you will understand the American perspective. You must decide for yourselves what is right."

That night I told Chris about the afternoon's events.

"It's so ironic, because I have taken great care to stay away from contentious issues."

He raised his eyebrows.

"Okay, I haven't been completely successful with Tibet or Taiwan, but I have certainly avoided all discussion of Tiananmen Square," I said. "But that's not the point. Here I am, finding myself in this situation, and the class was about *American* history, not anything even remotely related to China."

"It's a fine line," he said. "It's their country and their laws, and we have to respect them. But you also have to be true to yourself."

"What do you think about Qingdao Cathy?" I asked him.

"Well, she's in a difficult position," he said. "They all are. They are indoctrinated, but they are immature."

Yes, I thought. I had been too rough on her. I had told her to form her own opinion as if this were a simple thing to do. But now I saw that she truly had to wrestle with this. The easy choice intellectually was to choose to believe what her books and schooling had taught her. But she was making a more difficult choice: to maintain that separate sphere of free thought, to allow herself to form her own opinions. Opinions would only create a distracting buzz obscuring what she needed to recite; thinking for herself would muddle the regurgitation she needed to do to pass the tests. And failing tests is toxic in China.

The next day she slumped down into a seat in my office.

"Mrs. Arrington, I know you said that change is good. But it makes everything more complex! And what if I write down the wrong answer on the exam?"

"I know," I told her. "I was too hard on you. I know you could take the easy way and not bother to think about these matters, not bother to form your own opinion. But you aren't doing that. You are choosing instead to think freely. I want to tell you that I see that. I admire that. And I think it takes courage. I think you are courageous."

She sighed. "Thank you."

Not more than a few days later Dawn, a quiet and studious double major, came up to me after class.

"Mrs. Arrington, I was wondering what Americans thought about Marxism," she said.

Why is everyone bringing up Marxism this week when it hasn't been mentioned for two years? I thought.

"Well," I said carefully, "Americans think that Marxism was a popular theory in the past, but that it has been proven a failure. Look at the Soviet Union or Eastern Europe. We believe even China has moved away from Marxism and became more successful when it did so."

Dawn looked at me incredulously. "I don't think so. What you are saying sounds so strange. In my mind, Marxism is a holy theory. All of us think so."

❀

The following week I had lunch with Seven and Miriam, my two former students interested in international relations.

"So, do you think China is still Marxist, or is it capitalist?" I asked in blunt American style. I was particularly interested in Seven's opinion, since he was a party member.

"No, we are no longer Marxist," Seven said. Miriam agreed.

"But they taught you in school that China still follows Marxist thought," I said. "Don't you believe what they taught you in school?"

"No, we don't believe it."

"But why does China teach something that isn't true anymore?"

The two of them laughed and looked at each other.

"I think they do this to keep the society stable," answered Seven. "You see, they taught us Marxism for so many years. They taught us that Marxism and communism were a kind of paradise. That capitalism was evil. So they can't just simply say that now we are capitalist."

Miriam added: "That would be like saying that they were wrong before. That the party was wrong, or that Mao was wrong."

"Besides," Seven said, "in China theory is not so important. Practice is what matters. We only care about what works. What we are doing now in China is working. So we don't care what it is called."

"But you do call it Marxism."

"Yes."

"Even though it is not Marxism."

"Yes."

"So the whole country is agreeing to lie."

"Well, yes." They laughed somewhat embarrassedly.

"But China has so many students, and they must all study Marxism for so many years, even though it is no longer practiced," I protested.

"Yes," Miriam said. "We students must study so many things that are really not very useful. We are just forced to learn them."

"But this case is different," I insisted. "Students must study Marxism, but they are not taught that this is a theory used in the past. Instead, they are taught that China still subscribes to Marxism, that it is the Truth. That China is still Marxist."

"Yes," said Seven, "I once heard a joke about this. The president of Russia was driving a car, and he signaled left, then turned left. Then the American president drove down the same road. He signaled right, then turned right. Finally the Chinese president drove down the road. He signaled left, but actually turned to the right."

I laughed. "But Seven, you are getting ready to take the postgraduate exam to study international relations. You must pass a test in politics."

He laughed. "Yes, I know. So now I am studying Marxism all over again."

"But . . ."

"But I know, I don't believe it. So I won't put my own opinion on the test, or I will fail. I must put down exactly what the textbook says."

He sighed. "You see, it's like we have to have two brains—one for the textbook and The Exam, one for our own ideas. Now you are starting to see, it's difficult to be a Chinese student."

Miriam added, "Really there are three kinds of Chinese students. The first kind doesn't have their own ideas at all. They simply accept what the textbook says. The second kind doesn't believe it, and gets angry. They don't like our government at all. You probably don't know about these students. They won't talk this way in front of you, since you are a foreigner."

She continued. "The third kind of student is like the two of us. We recognize that the textbook is often incorrect and we have our own opinion."

Seven then asked me about human rights. "So if your government is always lecturing China about human rights, then I want to know what your standard for human rights is. What is it that China is not doing?"

I intensely disliked these questions. How was I to explain why my country felt it must lecture other countries?

"Well, this is difficult," I told them. "I'm not an expert in human rights. But you should know the history. For many years America didn't worry about what happened inside other countries. But World War II changed that. We found out that six million Jews were killed. We felt guilty that we hadn't done anything about it. We learned a lesson: you must stand up for what is right, you must speak out. Our thinking changed. After that, the United Nations adopted the Universal Declaration of Human Rights."

I thought for a moment. "I think Americans are fundamentally different from other people. You Chinese are a country because of your common culture, language, and civilization. We Americans don't have these things. We all came from different cultures and spoke different languages. So what makes us a country?"

I paused. "We are the only country founded upon an idea."

"Freedom," said Miriam.

"Yes, freedom. So when Americans look at China, they say, you don't have freedom of religion, you don't have freedom of speech, you are not allowed to criticize your government. And we believe these are human rights."

"But we've never had these things. We are so used to it being this way. We wouldn't know what to do if we had so much freedom," said Miriam.

"Americans think that what you believe in your heart, what you believe in your head, this is what makes you who you are. This is your identity. It is not what you were born or who your family is. It is your ideas that make you who you are."

Even as I said it, I thought about our conversation ten minutes earlier, where we had discussed that you could not have your own ideas in China. This system of textbook memorization and recitation filled up the whole room, leaving not a corner of fresh air to breathe in your own ideas. Except for those students who would not let themselves be suffocated.

I had thought before that the lack of creativity, lack of opinions, lack of ideas, was just a natural consequence of the exam system, which a country this large had to have to allocate its limited university slots. But after discovering that Marxist thought was still taught, that the government was afraid of dissenting students, I realized that the education system was not so innocuous. The government used it to control the thoughts and attempt to win the minds of its youth. But while Marxist dogma was being ritualistically recited in classrooms across China, individuals brought their vegetables to market, entrepreneurs opened up shop, and young couples saved up to buy a house.

❀

I had done considerable thinking and writing about the Chinese education system and how it stunted creativity. The paradox was that my own life in China was the polar opposite.

In my professional life, teaching, I had absolute freedom. We were given no guidance other than a course title and a textbook, the use of which was optional. I thrived in this environment. I could put my whole personality into my teaching. In my case, this meant encouraging critical thinking, talking about international affairs, discussing Chinese history, religion, and the cultural differences between China and America. I put myself out there entirely and, as a result, grew quite close to my students, who I hoped sensed my authenticity.

In my life home schooling our children in the evenings, I also had complete freedom. My curriculum was wide open, apart from certain things, like the three Rs, which they needed to know. I felt surges of inspiration as I planned our home school around literature, and felt my own creativity fed by the books we read together. As I thought about what I really wanted our children to learn—foreign languages and cultures, history, theology, language arts, values—I was excited by the education we had the chance to provide for them.

Then there was my own reading and study, in which I also had complete freedom. No syllabi, no grades to worry about, no course requirements. Over the past two years I had read about Chinese peasants, Saint Augustine, the history of Chinese characters, Irish monasticism, and the development of the English language. My instructors—through their written words—had been Barbara Tuchman, Margaret MacMillan, Jonathan Spence, and so many others. My life in ideas was extremely satisfying, so much so that I was eschewing thought of getting further degrees with the idea that it would impede my education.

It was not surprising with such freedom that creativity was flowering in my life like never before, and my life spilled out into writing continuously. My only temperance was watching my students wilt under this system, and wishing I could take Christina, Amy, Kimberly, Seven, or even Qingdao Cathy along with me.

But essentially, this life allowed me to be completely myself. I felt that I was being the person I was created to be, doing what I was supposed to do. I wasn't doing anyone else's work. I wasn't spending my days nine to five doing paperwork or other nonsense that in the greater scheme of things didn't make a bit of eternal difference—and I had had numerous jobs in which I had done that. Okay, most of my jobs.

I wasn't sure I could ever go back to that kind of life. In fact, now that I thought about it, I knew that I could *1,000 10,000 times not* ever return to that life.

Chapter 33

关系
RELATIONSHIPS

An invisible red thread connects those who are destined to
meet, regardless of time, place, or circumstance. The thread
may stretch or tangle, but it will never break.

—Ancient Chinese proverb

❁

"YOU OWE ME," SAID CHRIS, AS WE HEADED TOWARD FUZHOU A FEW
days after Spring Festival in February of 2009. This trip was not
his idea and I had to assert the full strength of my will to get him to grudgingly agree.

The fall semester had been a busy one. Chris started a master's program, adding graduate coursework to his already full teaching schedule.
Katherine moved on from the kindergarten that had grown so familiar to
begin first grade at the Ying Sheng Road primary school. She did amazingly
well—excelling in math and holding her own in Chinese. Grace and Andrew remained at the kindergarten and I continued to teach. Before we
knew it, the semester was over and Chinese New Year was upon us. After
traveling in Southeast Asia and Hong Kong, we were now on our way to
visit Grace's foster family, despite Chris's objections.

"They were her foster family!" I would say in the months leading up
to our trip.

"So they say," he would retort. "We don't know their motives or even
if they are who they say they are. To them, we're probably just a meal ticket.
The rich foreigners."

My husband, the former soldier, had a keen sensitivity to security.
Fuzhou, deep in the interior of an undeveloped province, even out of reach

of the long arm of McDonald's, raised his hackles and brought out his protective instincts.

To add to his suspicion, while arranging the trip with the travel agency, they informed us we would be required to pay 1,600 yuan to visit the orphanage. It was the standard fee for families returning to visit with their adopted children. We felt offended. We thought that since we were in town anyway, it would be nice for the orphanage to see one of the babies they had had official custody of. But it felt like all they wanted was money. Since Grace had never even lived in the orphanage, we dropped it from our itinerary.

Finally arriving in Fuzhou city, we had lunch, then set out for Hanlu village. The mere fifteen-minute drive didn't seem to account for what felt like a two-hundred-year backward step in time. We followed a one-lane paved road until it dissolved into dirt footpaths leading into a maze of homes and decrepit barns.

Suddenly, firecrackers started going off and a huge crowd of villagers began to cheer. We had arrived.

When we were in the midst of the long adoption process, long before we received our referral, while I endured the long wait by reading about China and adoption, I had also prayed a prayer: that our daughter would be cared for in a loving foster family, not an institution.

It was at this moment I knew that my prayer had been answered.

I recognized her immediately. She was wearing a yellow sweater with her long black hair pulled into a ponytail: the foster mother. Although not even five feet tall—barely taller than Katherine—she impatiently strode up to the van, her eyes searching and in turn dismissing all of us, until she saw Grace. She scooped her up without hesitation, without a hint of awkwardness, as if she had been waiting forever to do just that.

The foster mother, who we called Mama, led the way into the house holding Grace; the rest of us followed. The living room was spare of furniture: bare cement floors, a table with narrow benches, a bureau, a poster of Mao on the wall.

It seemed the entire village streamed in after us, everyone so eager to see Grace.

I picked her up so she could see.

"Look, Grace. All of these people are here to see you. They are so excited. They loved you and missed you so much. They are all here for you. Everybody is here for you."

Grace had her head down, peering out the top of her eyes at all the people. She felt shy, yet was unable to keep from grinning. After all, this was a girl born for the stage.

The house seemed full, but people just kept coming in. I looked at Chris, busy taking pictures.

"What do you think?" I asked.

"This is it," he said, his voice catching slightly. "This is the real deal. This is where Grace was."

The whole afternoon was a blur of faces.

Most of our time was spent outside sitting on benches, a throng of people around us: women knitting sweaters, men smoking, children laughing and wanting to see every picture Chris took. We snacked on apples and oranges and sugar cane. There is something absolutely pure about being in a Chinese village, like stripping away all clutter, all veneer of Westernization and modernization, and reaching the prime number of Chinese culture, the most basic unit.

Andrew felt uncomfortable at first. The opening firecrackers had frightened him; he stayed glued by my side.

"Let's go back to the hotel," he pleaded. "Everybody is looking at me."

But the girls fit in immediately. We took a stroll around the village, visiting its primary school and the village shrine, which showed an angry black god and several freshly burnt incense sticks. Our girls held hands with the other children. Chris and Baba (the foster father) walked slowly behind.

The family insisted we stay for dinner. Mama and Second Eldest Brother disappeared into a shack out the back door, whose roof would not have kept out rain, to begin preparing the food. Grace spent most of the afternoon with Eldest Brother, the one I had exchanged text messages with, sitting on his lap or holding his hand. During dinner he fed her chunks of tofu with chopsticks. Second Eldest Brother continued to bring more dishes to the table: boiled lotus, chicken feet, mushroom and tofu soup, glutinous rice balls, stir-fried noodles. We finally departed for the hotel, promising to return in the morning.

The following day the children and I ate breakfast while Chris went outside the hotel to take some pictures. He returned quickly.

"Everyone was staring and pointing at the foreigner," he said. "Come on. Let's go back to the village where they know us."

"Back to *my* village, right?" said Grace.

"Yes, Grace. Back to your village."

Our second day was much quieter. The crowds from the previous day had returned to their work in the fields. Andrew made friends with two local boys and played with them outside. Chris and I were finally able to spend some quiet time with just the foster family. I gave Mama a book of photos we had chosen that showed Grace over the past five years.

Opening the book, Mama stared at the first picture, a photo of Chris and me in the government offices in Nanchang, holding Grace only a few moments after receiving her. Grace was bundled up in a red outfit, her bald head covered with a red hat.

Mama stared at the photo and pointed excitedly at the picture of Grace. "I bought her that outfit. I dressed her in those clothes the day the car came and took her away."

Baba looked over her shoulder. "Yep, that's her all right."

The book had about thirty photos, but Mama never turned away from the first one. She just kept looking at the photo of Grace in the red outfit.

"Please tell us more about your life with Grace," I asked through our guide.

"She was always trying to walk," she said. Mama put her hands on the walls and mimed Grace walking, then moved the benches into a line, showing that Grace would cruise her way out the door.

A small bamboo chair that wasn't there yesterday had been placed in the living room next to the front door.

"She used to sit in this chair. Then she would actually climb out and stand on the chair, and yell out the door for people to come and get her."

She laughed.

"Eldest Brother would often take her outside, as I was quite busy. She really loved Eldest Brother."

I looked around, suddenly realizing that we hadn't seen Eldest Brother yet that day.

"Eldest Brother went back to Hunan province early this morning to return to work. He was supposed to go back right after Lantern Festival, but he stayed a few extra days because he knew Zhi Chun (Grace) was coming."

I felt sad that we didn't have a chance to say good-bye to Eldest Brother. But I was happy he and Grace had spent so much time together yesterday, and amazed at how much their bond had been renewed.

With most of the villagers gone back to work, I could ask more of the questions I wanted to ask. Where did Grace sleep? What did she like to eat? How old was she when she came to live with you?

Mama informed us that Grace was actually three months old when she came to Hanlu village. The orphanage director asked Mama to take care of her because she was sick and malnourished in her first foster family. We found out that over the years Mama had cared for about eight or nine orphanage babies; Grace was her third. She currently received 270 yuan a month, which wouldn't even cover a night's stay at our hotel in town.

As she went back into the kitchen to begin preparing lunch, Chris and I had a few quiet moments together.

"Grace's love of people," he said, "I think she got that here."

I nodded. I had seen not a single toy in that house that always had a baby in it. I'm sure that's why our Grace always thought people were the best amusement.

❦

I had one more errand to accomplish before we left Fuzhou. When we had adopted Grace, the orphanage director brought me and the other families to the finding locations of our daughters. Grace's finding location was listed as the Hongshizui Residential Commission, and the person who found her as Huang Hui Zhen (pronounced Hwahng Hway Jun). This building was located near the orphanage so it had been the first stop. I had quickly hopped out of the van and taken a few pictures.

Later, when the adoption research service went to Fuzhou, they sent me a picture of a different location, explaining that the residential commission had moved since Grace was found there, and that their picture reflected the original site, and thus, the actual place where she had been found.

Because of this discrepancy, I wanted to go find this place myself. For this place was where Grace's life took a sudden and drastic turn away from the life she was supposed to have. This place was the last meeting place, the last point in common, between the life she had now with us, and her unlived life.

Better yet, now that I spoke Chinese, I wanted to find Huang Hui Zhen. Only this woman could tell me where Grace was really found. Our daughter had a beginning, and this place and this woman were the only connection we had to it. I felt I owed it to Grace to get as close as I could, to find out as many facts as possible while I had the opportunity.

We dropped Chris and the children off at the hotel, and the guide and I went to look for the Hongshizui Residential Commission. Baba accompanied us, since he was more familiar with Fuzhou than our guide. Baba hopped out of the van once we reached the Hongshizui district and began asking various people on the street where to find the residential commission. I watched him from the window of the van, watched as he was repeatedly rebuffed or even ignored, perhaps because of his simple clothes, disheveled hair, or his country dialect. He didn't seem to mind. He just kept walking, disregarding his slight limp, looking for the next person to ask. After walking around the block and into several dead ends, he finally found it.

"This is it," he told me. "This is the place."

I looked out the van window. I was looking at the exact same spot the orphanage director had taken me to five years before: a building on a small spur leading into an apartment complex.

Why would anyone leave a baby here? It was not particularly crowded, not a park or a market, nor on a main street. Not only that, but two babies in our adoption group had been found here, the second one only two days after Grace. This just can't be it, I thought.

Baba and our guide went inside the residential commission to ask for Huang Hui Zhen. A few minutes later, our guide came out to talk to me.

"She used to work here, but she doesn't anymore," he told me.

"Can we contact her?" I asked.

"You want to call her?"

"Sure, why not."

He went back inside to ask for her phone number. A few minutes later he came out.

"I have her number and I can call her if you really want me to."

"Yes, I want you to call her."

"But what exactly do you want to say?"

I paused. "I want to know the circumstances around her finding Grace. I want to know what Grace was wearing. I want to know the time of day she was found. I want to know if she was crying or cold. I want to know if there was any kind of note. I want to know if she was in a basket or a box, or some other kind of container."

I took a breath. "These are the things I want to know."

He sighed. "Okay. I'll call her."

He dialed. The number was no longer in service.

"No luck," he said.

"Let's go in and ask them if they can get her current number," I suggested. He followed me into the office. The two ladies working there began calling their associates and former workers, trying to get Huang Hui Zhen's phone number. While one woman was on the phone, her curly-haired colleague talked with me.

"How long ago did you adopt her?" she asked.

"Five years ago," I told her.

"And how is she now?"

"Hen hao," I said. Very good.

"Ting hao," said the guide simultaneously. Great.

I appreciated her asking.

The woman got off the phone and announced, "I got her phone number." The curly-haired woman picked up the phone and dialed.

"Is this Huang Hui Zhen?"

I could tell that it was. The curly-haired woman spoke rapidly, asking Huang Hui Zhen if she remembered finding a baby in front of the residential commission five years ago. She listened for a while, nodded, then hung up.

"Huang Hui Zhen didn't find this baby at all. Five years ago she was the director of the residential commission. Since the orphanage is in this district, when a baby was found its paperwork crossed her desk and she signed it. That's why her name is on your document."

I sat back in my chair.

What was I to do now? I had pushed this issue as far as possible, but had come up with nothing. There was no one else to ask, except the orphanage, but since I had spurned the official visit, that option was closed.

"I guess we can go now," I said to the guide.

We got into the van and drove away. I took a quick look back at the quiet alley and the building. For five years I had pictured this place as my daughter's finding site, and that woman as her finder. Now all I knew about the Hongshizui Residential Commission was that my daughter was *not* found there, and as for Huang Hui Zhen, she was just a minor government bureaucrat. I had come searching for facts and instead had found that the few facts I had were false. I felt slightly dazed and absentmindedly said good-bye to Baba as I realized we had arrived at our hotel.

When I returned to the room, I told Chris about my experiences.

"It doesn't matter," he said. "Would you trade the last two days for that? They are worth far more. We have relationships now."

Relationships. The Chinese word for "relationships" is 关系, *guanxi* (pronounced gwahn-shee). The second character shows silk, and means "tie or bind." This is not surprising. Chinese lore depicts relationships as a red thread, binding those who are destined to meet.

关
RELATION

系
TIE

RELATIONSHIP
(simplified)

But the first character, 关, held no meaning for me. What did those strokes and dashes have to do with relationships? I was stumped.

As usual, when perplexed by a character I turned back to the traditional form. Typing *guan* into the computer, the database pulled up 關. A gate, 門, and in its center, silk 絲.

RELATION

系

TIE

RELATIONSHIP
(traditional)

I stared, stunned.

There I was, once more, standing at the gate. But this time was different. This was no ordinary gate. This was a gate with silk in the middle. A silk thread pulling me inside. A silk thread taking this American family and inviting us inside the gate, giving us seats at the table.

I did not have the facts surrounding her birth or her finding to give to my daughter. And ultimately, I could not give her the culture or the life she had left behind. But I could give her something else. A whole village that remembered her. A knowledge that she was not just Chinese, and not just from somewhere in Jiangxi province, but she was from a certain place. Not words on a map but a real place alive with the faces of those who lived there and loved her. I could give her relationships.

EPILOGUE

❀

IN 2010, AFTER FOUR YEARS IN TAI'AN, WE MOVED TO BEIJING. IT WAS TIME. Our small apartment was getting smaller as our kids grew bigger. Grace was falling behind in a first-grade classroom packed with more than eighty students. And we were simply ready for some broader horizons.

In moving to Beijing, we were following the trail already marked by many of our students. Amy had been here a few years already. She is finishing up her master's thesis on the Native American writer Louise Erdrich and applying to Ph.D. programs in comparative literature. Recently she sent me a photo of her family taken when she returned home to her village for her brother's wedding. Though fully accustomed to her Beijing life, she is still a traditional Shandong girl, and manages these various parts of identity beautifully.

Qingdao Cathy also moved to Beijing and, like Amy, attends Beijing Language and Culture University. She had her heart set on getting a master's degree in linguistics, but her scores weren't high enough. She had to settle for a degree in teaching Chinese to foreigners.

One day I met her for lunch. She complained about the subway ("It's always so crowded and I can never find the elevator!"), the weather ("It's so much colder here than in Qingdao!"), and life in general ("Still, I have no boyfriend!"). And she wasn't getting along with her new roommates.

"Sometimes I practice reading in English, other times I practice reading in Japanese. Then my roommate said she couldn't tell which one I was speaking. Now, I regret that I ever complained about the accent of my roommates back at Taishan Medical College," she said.

Then she sighed and looked at me. "Finally, I have the chance to talk freely!" she said.

We're glad some of our students are with us in Beijing, for we had to leave so many friends behind. While we were still in Tai'an, Zhang got married, and like a good Shandong girl who was marrying later in life (late twenties), she got pregnant immediately. We continued our tutoring sessions throughout her pregnancy, but after the birth of her son, they stopped for good.

But our relationship was already beginning to show signs of strain while she was pregnant. This pregnancy was a long hoped-for event for Zhang; when it finally happened, she fell back hard upon her own culture. Having experienced two pregnancies myself—double anyone else she knew—I felt myself rather a comparative expert in such affairs. When she discarded my ideas as too Western, or too foreign, or just simply too strange, I felt dismissed. When she gathered her Chinese friends around her and solicited them for advice, I felt sidelined.

Looking back, I realize I came on too strong. Suggesting something like natural childbirth, which would require her to go against an entire entrenched bureaucracy as well as the advice of all her well-meaning friends, was simply too much. I should have been more sensitive. Nonetheless, it saddens me that something that should unite cultures—motherhood—in our case caused our paths to diverge.

Mr. Jia hasn't changed. We had a health scare before we left Tai'an, and he was hospitalized for several weeks with heart trouble. (And the year we moved to Beijing, my father was hospitalized with his own heart trouble.) Mr. Jia recovered and returned to his smoking and drinking. "I'm too old to change," he said. He called us once in Beijing, a few months after our arrival. I could tell he missed us, just as much as we missed him.

We gained a lot by our move to Beijing. Our living space expanded. Our children now have a far better teacher-student ratio, and classrooms that get heated during winter. We have the opportunity to attend cultural events and eat Western food on occasion. Teaching at a national university, we have students from Hong Kong to Tibet, Taiwan to Sichuan. In Shandong we learned about the ordinary China, the traditional China, the China that drew its meaning from the past. In Beijing we are learning about China's diversity, its contradictions, and its future.

But our time in Beijing has also shown us the beauty of what we left behind in Shandong. We left behind a pack of local neighborhood kids that our children ran around with. We left behind our church with its bare cement floors and out-of-tune piano. We left behind The Trash Lady.

In Beijing we're not given a second glance because it's a cosmopolitan city. In Tai'an, we weren't given a second glance because they knew us. We've realized that we left behind a community that opened to allow us a place, and that was what made it home.

A Note on Sources

✿

THIS IS A MEMOIR, BUT MANY CHAPTERS REQUIRED EXTENSIVE RESEARCH. Unless it interrupted the flow of the writing, I tried in most cases to refer to books and other sources directly in the text.

The opening quote is from Zhang Ailing (1920-1995), who was known in the West as Eileen Chang. Both her personal life and her love life were filled with turmoil, which is reflected in her fiction. She wrote the short story, "Lust, Caution," which was later made into a film by Taiwanese director Ang Lee. One can see the emotional depth with which she wrote in my one sentence paraphrase of her motto. This quote is referenced in the book *Transformation! Innovation? Perspectives on Taiwan Culture*. Also in chapter one, my mention of Chinese historical and more current literacy rates comes from an article in the *International Herald Tribune* (February 12, 2001) by Ted Pflacker.

The Chinese language, particularly the written Chinese characters, is more than just a theme in the book; it was the lens through which I approached Chinese culture. I used several sources in researching their ancient meanings. The websites www.zhongwen.com, www.chineseetymology.org, and www. chinese-characters.org were immensely helpful. In addition, *Picture Chinese: Art as Language* by Sukming Lo (San Francisco, CA: Long River Press) and *Reading & Writing Chinese*, by William McNaughton (North Clarendon, VT: Tuttle Press) helped me understand some of the nuances and mysteries of the Chinese language.

Lin Yutang's classic *My Country and My People* is still the gold standard for a book about Chinese culture. My version was published by the

Foreign Language Teaching and Research Press (Beijing), and I refer to it throughout the book.

The statistics on the college entrance examination in chapter six came from an opinion piece published by *China Daily*, titled "Time to Revisit the Exam System." I found it useful to read the opinion pieces in *China Daily*; they helped me keep my pulse on current debates within China.

Andrew Loo published a series of books on Chinese *chengyu* (Hong Kong: Silk Road Press). Within that series, *The Plant World* gave me insights into the *chengyu* mentioned in chapter nine. My knowledge of the history of Mount Tai in chapter eleven mostly came from *Shandong: Home of Mount Taishan* published in Beijing by the Foreign Languages Press. Such books are difficult to find outside of China; I purchased my copy at the Xinhua book store in Tai'an.

In chapter twelve I referenced the journals of Captain Cook, in which he first mentioned the word "taboo." His journals were first published in 1777 under the title of "A Voyage to the Pacific Ocean." And finally, in chapter thirteen I traced briefly the history of the term for God in the Chinese language. The occurrence "Shangdi" on Shang dynasty oracle bones is well known and documented. My reference to Shangdi appearing thirty-two times in the Book of History came from Wikipedia.

ACKNOWLEDGMENTS

✤

WE COULD NOT HAVE COME TO CHINA HAD MARTHA CHAN AND ERRC not agreed to take us on. And we could not have stayed in China without the love and support from so many people. Among the too many to thank, I must mention Mike and Jill Roderick and Brad and Kathy Gavle, as well as Sonlight Community Church of Lynden, WA and First Baptist Church of Hinesville, GA, for sending packages of goodies from home that buoyed our morale immensely. In addition, Rex and Audrey Warolin, Dave and Sue Johnson, John and Bridgette Moelter, Allan and Nancy McQuown, Dale and Marylee Bell, Connie Hoag, Bill and Kristin and the whole Smoot family, sustained us spiritually and otherwise.

In Tai'an, we will never forget Mr. Jia, Xue Li, and Teacher Liu, our minders in the foreign teachers' building (and who together made up the composite figure of Mr. Jia). They made a home for us in China, and through their friendship and acceptance, opened the community to us. We are immensely grateful.

At Taishan Medical University, so many went out of their way to accommodate a family with young children. Kathy Lee and Sally Zhang in the Foreign Affairs Office were always there for us. Richard Zhang arranged our teaching schedules so that we could pick our children up from school. Zhang Hui Juan, Zhao Yan Ping, and Chen Ning Ning were both my Chinese tutors and my good friends. They patiently answered every time I had just one more question. We were fortunate to land in a place in which both the local kindergarten, the Taishan Medical University Affiliated Kindergarten, and the primary school, Ying Sheng Primary School, not only allowed foreign children, but encouraged them and us. Without supportive school systems for our children, we would never have made it past a few months. Our debt to them is enormous.

Our students taught us more than we ever taught them. We grew especially close to English Majors Grades 2005 and 2006. They displayed the seriousness, earnestness, and eagerness of those who are the first in their family to go to college. Almost without exception, they were raised in one of Shandong province's many small villages and were born with few advantages. Their university places were earned by sheer hard work. I doubt we'll ever teach another group like them. They are special.

I would be remiss if I did not mention my seven classmates in the beginning Japanese class at Waseda University in Tokyo in 2000–2001: François Flahaut, now a policeman in northern France; Bettina Haag, married and living in Germany; Liang Wenxin of Dalian University of Technology; Zhao Liang of Xi'an Jiaotong University; Ruby Duan, of Taiyuan (Shanxi province, China), Tokyo, and now Denver; Shentu Baoqing of Zhejiang University; and Garlum Lau, singer, songwriter, and writer in Hong Kong. This class was my introduction to China, and I was privileged to have been introduced to China by its very best.

Ruby was the first Chinese I met, and I was her first American friend. We are endlessly amused that we are now living in each other's countries. She read the manuscript, and patiently answered many e-mails when I was confounded by some aspect of Chinese culture.

This book began as a series of e-mails to our friends and family back home, and would never have been turned into a manuscript without their encouragement. My publication journey began when Allison Zimmer, intern at InkWell Management, picked the manuscript out of the slush pile and showed it to literary agent Alexis Hurley. Alexis believed in it from the beginning and refused to give up. She found the perfect home with editor Stephanie Gorton at Overlook. Because of these two brilliant women, full of editorial wisdom and sage advice, a manuscript was transformed into a book.

This is a book about family, and we are blessed with large and supportive families. My mother-in-law, Charlotte Wolf, took me along with her to China, my first trip, from whence it all started. The entire Arrington clan has always been a deep well of support for us, and we're grateful for each one of them. Though we've seen them so infrequently over the years, distance has never strained those strong family bonds.

My mother, Marlene Van Dyken, is my model for all things interpersonal. If I could ever befriend the friendless, care for the uncared for, encourage those who need an extra boost, or simply make everyone feel at home as she does, I will have arrived. For her, it seems effortless. My father, Roger Van Dyken, likely planted the seeds for our journey to China when he laid out maps on the living room floor of my childhood home and planned our family sabbatical to Europe, where we barged the canals and waterways of Europe for eighteen months. Through my parents I was given the unique perspective of being rooted in small-town America yet having windows open to the world. My three brothers, Justin, Danny, and Jonathan, and my two amazing sisters-in-law, Jaime and Kathryn, enveloped us into our family circle every time we came home.

Finally, and most importantly, my husband Chris, who actually said yes when I suggested we move to China. Together we have shared fifteen years are raising five children: Christopher, Michael, Katherine, Grace, and Andrew. Though Christopher and Michael were grown and didn't accompany us to China, I remain forever indebted to them for the privilege of being their mother. Katherine, Grace, and Andrew have certainly been more immersed in Chinese culture than either Chris or I. We are so proud of their courage in Chinese school, their ability to make friends in any culture, and their perseverance through many crosscultural struggles. Living in China together with them gave our experience depth and richness it never otherwise would have had. Without them, I likely would never have felt compelled to write it all down.

And one extra thank-you to Grace, for giving us China.